Spirit World
Diary of an Urban Shaman

Raym

Global Healing
PO Box 1611
Byron Bay
NSW 2481
Australia
www.global-healing.com

First published by Global Healing as "Diary of an Urban Shaman" 2013
Copyright Raym Richards © 2013. Republished and expanded as "Spirit World" © Raym Richards 2016, 2017, 2018, 2019
All rights reserved.

Without limiting the rights under copyright reserved above, no part of this publication may be reproduced, stored in or introduced into a retrieval system, or transmitted in any form or by any means (electronic, mechanical, photocopying, recording or otherwise) without the prior written permission of the copyright holder and publisher of this book.

Printed by Ingram Spark

Edited by Valery Isherwood
Proofed by Chicchan Richards
Designed by Global Healing
ISBN 978-0-9577935-6-9

Contents

Introduction 5
Prologue 6
Possessed 8
Demon 13
Virgin Sacrifice 18
Sex and Death 23
Spirit Guide 29
Alien Abduction 33
Haunted 38
Disco Inferno 43
Templar Knight 47
Miracle Man 52
Zero Point 58
Cursed 64
Talisman 68
Waif and Strays 71
Space Cadet 74
Braided 78
Karma 81
Boy 84
Hive Mind 87
The Tower 93
Old Soldiers Never Die 96
Slayer of the Beast 99
Long lost sister 102
The Dark Lord 105
Fear of the dark 109
Ceremony 112
Long-term relationship 115
Time-Traveller 118
Contact 121
The ramifications of unconditional love 124
A hidden cause of chronic fatigue 127
Home visit 130

Spirit World

A wolf in wolf's clothing	133
The mystery of repeated traumas	135
Past Life skills	138
A hidden cause of anger	140
A dancer's dilemma	143
A block to intimacy	146
A Pull in the fabric of Time	149
The Goddess unveiled	152
Running with the wolves	155
Open heart surgery	158
Black dog	161
Seeing the wood for the trees	164
A healer's choice	167
Mistrust of men	169
The awful answer	172
Vietnam veteran	175
Day tripper	178
Lost Soul	181
Bring in the Clowns	184
Death and Birth	187
Forbidden Love	190
Heaven and Earth	193
All that Glisters is not Gold	196
And the blind shall see	199
CIA interference	202
Sorry Business	205
A Christmas present opens a Christmas past	208
A big man	211
Predator	214
Dead twin	217
Slave to love	220
Birth of a Guru	223
Reflections of Spirit World	225
About the Author	227

Introduction

My interactions with the Spirit World as a contemporary shaman are captured in these true life stories. These stories offer an accurate depiction of what can happen to every-day people during the safely expanded states of consciousness triggered by my Crystal Dreaming™ technique.

Crystal Dreaming™ creates a safe drug-free opening to the superconscious for anyone, enabling them to have a firsthand, often visceral experience, of other realities, times and places through their own fully conscious bi-location.

Take your time reading this book. I encourage you to take a break between stories and feel into their content and how they have affected you. After reading the whole book, revisit stories at random for a deeper understanding of their content.

Please explore "Reflections of Spirit World" at the end of the book for contemplation of the knowledge you have absorbed through reading this book.

This book gives an insight into the Spirit World, our enormous potential as infinitely powerful sovereign beings of light, the inter-connectedness of all things and the power of unconditional love and forgiveness in self healing.

I encourage you to read it aloud, share it with your friends and pass it on when you have finished reading it.

It could offer invaluable help for a loved one.

Raym November 2017.

Prologue

I am holding a green glass ball in my hands and it is heavy. I feel what seems to be energy from the ball pulsing through my arms. I am beginning to sweat and my body shakes as I move the ball in front of my body. The ball in front of me starts to glow faintly. Everything in the room around me drops into soft focus and the chatter of my friends becomes a background hum. I feel apprehension, even a little fear. This should not be happening to me, I don't believe in this New Age crystal nonsense.

It is 1994 and I am at the fulcrum of my life. I am at a friend's dinner party and I have been handed a curio, an obsidian ball that looks like a fishing float but is much heaver. In minutes, this Mount St Helen's obsidian changes my life forever. I am not having a "healing crisis" - in fact my life has never been on a more even keel. After a twenty-five year career as a performance artist which took me from the fringe to the mainstream, I am finally over the struggle of creating and into a still place with my art. There has been a lot of change in my life recently, all of it good. I have a blank canvas in front of me and I feel content, so now the Universe steps in and takes the opportunity to shake things up a bit.

A tunnel of light opens up before me in the ball. I glance at my friends expecting them to notice my face illuminated from the ball, but they chatter on laughing, oblivious to what is happening to my body. We are no longer experiencing the same reality.

As I gaze into the ball I am sucked into a vortex of light and I move into a beautiful space, indescribable in its peace and love. I burst into tears, knowing in the back of my mind that my friends are probably wondering what is happening to me. But I no longer care: I am in a state of absolute bliss.

Beings step forward from the light around me and embrace me with their infinite joy.

Dudes, I telepath. *You have definitely got the wrong man. I don't believe in this stuff.*

I realise immediately that this is like saying I don't believe in the sun. It just IS. And it is time for me to wake up to the truth of my own infinite being - which I do, in seconds.

In this precious moment, my journey of realisation as a complete being begins. The beings I am with gently remind me why I incarnated and I release my egotistical resistance to the truth of their guidance; they explain the workings of the Universe and we discuss my future.

When I return to the reality of my friends' dinner party I can see the energy around each person in shimmering colours. I meet my wife's concerned and loving eyes and smile. Noticing a line of soft pink energy connecting our hearts and I start crying again.

Spirit World

I see more than I could ever have imagined existing in this small physical space that contains us. Then I see beyond, through the walls, into All There Is and I am overwhelmed by its beauty.

In this moment I cease to be an artist and become so much more. I am no longer all I ever thought I was. I am nothing and everything. I feel everything and it is overwhelming. I am both terrified and ecstatic.

I see into my own future and grasp that it will take some time before I can share my experience with others. I see that in due course I will be able to help many people, but that seems irrelevant right now as my own profound initiation has begun and it is all-consuming.

I take a deep breath, smile reassuringly at my friends and step into my new life as a shaman.

Possessed

The time is now.

I am in no time-space with my client and I am trying hard not to confront an already angry and abusive Earthbound spirit that has attached itself to her. Cursing me in Afrikaans he reaches through my protective energy shield and starts to throttle me. This should not be possible, but it seems to be happening and it really hurts.

I can feel his hands clamped around my throat. This is turning into the most visceral other worldly experience I have ever had. Choking, I telepath...

I am not a threat to you. What are you so angry about?

I am blasted by another outpouring of abuse. I need to stay cool, but I am beginning to feel light headed. I feel tapping on my shoulder, I look to my left but there is no one next to me. Now I am really confused, the other Earthbound spirits are still attached to my client, what is happening to me?

Then I get it, my assistant is trying to bring me back into the physical, so I quickly return to full consciousness. When I open my eyes I realise that my client, a tiny woman, has lifted up my muscular body and has me pinned against the wall. Her face is right next to mine, her eyes are wide open but her eyeballs are rolled back so I am staring straight into the whites of her eyes as she rants on at me in a deep male voice.

Her mouth is flecked with foam and my assistant who is trying to prize her fingers off my throat has gone a lovely shade of white, a colour that matches perfectly her blouse and bleached and braided dreadlocks.

If her grip is not released very soon I will pass out. As my vision becomes grey around the edges, I wonder how I got myself into this mess.

I live in the old part of the city, I like its character and the people there. As I cycle across town to "Inner Journeys" my crystal shop, I become an observer. I sense the vacant ones, people wearing grey suits with matching grey auras. I stop at traffic lights, they hurry past and I look into their eyes. They are like windows into abandoned warehouses, empty, dark and slowly crumbling inside. They look utterly lost and hopeless. It seems to me that there is no-one home - or worse, there is someone else there.

My crystal shop and session room sit in the borderline part of the city because the rent is reasonable. It's the kind of place that starts out being inhabited by artists, musicians and students and ends up being taken over by architects, real estate agents and lawyers who then complain about the character of the place that they bought into. This part of town is the nexus for transformation, so for now, for me, it is a good place to be.

Spirit World

There is community here, people look out for each other and there is an easy going atmosphere that comes from having not much money, not too many worries and plenty of time.

So it was that I started receiving calls from other alternative shops in the area, they all talked about the same person. A slightly built woman who needed my help. I knew it was only a matter of time until she showed up.

Sometimes in my business you need assistance. I have two apprentices, both mature and very groovy women. They are similar yet very different. Both have bleached blonde, braided dreads and dress like they are about to rock on to an all night rave after work. Secretly I call them Topsy and Mopsy.

Brianna, is your Earth Mother type, large and well built, she exudes nurturing feminine power. She is lesbian and proud of it and has trained in martial arts, as well as esoteric disciplines. Bryony is smaller and has a lighter build, she could be Brianna's sister from another life. Her birdlike features give a hint of the sharp mind hiding under her dreads, like Brianna she has studied extensively with other teachers. She is an excellent Tarot reader and a natural trance channel.

Both women look many years younger than their age because they are so happy. They are enjoying their lives, so looking after their bodies comes naturally. These powerful women are my guardians, my front door filter, they run my crystal shop and keep the tyre kickers away from my session room. No time-wasters make it into my sacred space for a journey. Just the genuine spiritual seekers and those in need of help.

Today I am thankful that Brianna is my assistant. Sometimes things can get physical with this kind of case, and I prefer to have another woman in the room if my client is female.

I can feel my client coming towards the shop before she arrives. The energy around her is big and very prickly, although the woman who walks through the door appears to be the opposite. This tiny, thin woman tells me her story.

She has had a violent temper for as long as she can remember and lately it is getting worse. It seems the happier she becomes in her relationship the bigger this rage inside her gets, disrupting her life on a daily basis. She had been placed on an Apprehended Violence Order (AVO) for biting off a chunk of her husband's ear during a bout of uncontrollable rage. It is clear to me that I am probably dealing with a case of possession. As she is coherent and calm I decide to move straight into our session, her name is Mia.

My aim is to find out when she gave permission for the spirit to attach itself to her and work from there. Laying in a powerful mandala of crystals we both travel into the space between worlds, I telepath Mia the following affirmation:

Body I command you, show me the moment this started.

Immediately we are standing in a country area by the side of a dusty dry road surrounded by lush, green vegetation. We notice a little girl in front of us playing on her bicycle, she seems happy and carefree. She is not concentrating, daydreaming as she navigates rocks and pebbles on the roadside. Mia confirms it is herself as a child and I suggest that she step into the child's body.

The child is near a corner, I feel the rumble of an approaching truck, but she does not notice it at all. The truck driver is speeding and as he swings out on the corner he almost loses control as his load shifts. His heavy vehicle is old and unroadworthy. I catch a glimpse of the panicked driver, dropping greasy food on his lap as he clutches his steering wheel with both hands. There is no way he will even notice the child.

He collects her with his front fender and knocks her under the nearside front wheel, fortunately it is only her legs that go under and because as he is turning only one wheel runs over her. The bike is destroyed and the frail little girl is left wailing at the side of the road as the truck driver continues on his journey in a cloud of dust and small stones, totally unaware of what has just happened.

How are you feeling? I telepath the girl.

I am in agony. Somebody stop this pain. Please someone. ANYONE!

We are at the point of attachment. The point when she gave permission for ANY being who wants to step in and help to do so.

She did not say or think;

...will the beings who love me unconditionally please help me.

I do not know many people who would have the presence of mind to do that, let alone a little girl with two broken legs, lying on the side of a deserted road in the bush.

Unknowingly she has issued an open ended invitation and in effect a contract for any beings, particularly confused dead people (Earthbound spirits) to come to her aid, and they do. But there is always a catch, they are looking for a place to stay, permanently.

I witness several energies come flying through the ethers and attach themselves to her, offering succour. They cringe to one side clinging on to her solar plexus for dear life as a large dark form approaches and attaches itself firmly to the back of her neck. I don't know how, but it eases her pain, maybe it takes on some itself. Her pain lessens and her wailing changes to deep sobs as she waits for someone to find her.

I take her into no time-space and suggest she transmits the following thought-form:

I challenge any being that is under the illusion that it has power over me. Show yourself to me now, or forever hold your peace.

Of the dark forms surrounding Mia the largest comes forward. I have an overriding sensation of intense and explosive anger.

I am not yet able to make out its form but rather than arguing with Mia it is headed straight for me. As it materialises in front of me I perceive that it is male, human, muscular and dark skinned.

He talks to me in a language I do not understand.

Neuk af wit seun! It sounds like Afrikaans.

Talk to me in English mate, I don't understand you.

What the fuck do you want white boy? Why don't you fuck off back to where you came from and mind your own bloody business? Even his thought forms have a strong accent.

He towers over me and he is a big bloke, he is strong and has a lot of will power. Suddenly he reaches through my protective auric field and starts to throttle me. I feel the tapping on my shoulder and remember that I asked my assistant to tap me if she feels I should return to my body for any reason.

I return to full consciousness as quickly as I can and realise that things are going pear shaped fast, this session turning into an all in wrestling match and I am about to pass out. I must stay calm and act...

Think, breathe. Think.

This petite woman with her white bulging eyes now has the strength of an ox. I manage to get my fingers under hers and create some breathing space as my assistant grapples with her. We must not hurt her. I am now speaking out loud talking directly to the African presently in possession of her body.

"What happened to you, I want to know."

"What do you care? You interfering bastard." A deep and thickly accented voice booms out of Mia's tiny chest.

"Maybe I can help."

"Bullshit. You fuckers left me for dead, in this dark shitty place. The mine caves in and you just fuck off! You bastards just left me. And I died. FUCKERS!" he shouts

I am already preparing excuses about a play rehearsal for my neighbours.

It sounds very weak but I say, "I am sorry to hear that."

"Fuck off!" His grip tightens again but now fully conscious, I respond quickly.

"What year is it?"

'What?'

"In the mine, what year is it."

"1951, who gives a shit?"

I do, and I am doing some rapid mental calculation. If he was mature man in 1951 there is a good chance his wife is also now dead, if he had one. I sense a way of getting through to him, helping him. He is definitely not going to go for any flaky New Age fluff, that's for sure.

"Do you miss your wife?"

He is poised on a knife edge between intense rage and deep grief. Fortunately for me, as my assistant is beginning to flag, he leans towards the latter. His pause tells me he loved this woman.

In this space between anger and grief I seize the moment.

"Across time and space, I call on this man's wife, I call on this man's wife, I call on this man's wife, please join us now."

I do not need a translator to understand what is happening as he releases his grip and breaks down, sobbing.

"OK you can go with her, you can go home and find peace, go home to light now. Go in peace"

One word of Afrikaans leaves Mia's lips as he leaves her body and it completely relaxes.

"Dankie…"

I help the other attached spirits find peace and after cleansing and protection exercises Mia returns to her body and reclaims it. She tells me she grew up in South Africa, so it all makes sense. This dead African miner had become a confused and distressed Earthbound spirit. Refusing the opportunity to go home to light when his ancestors came for him he was stuck and looking for a safe and pleasant place to hang out when she called for help.

He had been with her since her childhood accident, affecting her moods and thoughts. He had become possessive, resenting her love for her husband. Now that he has left everything will change for my client.

We say goodbye and my shaken assistant ushers her out. I give thanks to my non-physical team, and think how silly I will look wearing a neckerchief in summer. For a few days my throat will be very red, I hope it won't bruise.

Demon

I am in a dark and hot place and it does not feel pleasant, I know my body will have a thin film of perspiration all over it, particularly around the neck. The thing is, I have left my body a long way away, in a place we usually believe is our primary reality. Today things are different.

It takes me a few moments to acclimatise. It is stinking hot. I could be close to a bushfire or a furnace, the ground around me is rough and dry, a dusty, rocky, level surface. Next to me I can see my client. If I am feeling warm and apprehensive, she must be feeling hot and terrified.

In front of us is a huge dark form, hard to make out at first, but definitely not friendly, definitely not human and definitely not alone. Things are not looking good and we are just at the start of our journey together.

Hoping that she won't collapse into utter, unmanageable fear and total vulnerability, I wait patiently for her to notice that I am standing right next to her. I hope she won't start screaming, we have had enough complaints from the neighbours back on Earth, and my shop lease is up for renewal.

I am mindful that I should not control this situation too much. Although to some extent I am capable of manipulating the reality around us to suit my purposes. It is important that my client overcome the challenges before her of her own free will and without too much interference from me.

If I intercede too much I will get involved in her Karma. Not a good idea, as I have enough on my own plate right now, thank you very much.

I know my client is beginning to access levels of fear which are way beyond her experience or expectations. I am alert and ready for action, I have trained myself to deal with fear as a companion, one that makes me alert but does not control me.

My client notices me.

> *Fuck, I am shit scared* she telepaths staring wide eyed at the apparitions surrounding her which she has suddenly seen clearly for the first time.

> *That's three negative power words in one very powerful sentence. Couldn't we just play safe, remove the negatives and stick with 'I AM'?*

Too late.

Feeding off her fear, the being in front of her has grown in stature and is materialising into a fully formed, red eyed, horned and salivating Demon of the aggressive variety of the first order. It reaches forward and grabs her solar plexus and starts squeezing and twisting it with its dark claws.

It is laughing at her.

This is all moving far too quickly for my liking, I need to create time to think.

Spirit World

I know back on Earth, right now my client is squirming and writhing in pain on the futon next to mine, I trust my assistant is doing as she promised and looking in on the session. For once I hope my little shop is not too busy.

Tell it how beautiful it is. I suggest

"What? You are jo..." her sentence is cut short as the being in front of her uses its other hand to claw deeply into her side. She starts moaning, I hope it's not too loud.

I need to take control, *Say after me, Beray sheet eyer esher eyer. Beray sheet eyer esher eyer.*

She gasps the affirmation out loud and for one short moment the being in front of her hesitates, totally dumfounded.

In this moment I have a chance to collect my thoughts.

My client had been referred to me by a student, offering discounted practice sessions to gain experience, she was attracting people in need who were short of cash. The woman next to me had come to her in great physical pain. Pain which several doctors were unable to diagnose or treat with any success.

She was an initiate of an international religious group who did good work feeding the needy and offering them support. She had reached the rank of temple priestess and was respected in her community. She was authorised to create and lead ceremony and had become a high priestess. She was devout, chanting and praying from the early hours each morning, immersing herself totally in her practice.

Yet despite her good work and practices she was coming under massive psychic attack.

In her session with my student it became obvious that she was being attacked by powerful non-physical beings who meant to do her great harm. She was referred to me.

When she arrived for her session she was in so much pain she could barely walk, supported either side by two novice priestesses, her hands were cramping up like claws and her back and legs convulsing with muscle spasms.

She had come for a shamanic journey with me in which she might see exactly what was happening to her.

I had already prepared a clear and sacred space for the journey. I had travelled this route a thousand times before. As we lay down next to each other I looked over at her for the tell tale signs of deep trance. She closed her eyes and they rolled back, leaving only the whites of her eyes visible through her rapidly fluttering lids.

Deliberately opening a portal through which we could step into no-time-space and hence into all-time-space, I closed my eyes. We both slipped into an altered state of consciousness easily, allowing the mandala of crystals that surrounded us to do its work.

I joined her immediately, but the speed and ferocity of the attack took me unawares. We did not arrive where I expected and I was in danger of becoming fearful myself. I needed to buy time.

Ask it what it wants.

To destroy me.

Why?

Because I am weak, because it can, because it gives it pleasure...

When did you give it permission to be here?

What?

There is always permission, when?

I see myself carrying out ritual and ceremony, I am in training. My teacher is not being totally honest with me. I am making promises in a language I do not understand, this is the moment I gave permission.

OK, tell it not to be afraid of you.

"*Don't be afrai...*"

The great beast's laughter is deafening, it claws and wrenches at my client, and its smaller friends in the shadows move forward to join in. My client is in torment, and I know by now that the neighbours will be making a note to call my landlord. Again.

I reluctantly step forward, closer to my client. The violet white light that surrounds me buzzes and hums with a focussed life force; for now I am containing the energy into a bubble that surrounds my body for about a metre. It pushes the smaller demons back into the shadows, but not the big one. It still has tight hold of my client and will not be distracted by me, or my light.

Say again out loud, 'Don't be afraid I promise not to hurt you.'

I know my client is in agony and I will her to ride it out.

'This pain is an illusion, it has no power over me.' Say it.

She repeats the affirmation out loud and it is like a red rag to a bull. We both sense this beings thought-forms:

How dare you challenge me!

This being has probably not been challenged for eons, it is used to getting its own way. I am deliberately trying to cause it confusion. It is enraged but beneath that there is the tiniest twinge of doubt. This is our leverage, our way in.

It directs its attention towards me.

I am ready, but I do not intend to harm you.

And I am ready. I have quietly called in my power, I am centred and ready for anything. The time I bought a few moments ago has served me well. I am ready to experience whatever this thing has to offer, without rising to its bait of becoming angry, or worse and far more dangerous for me, becoming fearful.

It senses my readiness and backs off, focussing again on my client.

In this moment my client draws strength from me and my actions, she recalls my advice before our journey started, that this could be her true initiation into the priesthood. She had been initiated through ceremony, now she was to experience her true initiation as a high priestess. It is time to confront her deepest fear. This is her baptism of fire.

> *You no longer have my permission to be here, our agreement is dissolved, the contract between us is complete, you may go in peace.*

As she repeats this affirmation she starts to believe it. I also sense my assistant back on Earth, looking down on us and smiling, she knows the power of this statement if it is made out loud and from the heart.

Now the great beast is shrinking, still malevolent, it starts to doubt its tenure. But it still has hold of my client and is still causing her pain.

> *In you I see great light. In you I see great beauty. Don't be afraid of me I promise not to hurt you. I am not angry with you.*

Although still squirming under its steel like claws, she senses she is beginning to win.

> *You are beautiful. Don't you remember how beautiful you are?*

Confusion. The Demon is genuinely perplexed, my client is gaining strength.

> *Look inside, tell me what you see...*

Even though I have seen it many times what follows is still beautiful and moving. As my client repeats the affirmation I know she is up for a life changing experience.

And so the great beast looks within.

In the pain, sadness and anger that is within it, it senses a spark of light at its core. As it focusses on it, the light expands and becomes a supernova that totally envelops it and the surrounding space. We and it are breathless at its own realisation of what it truly is. It is a beautiful being of light. It is an Angel, lost and now found.

> *Go home to light now, take the others with you, go home and find peace, you are forgiven. Go in peace.*

It is so joyful it swoops over us and the smaller beings, its gratitude is palpable. As it leaves my client's body completely relaxes and she is pain free. I know by now that she is completely drained, and decide not to take her further into the circumstances surrounding the Demon's contract with her.

I take her through exercises to cleanse, refresh and strengthen her energy bodies and we return to the futons we are lying on, upstairs in my shop.

She is utterly exhausted and tearfully grateful for the session. The acolytes she came with are also tearful and happy at her recovered condition. Not much explanation is needed, I accept payment and she leaves.

I decide not to share all I saw in the journey: The priest who tricked her, his misogyny, and the arrangements he had made for non physical beings to feed off the energy in the temple for their own ends and their fear of her growing personal power. That I will leave for another session, when she realises it is appropriate.

I lie back on my futon and give thanks to the crystals that surround me and the loving non-physical beings who work with me. I feel at peace. I have done my best for my client, she is now and will remain pain free. I feel tired but content, everything in my world is perfect.

My assistant knocks and pops her head around the door of my session room.

> "Its Mrs Jenkins from the tea rooms next door, she wants to have a chat about the screaming she thought she heard coming from your room."

Virgin Sacrifice

The thing about time travel is the intensity of new smells - sometimes their strangeness can be overwhelming; earth mixed with animal dung from now extinct species, rich cooking aromas filled with forgotten herbs and spices, woodsmoke from trees that no longer exist and the ever present tang of sweat from a native people whose diet is vastly different from our own.

All of this immediately creates a very tangible atmosphere, a far cry from the session room in the busy city, where my body now lies.

A friend of mine, a doctor, once told me that he believes smells completely bypass the conscious mind, often triggering an emotional response to a long stored and deeply hidden memory. I wonder if my client is beginning to remember what happened to her and why she has been drawn here.

I am walking with her in an ancient Central American culture thousands of years in the past, possibly Aztec, Toltec or Mayan. It is a hot, steamy environment but as we have arrived just before dawn, there is a slight, cool breeze as the mist hugging the young jungle trees around us begins to evaporate.

I am enjoying being in another time and place, smelling things I have never smelt before, walking through an ancient, vibrant culture. The detail in everything I see is astounding and fascinating. It is a sensational experience and I realise just how much I love my work as an urban shaman.

As time travellers I have advised my client we cannot be seen by all but the most accomplished of shamans. Even then they would have to be in a deep trance state and focussed on finding us. So I feel relaxed as we walk through the happy crowd of small, dark haired, olive skinned locals.

It is a morning of great celebration, we sense something very special is about to happen. Some people have obviously been up all night, others look fresh and excited. Children play freely around us, just as they would at any party anywhere, simply happy that a party is happening.

I have a pretty good idea what is about to happen but I must be patient and allow my client her own realisation, without any interference from me.

I am waiting for her to recognise who she is. I have already picked her through the unique signature of her energy body. It varies from lifetime to lifetime but it always has an identifiable consistency. I found her easily.

She is in the group in front of us and she is the centre of attention. So many smiles and so much love is directed towards her it is palpable. She is beautiful: a young woman, almost naked, she is adorned with feathers, body paint and gold jewellery. Her eyelids and lips have also been coloured, it is her special day.

The magnificent structure she is being led to is a great stepped pyramid. Iridescent birds swoop low over the crowd and monkeys chatter and call in the surrounding forest, even they seem excited.

She still has not recognised herself as her body is quite different from the plump middle aged one she has left in my session room, over my small crystal shop, back in the twenty-first century.

I have given her enough time. I know, like me, she is fascinated by the very tactile experience we are having, walking and breathing amongst these diminutive, happy people. It is time for me to step in.

Which one are you? I telepath her.

Am I here?

Sometimes my patience grows thin, I feel like saying, "Of course you are here, why else would we have arrived here, when you asked to be shown the root cause of your life long issues?" But over the years I have learned to be tactful.

Have a look around you. See if you can sense which one is you...

Wow is that me? She is gorgeous.

Totally. I think, but I keep that thought to myself.

OK if you want to you can step into her body now. Tell me what she is feeling.

A few moments pass then she responds, perplexed....

Well, you would think she would be happy it's obviously her birthday or something, and everyone is so happy for her, but she feels anxious and sad.

How does her body feel? Another long pause.

It is completely numb, I can't feel a thing. She is chewing something that deadens all physical sensations.

OK, just as I suspected. My client is in for a rather unpleasant surprise. I have been in similar situations many times before so I am prepared for what is coming. It may not be pleasant for my client, but if she follows my advice she will be able to break a pattern that has been dogging her for almost forty years.

Every other therapist she had seen (and there have been many) was looking for the cause of her low self esteem in her childhood or early life, I knew it went much further back than that. Today she has an opportunity to change everything, but she will need to be very brave.

We are climbing the steps of the great pyramid and above us at the top stands the high priest and his assistants, they look totally awesome. They stand straight and proud, and they look towards my client with much love and gratitude.

She is being helped by other semi-naked young women as she stands next to a large slab of stone and they gently lay her down. The whole temple faces due east;

silence envelopes us as the priest raises his arms to salute the rising sun; even the monkeys are quiet.

The sky is red now and turning yellow, dawn is close. I do not need to know the ancient language he speaks as he invokes the gods and goddesses of his culture and picks up a large curved blade.

As she lays on the slab and awaits her fate I am relieved that she will feel no physical pain. I ask my client how she feels.

Get me out of here! She screams in my mind. An understandable reaction given the circumstances.

How does the girl feel?

Fucking terrified, what do you think?

It's important you feel exactly what she is feeling now. Tell me what is happening for her, why is she here?

She is a virgin, she has trained for this since birth, it is a great honour to be selected for this role, but she is terrified and knows she shouldn't be. She is supposed to be feeling strong and full of joy so that she can complete her life's work and her job here.

And what is that?

Her job is to leave her body and stay here as guardian spirit. She is to become an umbrella protecting her people and their crops for the next year, until another virgin is sacrificed and the cycle is repeated.

Oh shit. He going to put the knife in my chest, thank God I can't feel it.

The sun breaks the horizon in a blaze of gold illuminating the very top of the great stone structure first. As it moves downward towards the slab, the priest, with great deliberation and ceremony, opens her chest with his razor sharp knife.

The people gasp as he pulls out her still beating heart and offers it to the rising sun. They are not shocked by his act, they have seen it many times. It has happened every year since they played as children at the foot of the towering pyramid.

What they are shocked about is the way her body resists his actions and the scream of absolute terror that leaves her lips and echoes around the valley, as her still beating heart is held before her.

This is not as it should be. There is consternation amongst the crowd. Every shred of joy has evaporated like the early morning mist. It has been replaced by apprehension, fear and confusion.

How could she let us down like this? Their group thought-forms are unanimous.

People start crying, fearing the bad crops and famine that will inevitably follow this major catastrophe. Picking up the immediate change in energy the children follow suit and soon the scene looks like a serious disaster has just happened, which it has.

This ancient culture runs on ceremony. Their priests and priestesses have a very good and workable understanding of the afterlife and how to navigate it. The lack of a conscious, overseeing, trained spirit will be dire. For the first time in his life the high priest is dumbfounded.

My client is now experiencing everything her past life self is going through on a very emotional level and I know she will be sobbing loudly and uncontrollably, in my session room above my crystal shop back in the twenty-first century. I prefer to keep the sobbing to the minimum.

What are you feeling now? Through her sobs she telepaths.

Fear... despair... great sadness... unworthiness. I have failed my family, my community and my teachers, and they know it. I feel totally shit-house. I am an utter failure.

Do you recognise this feeling?

Ooh yeah. I sure do.

Are you ready to be free of it?

Absolutely.

OK, step out of her body and stand next to me.

As she steps out and stands next to me the chaotic scene around us fades into washed out colours, sounds and smells and for the moment it continues.

Call on your family, teachers and community from that time, ask them to stand before us now.

As she does so, we move into no time-space. We could be in a large hall or open field, there are many people here.

Repeat after me... Across time and space, of my own free will, in full consciousness, as the Universe is my witness, I humbly beg your forgiveness, Please forgive me for letting you down.

The response is immediate and conclusive, waves of love and forgiveness wash over us both. Even I start to feel a bit teary.

My client breaks down again.

Thank them and tell them they can go in peace.

She does and they fade away. My client turns to me and sobbing, thanks me with all her heart.

Not quite done, now it's time to forgive yourself. Are you ready to do that?

She agrees and I give her the appropriate affirmations. In forgiving herself she finally releases herself from the trauma in this past life and its affect on her present life. This is the breakthrough I was hoping for when she booked her session and briefed me over the phone a few days earlier.

After taking her through cleansing and purification exercises we return to our bodies in the twenty-first century. She is exhausted and still sobbing, I pass her a tissue as she sits up and I move her away from the mandala of crystals that surround us. I give her a grounding stone to hold, it will help her consciousness return completely to this time-space.

If I leave her sitting in the mandala it will take longer to get her back into her body. It takes her a while to calm down. I have a tendency to appear curt with clients, it's not that I don't care about them, it's just that I don't think it serves anyone to get stuck in the emotions that their session has brought up.

If things are released they are released, time to move on. My debrief is short and sweet.

"You understand what happened there and how this will affect your life now?"

"I do... How did you do that. How did you take me there."

"Actually, you took us there I just created a space where it could happen safely."

"That was utterly amazing. I am totally lost for words. How can I ever repay you."

At this point another person might ask for a substantial amount of money and I must admit sometimes I am tempted, but I am mindful of my Karma.

"Just pay the standard fee to my assistant downstairs."

"I want to do more, really."

"Buy yourself a few crystals downstairs if you like, or better still, give some money to your favourite charity or do some community service."

She undertakes to do all three and leaves. I thank the team of loving spirits who work with me and clear the space in readiness for my next client.

A minister of religion has approached me to help him unravel a repeat pattern in his life. By the sound of things I suspect we will be headed for a showdown in Ancient Egypt. They were a very smart crew in that time-space without a doubt, Master magicians each and every one, or so it seems to me whenever I visit. I sense it will be a complex case, but hopefully not too noisy.

I wonder what his congregation would think is they knew he was seeing someone like me. None of my business I suppose, just a passing thought. I am already looking forward to my swim at the end of the day.

Sex and Death

I arrive at my inner city shop on my pushbike, totally windswept and disheveled. It seems like any other day as I prepare for work in my practice as a twenty-first century urban shaman. The shop is bright and fresh. I visit my upstairs session room which is clear, the crystals in my mandala clean and sparkling and unusually, when I return, both my assistants are present. They look particularly resplendent in their matching bleached blonde dreads and as always they look ready to party. The perennial thought drifts through my subconscious as I greet them - how do they always manage to look so cool?

I sense an unusual air of excitement in their demeanour this morning, something is out of the ordinary, they do not normally show up as a matching pair and rarely wearing so much extra glitter. I am bemused and intrigued. I am not sure what could be causing this double flurry of excitement, it certainly is not my flushed and scruffy appearance.

"Why don't you make more of an effort to look like a shaman?"

Bryony, the sharper of the two asks as Briana smiles behind her. She should know by now that I like to be inconspicuous, one of the reasons I left my dreads on the barbershop floor a few years ago. I sense some irony in her question as she already knows the answer.

"Shamans come in all shapes and sizes and I don't like clichés," I respond starting towards the stairs to my session room and inner temple.

"Aw c'mon, you could a least wear a fancy hat!"

"With a feather!" Briana laughs.

"Yeah, sure. Who is my first client?"

"Her name is Mo, no one special."

They giggle like two school girls and I know something is up, but can't be bothered to give it any energy.

"Well, send her straight up, I'll be waiting for her."

Mo is ushered into my room with both my assistants elbowing each other to open the door for her. She is an athletic looking middle aged woman, fit and lean, she must have been an absolute stunner a few years ago. I sit down with her for a brief chat before our session as my two assistants fall over each other leaving my small sacred space.

Mo's story is an unusual one, in recent years she has become interested in the occult arts, particularly astrology. Her studies led her into a deeper understanding of Chiron the wounded healer, a being she felt a great affinity with. She tells me that whilst meditating on Chiron he appeared before her in the room and proceeded to seduce her, making passionate love to her, bringing her to several intense full body orgasms.

This happened twice over a period weeks and she enjoyed it enormously. Her challenge is that since that time, several months ago she has been feeling drained and tired. She confides that she also has a compulsion to masturbate. Something she mimics onstage, but rarely found the need to do for real.

"What are you, an exotic dancer?" I ask.

"More cabaret," she smiles "song and dance."

"OK we will look into it, but with any first Crystal Dreaming session we need to let the process take its course, there may be other things we need to deal with first."

"That's fine by me, lets do it!"

We lie in the crystal mandala together and I make the appropriate affirmations. We close our eyes, the crystals do their work and immediately we find ourselves in another time and place.

This is cool.

Mo telepaths as we stand together in a busy market square, there is an air of excitement, prior to some special event.

We are time traveling, they cannot see us. Let's wait and see what happens, we are here for a reason. For now just soak up the vibe.

I telepath Mo.

I am!

Her eyes are popping as she looks around, absorbing the sights, sounds and strange smells that surround us. We breathe in a mixture of animal and human excrement, stale sweat and unwashed clothes mixed and other, now mostly defunct, aromas.

We are somewhere in Europe, in a cobbled town square hundreds of years in the past. A woman is being dragged across the square in front of a jeering crowd, by men wearing steel hats. Mo realises it is herself in a past incarnation.

This is all new for Mo, but for me it is almost a cliche. I have witnessed similar scenes, with many other clients. Human beings can be very cruel to one another and many healers rediscovering their path now, remember experiences like this.

The woman being dragged across the town square is in bad shape, she is bruised, battered and bleeding. She has obviously been tortured, probably raped. There are bloody gaps in her mouth where teeth used to be, she is missing fingernails and she has been branded. Her clothes are in tatters and she looks totally exhausted, but there is defiance in her eyes.

The soldiers are pulling her towards a high stake with chains surrounded by faggots of wood, with more bundles off to one side.

"Confess!" the crowd yells at her.

"Witch... Enchanter... Heretic!" they are whipping themselves into a frenzy.

A podgy, pious and grubby looking priest bends over her, his loose flaccid skin hanging off his anaemic face.

"Accept the Christ and the Catholic Church as your one true saviour or face the fire of eternal damnation." His foul breath suffocates her as she stares back up at him.

"Never!" She spits blood as they drag her and chain her high on the post, which will be her last resting place.

The crowd cheers as they set light to the bundles of wood around her feet and her death is agonising. I know Mo will be feeling the hot smoke scorching her airways and lungs as her skin blisters and she tries in vain to stifle her final screams. She coughs and chokes, it is not a good death.

I am ready for her as she leaves her body.

I hate the Catholic Church! I hate it! I did no wrong, I was a healer, herbalist, and midwife. I helped others. The priests were scared of my light. That was it, scared of my light...

OK its over now, its over.

It takes me some time to help her realise that if she wants to be pain and trauma free then forgiving the Catholic Church is her only option. We also dissolve any affirmations she made at the moment of her death regarding never using her power as a healer, ever again.

I always wondered why I never trusted Catholics, and I come from a Catholic family!

She is regaining her composure.

I take her into no time space and ask her to be still, I sense there is more. I lead her in the following affirmation:

I challenge any being that is under the illusion that it has power over me, show yourself to me now or forever hold your peace!

I feel a surreptitious and furtive male presence in the shadows around us.

Don't be afraid, we promise not to hurt you.

He steps forward into the light that Mo and I are generating.

I see a young man in his prime, he is dressed in the kind of work gear worn by tradesmen on building sites, although his shorts are very short, by modern standards. He looks very sheepish, I wonder how he appears to Mo.

OK mate, what are you doing here?

Just hangin... He telepaths looking even more uncomfortable.

What year is it? I ask, knowing he will be stuck in the year he died.

1973, he responds.

You realise you're dead?

Yeah I guess so, some idiot sparky left the power on and I copped it, big time.

Who are you and where are you from?

My name's Ron. I'm a plumber from Bondi.

And what are you doing here Ron?

No harm mate, just hangin'.

Confused dead people are always looking for a comfortable place to hang out. They need permission, a contract or agreement given by the host, for this the most common form of spirit attachment, to take place.

I want to help Mo understand what has happened but I suspect the knowledge will not be very palatable for her.

Who is this dude? And how did he get here? Mo is not impressed.

You are about to find out. Repeat after me:

Body I command you show me the moment I gave permission for this man to be here. Show me now!

As I suspected we find ourselves back at Mo's well appointed pad, some time in the recent past. It is late at night and she has been studying. Astrological charts and books surround her on her soft leather settee. She is obviously tired and lies back closing her eyes. A naturally relaxed and sensual woman, she runs her tongue across her open lips as she thinks to herself...

Chiron, what kind of man were you?

Our friend the plumber drifts into the room through the open window and stands before her, he appears naked.

You called me and I am here, he telepaths. *Do you want me?*

In her half waking trance state she sees him clearly, not only is he in great shape, he is a big man in every sense of the word. His long sun-bleached hair falls in loose curls onto his broad muscular suntanned shoulders. To me he looks every inch the Bondi surfer.

I thought you were a centaur? she telepaths vaguely.

I am Chiron. The centaur thing is just a myth. You can see why. He responds looking down, with a cheeky grin.

I certainly can... Mo's eyes widen.

Not sure whether she is dreaming or waking, she allows him to kiss and caress her, before long she too is aroused. They make intense and passionate love. Mo's orgasms build one on top of another into a noisy and explosive crescendo.

*Mind if I stick around? h*e telepaths as she drifts into a deep and timeless sleep. She responds, vaguely, barely aware of her thoughts.

Sure, why not, that was great.

So the contract is issued and their relationship begins.

I can see by scanning the time-space around us that he visited her a few more times than she mentioned. What Mo doesn't yet understand is that through this Earthbound spirit's attachment to her, he can experience everything that she does, hence his creation of her impulse to masturbate, by influencing her emotions. He is fascinated by the female experience of something he had only experienced as a male. However, his parasitic nature is also draining her of energy, hence her tiredness.

Mo is realising this almost as quickly as I am, although for her it is a complete and utter surprise. She is very annoyed.

You arsehole! Lying bastard. The abuse that follows pours out in a mixture of Italian and French, but we get the drift.

Our plumber looks crestfallen. He is genuinely embarrassed and remorseful.

OK Mo calm down, you're not helping matters. This guy is an idiot but he did not mean to hurt anyone.

Fuck-wit.

We need to release him, so he can go home to unity consciousness. You can dissolve the contract by forgiving him and giving him permission to leave.

She takes some persuading but sees the sense in it. I ensure that he returns home to light and we wrap up the session by checking and cleansing her energy bodies, verifying she is clear and free from all attachments.

We return to the physical, she is refreshed and relaxed.

"Was all that for real?" she asks.

"Did it feel real?"

"Well…"

"How do you feel now?"

"Really good, thanks."

"See how you go, I expect you will be having lots more energy after this session and the compulsion you mentioned earlier will disappear."

"No kidding," she responds with just a hint of sarcasm.

"Let me know, if this is not the case."

"Sure." She thanks me and I show her the door asking her to pay my assistants, downstairs.

I cleanse the crystals she has touched, open a window and break the pattern of my crystal Mandala before following her downstairs.

Both assistants are waving and staring goggle eyed at a long white limo as it pulls away, presumably with Mo in it.

"Did you find the plumber?" They both giggle conspiratorially as they turn towards me.

"You know it's bad practice to probe too deeply into a client before a session," I reprimand.

"It was so..oo obvious. You got him?"

"Of course."

"Hey, there must be a bob or two in song and dance," I muse looking after the disappearing limo.

"You really have no idea who that was, do you?" They are both now looking at each other in disbelief.

"A singer?" I respond lamely.

"Don't tell us..." they laugh, "in your world there are only two kinds of music, Country and Western. Right?"

"Wrong! There is only one kind of music. Classic Rock!" I grin giving my best Jimi Hendrix air guitar demonstration.

My two assistants think I have just cracked the funniest joke in the known Universe, when in fact, I am being quite serious. The hysterical laughter, tears and runny mascara that ensue are somewhat of a mystery to me.

Spirit Guide

My assistants finish briefing me about my next client as she arrives. Nina is a well-known environmental activist who has been very public about the inspiration she receives from her spirit guide. He is a Native American who has motivated her to become a spokeswoman for the planet and the environment. She has come to see me because she feels, at the age of 65, that it is time to deal with her lifelong fear of water. She is unable to shower or have a bath let alone go anywhere near the sea.

Nina enters my crystal shop and my assistants make a fuss of her, their usual ebullience is tempered by respect and even deference, something I have never seen in either of them before. I can see that while Nina carries herself well but she also looks tired to the point of exhaustion, something I do not expect to see in someone who is working for Spirit from higher guidance.

Spiritual growth often leads to a sense of peace and detachment, insomuch as many of the challenges we perceive in this three-dimensional reality are revealed as fear based illusions. This does not mean that we do not engage in this reality and support the causes that we believe in. What it does mean is that the dramas attached to such activities no longer affect us. This woman looks quite affected by her work and I feel for her.

Prior to our shamanic journey together, Nina explains that she has tried many ways of overcoming her lifelong phobia but none has succeeded. Describing her spirit guide Bald Eagle, she recalls connecting with him in a workshop over twenty-five years ago. He has been guiding her ever since. He is passionate about the environment and is a great motivator for her. I expect that we will encounter him on our journey so it's useful for me to know a little about him. Already I feel uneasy.

Surrounded by crystals we embark on our journey. Unusually, she guides me and I allow it, intrigued by what might happen. We find ourselves in the bush at dusk, the smell of fresh woodsmoke drifts past us as we walk towards a small campfire next to a teepee. A man is sitting by the fire waiting for us: Bald Eagle is a fine looking man at the peak of his prowess, mature and strong. He is surprised to see me.

> *Who is this?* He telepaths. *Is he dreaming? Does he know where he is?*
>
> *He is not dreaming* she responds *he is in a trance with me and we are both fully aware. He says he can help with my fear of water.*
>
> *I have told you that it is not safe for you to look into this. It is best that you just learn to live with it.*
>
> *I know, but I'm sick and tired of it and I'm prepared to face any challenge to be free of it.*
>
> *You should not bring this man here, this is our sacred space.*
>
> *I thought you would be pleased to meet him, he is a shaman.*

He does not dress like one. Where are his badges of office? His totems? His tools? What ceremony has he done to bring you here?

It doesn't work that way these days, it's much simpler in the 21st-century.

Ha!

He does not seem impressed by this idea, but tolerates my presence. We sit next to him in the soft warming glow of the campfire.

How is our work with our Earth Mother going? It is important that you persist, tell me what has been happening.

They discuss her work and through his questions I become aware that he is leading her to do what he thinks is best. This is not the role of a spirit guide. Spirit guides are evolved beings that have returned to the Source. They are no longer attached to outcomes on Earth and surrender completely to the perfection of everyone's choices here.

They are able to do this because after death the fear-based illusion of separation we experience in a body dissolves. We become one with everything and everything is perfect. Bald Eagle however seems to be very attached to outcomes.

I find myself in a dilemma, I cannot proceed any further with this healing if this man is not her spirit guide. I need to ask a few questions, I wait for a suitable pause in the conversation.

Do you mind if I ask a few questions?

I sense he knows what's coming and is not happy, but does not want to lose face in front of his friend.

Tell me how you died.

His face creases with a pained expression. A battle, a painful, unnecessary, untimely death. I was in my power. I was not ready to leave, I had just dedicated my life to honouring the Earth Mother.

And where did you go after you left your body?

I stayed here of course! My work is not finished, there is so much to do. I can see that your people do not love the Earth Mother, they treat her with great disrespect. It will bring calamity, you must respect her as I do. She is losing her patience.

So, you did not return to your ancestors?

No, I did not, I'm not ready yet, they can wait.

Tell me, do you love this woman unconditionally?

I am her guide and teacher.

Do you love her unconditionally?

Together we honour the Earth Mother and bring peace.

Do you love her unconditionally?

What business is it of yours who I love?

He stands and faces me, a weapon in his hand.

If you do not love her unconditionally it is not appropriate that you act as her guide.

Just a minute. Nina intercedes *What's going on here? This is my spirit guide he has been helping me for many years.*

I'm afraid he is not your guide. He an Earthbound spirit who attached himself to you twenty five years ago, because you were looking for someone like him. You do have a great deal in common, but he has his own agenda.

I can see that Bald Eagle is getting agitated but he also looks quite sheepish.

Is this true? Are you my true spirit guide?

Silence.

It is appropriate that you two part company. His presence is interfering with access to your true guides. I cannot help you release your fear of water as long as he is here.

She becomes both angry and sad, I can see tears welling in her eyes.

Is all this true?

Together we are helping to restore balance. Our work honours the Earth Mother, we are helping her. You asked for a guide. I came.

But your love for me is not unconditional.

No, I never said it was.

I intercede. *You know you cannot stay here without her permission. It is time for you to leave.*

They talk and embrace. I call three times on his ancestors. They arrive immediately and are overjoyed he has chosen to leave with them, they thank me and depart.

Nina's face is a picture of confusion and despair. *What the fuck I have been doing with my life?*

Good work. But perhaps your focus will change a little after this session.

Damn right it will.

I give Nina time to compose herself and then lead her in the affirmation that will reveal why she is terrified of water.

Body I command you show me the moment with this fear started. Take me there and show me now.

We are walking next to a young girl dressed in the clothing of the early 20th century, her arms are covered and she wearing a long full dress. She looks hot even though it is quite a cool spring morning. We are in the thick of the hustle and bustle of a busy dockside and she is with her parents about to embark a huge ship. Everyone is excited.

We are both totally immersed in the alien atmosphere of another time and place. Cigar smoke, perfume, petrol fumes, sweat, horse manure and the all pervading smell of soot, emanating from the massive coal fired furnaces under the four red and black funnels of the great ship beside us. I hear Southern English accents amongst the watching crowd.

I try not to lead her. *Can you see the name of the ship?*

She can't but I can, and the pit of my stomach churns as gaze up at the rear of the ship. From where we are I see part of the port of manufacture Liverp... And above that the first four letters of the great ships name.

I realise that to be totally free of her phobia she will have to experience then surrender to the perfection of her own death. Death by drowning, in the arms of her parents, trapped in their cabin below decks, on the sinking Titanic.

Alien Abduction

What did he mean sky-devils?

My client Nadia telepaths as we take our leave of a helpful old Alchemist from a past life. We are on a shamanic journey and are in no time-space.

Rather than explain, I suggest she tells her body to show her when the crystal we have just discovered inside her body, was placed there.

Body I command you, show me the moment this crystal was placed here. Now!

Immediately we are in that moment and just as quickly my client starts screaming.

I do not have to ask do you recognise anyone because she sees herself as she is in this present life, but she looks a little younger. She has immediately stepped straight into her own body. She is in a cold sterile place on a shiny operating table. She is being pinned down by restraints on her wrists and ankles and small grey humanoid creatures with large dark eyes are probing, testing and opening her body, without any regard for her feelings.

I see them removing, then inserting something into the centre of her torso, she is barely aware of what is happening as she is in so much physical and emotional pain. I know she will want to know more later and I am already reluctant to take her there. However my priority now is to remove the crystal from her body so that she can be free of its influence and can, hopefully, stop screaming...

Nadia has been referred to me for a shamanic journey by another therapist who has been unable to get to the bottom of her behaviour during meditation classes. Keen to grow spiritually, she has been attending classes but has found whenever everyone else in the class enters a deep meditative state, her body involuntarily twists and contorts, her back arches and she is unable to relax. It has got to the point when she is too embarrassed to go to class but does not want to give up, so she has sought help from a healer.

After a brief interview we lie down inside the mandala of crystals which help us easily enter an expanded state of consciousness. Once she is in an altered state of consciousness I suggest she scan her own body as if she has CAT-scan or X-ray eyes. She is surprised by just how much she can perceive if she allows it.

Nadia is able to see straight through her body and perceive the energies surrounding it, our aim is to pick up anything that should not be there. We are looking for anything that looks unusual or uncomfortable, energies that are a natural part of her well-being will not show up during this process.

There is a long list of interesting phenomenon to be uncovered, a list that only my students and apprentices are aware of. In this process it is important that the client sees what they need to see, not what we see. The energy that is most damaging to the client's well-being usually presents itself first.

Nadia is a bit of a New Age fairy and she is delighted when amongst other things, in the heart chakra in the centre of the chest she discovers the most exquisite sparkling jewel-like crystal.

In her world, all crystals are positive, cool and groovy. In mine unfortunately, they may not be, depending on who put them there and why. We must find these things out.

Nadia is so enamoured with its sparkling beauty that she has no idea that it may not be there for her divine highest good. I ask would she like to find out more about the crystal and she agrees. Knowing that our body holds the record of all our experiences, everywhere, I telepath her the following affirmation:

Body I command you, show me the moment this crystal was placed here. Show me now!

We are standing in a dusty, dimly lit room in an old-style castle which appears to be relatively new. I can sense that Nadia is perplexed thinking perhaps we are on a movie set, I encourage her to explore her surroundings as I step back into the shadows. We walk from room to room through what looks like a primitive science lab with parchment scrolls, strange looking pans, bottles full of plants and other strange substances suspended in murky liquids.

A young boy is busy tidying up the place, putting these relics into some kind of order, we can sense his excitement. An elderly gentleman enters the room. A little stooped and tired looking, he looks like an archetypal magician. His rich purple blue robes are impressive though a little threadbare and long white beard is magnificent if a tad unkempt.

He is a man just past his prime, still in his power but aware that his time on this planet is getting short. His stern looking face and gruff demeanour hide a tenderness for the boy that is apparent in his eyes when the boy's back is turned.

Do you recognise anyone?

I telepath, trying not to lead Nadia into a realisation that is terribly obvious to me.

What do you mean? How would I know anyone here?

Feel their energy, does anyone's energy feel familiar?

It's the boy! It's me, I am the boy!

Her surprise and excitement are touching.

Let's see what happens next.

The old man leads the boy through a series of tests. The lad is a bright spark and answers all the riddles put to him easily. He is enjoying both the test and the fact that his answers are pleasing his teacher. The quiz goes on and gets steadily more difficult and complex as the teacher rigs up elaborate contraptions, watching the boy mix potions and create magic, using herbs, crystals and invocations.

Spirit World

Nadia is awestruck at her own past life knowledge and enthusiasm. We are about to arrive at the key moment in her recall.

The old man is explaining to the open hearted and naive boy that his apprenticeship is almost complete, and he will soon be ready to go out into the world and share his abilities with others, under the distant supervision of his teacher. He explains, that not everyone will appreciate his work and that some people may attempt to harm him, through jealousy or fear. He offers to give him protection and produces a magnificent crystal which, to the boy, appears very real.

We can see that it isn't. It is a projection, a thought-form conjured up by the old wizard to impress the boy. Whilst it may not be a "real' three dimensional crystal, all of its powers and programming are.

The boy's eyes widen as he accepts the gift and the old Adept gently pushes it straight into the centre of his chest. There is much more we could explore, the boy's life journey, the esteem he gains in his community as a great herbalist and healer, and the deep mutual respect he and his teacher have for each other as the boy grows into a man and the old man ages and passes on. However, we have seen enough.

I take my client into no time-space and suggest she call on the old Alchemist and ask him to join us.

Across time and space I call on my old teacher, I call on my old teacher, I call on my old teacher, please join us now.

The old man appears and as he approaches, Nadia starts to cry. Feeling the depth of their connection as they embrace, I give them space.

Ask if the crystal still serves you now.

No, he meant to remove it but could never bring himself to do so, he would love to take it back now, he knows it should no longer be here.

Give him permission to take it. Ask how its removal will affect you.

I will not have his protection but I am strong. Things are different now and it is time for me to be free of his influence.

The crystal is removed. I ensure Nadia fills the space where the crystal was, with unconditional love.

Thank him and tell him he can go in peace, your relationship is complete.

The old Mage telepaths me.

Thank you my friend, I have been wanting to do this for some time. You have done us both a great service, I can be at peace now. I sense you are aware of the other crystal, it seems to me you have enough power to deal with the sky-devils who put it there. Good luck.

He embraces Nadia and leaves, dissolving into light. I am pleased things have gone so smoothly. I know part of this journey is about my client accessing her innate healing abilities. No lifetime is wasted and she can reactivate these skills when she is ready, they will manifest as intuitive knowing.

I know that the next crystal, which I have already seen, may not have such a happy ending.

What did he mean, sky-devils? Nadia asks.

I suggest she scan her body again and this time she perceives the second crystal in her womb. She makes the appropriate affirmation and then the screaming starts...

Right now I must remove the crystal. It is not a positive influence, it was not placed there with her conscious permission or with unconditional love...

I suggest she step out of her body and into no time-space. Out of her body her experience will be less intense and she should be able to stabilise her emotions.

Are you ready to call on the beings who placed this crystal here?

She looks nervous.

The best way to deal with this is to reclaim your power and have them remove it.

She does not look confident. She knows I am talking sense but is still fearful, eventually she agrees.

Across time and space I call on the beings who placed this crystal here, I call on the beings who placed this crystal here, I call on the beings who placed this crystal here. Please stand before me now.

Three small blue-grey beings appear in front of us, their energy is cold. They are like the green ETs with large, dark almond shaped eyes that you see on popular T shirts, except these are grey. They are about 1.5 metres tall and have shiny skin, I have dealt with them and their kind, many times.

They have no emotions and care nothing for a person's feelings, on any level. We start the process of removal, which could take time.

I telepath Nadia the following affirmation:

You do not have my permission to leave this crystal here, you must remove it now.

The ETs stonewall her. They are not aggressive or threatening, just cold and neutral. They do not respond.

By the Law of Grace and Decree of Victory I command you to remove this crystal. NOW!

Still no response. It was worth a try, it works sometimes.

I call on your superiors, please be here now.

Now we are in business, their controllers arrive. Tall Nordic types, quite different from the little ones, they have the air of studious scientists, their energy is less cold, but not what you might call heartwarming.

Spirit World

You do not have my permission to leave this device inside my body. This is a free will zone and you know it. It is not possible to leave this crystal here without my conscious consent. Please remove it now.

There is a huddle and a discussion, I can tell they are not used to a mere human being aware of their rights. I also know that they must respect them.

They turn towards us, there is no apology or further discussion, they simply remove the crystal and start to leave.

I advise the following affirmation before they leave.

You may not return without my conscious written permission. So be it.

We ensure the area where the crystal was embedded is cleansed and repaired. Nadia concludes that the device was there to stop her meditating, remembering her abduction and the tests they carried out on her body. I do not disabuse her of that thought as it is partially true.

When we return to the physical, she tells me that coincidentally, several years ago she became unexpectedly pregnant. After a full medical examination she was told she could look forward to a healthy baby within the usual term. Several months passed and she woke up one morning and the baby in her womb was gone. There was no trace of it. She consulted her doctor only to be told that it was a phantom pregnancy.

I decide to end our discussion here and reassure her that now that the etheric crystal has been removed, she will be able to meditate. I call on my assistant Bryony to take Nadia downstairs for a cup of tea and some TLC. Bryony can tell, by the absence of my usual abrupt manner, that she needs extra support.

I hope that Nadia will not pursue the matter further. I could easily take her to an earlier recall, where she would see that the pregnancy was not phantom and was not created in the usual way, by human to human interaction.

It makes my skin crawl to think of what may have happened to the hybrid embryo, whether it is alive now and if it is, what kind of life it leads, in a totally loveless environment. I understand that in cosmic terms everything is perfect, however sometimes it's hard to surrender to the perfection of this sector of the Universe, but I try.

Haunted

I am being driven down a country road at high speed when without any warning my driver drops into a deep trance state. With his eyes rolled back and eyelids flickering rapidly I know there is no way he can be seeing the road ahead and further, the hairpin bend that we are about to negotiate.

"I can sense some dead people up ahead, they are stuck. There's been a car accident here, a few years ago. We should help them," he says calmly.

Great I telepath, *Could we not just pull over and deal with this?*

There is no response, I am too close to this third dimensional reality to get through to my friend through telepathy.

"Wayne! Snap out of it mate, you're still driving!" There is no response. I am starting to feel a bit anxious.

I have just a few moments to make a life or death decision, we could be about to find ourselves in the same situation as the people my friend has just sensed. I look at him again and can see only the whites of his eyes, staring blankly at the grey ribbon of road ahead.

I have to act and act now. I reach across to the steering wheel with one hand while the other hovers over the handbrake as I pray I am making the right decision...

I am with my sidekick Wayne, a gifted young trance channel whom I work with occasionally, when the need arises. We are known locally as the Dynamic Duo because of our willingness to tackle any weird spiritual occurrence. Far from being paranormal investigators we are paranormal interlopers. There is nothing to be proven or measured in any remotely scientific way when we work together. We just get out there and do our best to fix whatever it is that is terrifying people.

We have driven across town from my crystal shop and are traveling to a country property where some strange things have been happening. The new owners rang my shop asking for help and we are en route to meet them.

Wayne rocked up at my shop a few years ago; I knew he was coming, as several people had called to tell me a young surfer dude was looking for me. They said he had seen me in a vision and was trying to find me after seeing my photo on brochures and fliers around town.

Wayne was not your standard New Age crystal type, no hippie clothes, no wafting fluffy ideas and none of the conspiratorial arrogance that sometimes comes with blokes who have a little esoteric knowledge. Instead, a young surfer arrived telling me that he'd been dreaming about me and that he and I would be working together.

This kind of proposition happens a fair bit in my line of work, novices get the idea that I will somehow allow them to hang out with me and through osmosis they will pick up skills and knowledge that have taken decades (if not lifetimes) to reacquire. This is possible of course, for a few selected apprentices who have been through rigorous training and initiation with me. But someone straight off the street? Never.

Well, almost never. I agreed to facilitate a Crystal Dreaming session for young Wayne and in his first full shamanic journey with me he displayed great clarity and fearlessness, along with a 'knowing' that comes from extensive past life experience in this field. We talked at length after his session, unusual for me as I like to move clients through and let them figure things out for themselves. I am not keen on co-dependency, which is why I allow people to see me just a few times, and then only after they have experienced a session with one of my apprentices.

I could see the surprise on Briana's face when he left. My assistant, the large blonde, dreadlocked Earth mother, has seen plenty of people pass through my session room, very few get to talk to me at length.

"OK" she says arching her dark eyebrows, "what's so special about that kid? He's barely out of being a grommet."

"Well, for a start he's not as young as he looks, and the boy's got promise. He was clear as a bell, no past life trauma, no attachments and he is totally fearless. I took him there, and he was cool."

She can see I am impressed. "So he wants to work with you?"

"Could be fun," I respond.

She turns, shaking her head and muttering to herself, as she goes off to make us both a cup of tea. She obviously thinks I have lost my marbles. I haven't. Young Wayne has been studying with a variety of teachers since he was in his early teens. He started after some serious poltergeist activity terrified him and his mother. A sure sign, from my perspective, that he had great potential. That kind of thing never happens randomly and always around a gifted one.

He is now in his early twenties and he has had some good teachers. The first of whom came and cleared his house, recognised his potential and took him under his wing.

After a few more sessions together I become confident that he can deal with the most challenging of situations. From time to time I accept jobs outside of my session rooms so occasionally, without training him formally, I invite him along.

The only challenge in working with this young man is that he has it in his head that ours is a god-given gift and we should not charge for our work, only accept donations. Now this is fine if you are a young surfer living in a panel van but not so fine if you have spent many years building up a reputation and a business built on your special skills and profound understanding of a dying art. We reach a compromise, I will deal with the money side of things and he will accept a donation from me, which of course will be half of any fee I negotiate.

Our relationship ends up being that of the classic priest and priestess. He easily and sometimes spontaneously enters a deeply altered state of consciousness. He moves into such a deep state that logical thought is a challenge for him there. In this situation it is best to have the second partner not in an altered state, so that there is one clear and logical thinker in the team. I work with him and through him with tackling whatever it is that is scaring the bejesus out of my clients. I have checked and rechecked his clarity and I am happy to accept whatever he perceives as gospel.

The challenge is that today for various reasons I am not driving and he is. A big mistake when he is primed to deal with the situation at the end of the drive, not one half way through it, as he is doing now...

I am about to take hold of the steering wheel when a deep male voice booms out of Wayne's upper body. It is not his.

"Don't worry about the driving leave that to us." A perfectly enunciated English gentleman is speaking through Wayne as he keeps the car on course with only the whites of his eyes visible.

"Are you sure?" I mumble, by now my hands are trembling as we are almost on the bend and have not decelerated.

"Trust, my friend. Trust," the gent responds.

You must be joking. I think.

"We are not joking, relax. Everything is fine. Wayne is busy right now." The gent is reading my mind.

OK mate, go for it. I telepath. What have I got to loose? Only my life.

What I experience next is barely believable, we take the bend at speed and it is as if we have an all-wheel drive. The rickety, ageing panel van sticks to the road like glue. We get around the bend perfectly and are on the straight and narrow on the other side in the blink of an eye.

A few seconds later there is a gasp from Wayne as he opens his eyes, the car swerves violently.

"Jeez. Am I still driving?" he asks.

"Yeah, mate, sort of," I laugh releasing the tension that has built up in my chest. He pulls over and we both crack up.

It turns out he was able to help the dead family by the roadside, but they needed some persuasion. They thought it was New Year's Eve in 1966 and were really mixed up, after their sudden death. After a little persuasion they responded to Wayne's offer of help and were now safely returned to Unity consciousness.

We have yet to reach our destination, what awaits us there may be more unnerving. The family who rang for help had been having what they described as poltergeist activity around their property and it was freaking them out. They were new owners fresh from the city but they knew it was more than just wind, branches scraping on windows, creaking trees and doors slamming that was keeping them awake at night.

The youngest girl in the family was very sensitive and claimed she had seen a black man with a spear staring through her window into her room. She was frightened of him, although he had not threatened her.

For spirits to interact with the living it takes a great deal of effort and it is more often an intensely angry or misguided dead person out to deliberately frighten the living. They can't pick things up and move them around but they can work with other nature spirits and less evolved beings to create that illusion.

The description I had indicated a spirit or group of spirits with a great deal of willpower and focussed energy. As the black man did not attack the girl or deliberately try to frighten her, I suspected he wanted to communicate urgently, not necessarily harm her or her family. However, sometimes all sorts of other critters show up and invite themselves to the party.

We arrive at the property; it is an old place that the city money has bought into because of its stunning location, right next to a meandering, smooth-flowing river. The house needs work and I can see by the heavy earthmoving equipment that the owners plan to reconstruct the crumbling driveway to create an easier route to the house.

The family are grateful to see us. Sometimes in situations like this I am not really sure what to charge. We are not just helping the family, we are helping other sentient beings too. To a point Wayne is correct, this work is a kind of calling. I ask what I feel is appropriate given the time (and near-death experience) involved in getting here. They agree without hesitation.

Wayne and I walk the property and we both pick up unstable energies in the same area. There is a fantastic old tree between the house and road, it would normally offer shade and tranquility. Today it offers only shade.

"This is it," Wayne says quietly and I agree.

We find a comfortable spot and sit under this magnificent tree. Wayne quickly and easily moves into trance and starts talking.

"I've got a group of local indigenous people here and they are upset. They want to talk to the new custodians of this place."

"Tell them I can speak for them and will pass their message on."

"OK, they agree. They are happy to be talking with us."

"These are the spiritual guardians of this place, the ancestors who have chosen to stay here to look after the land; they are not Earthbound. They say the new driveway will damage the roots of this tree, which is sacred to them, they want it rerouted. It is not respectful."

"That shouldn't be too hard, anything else?"

Wayne gets emotional. "They are showing me what they did here, how much it means to them and how happy they were here. They are a good crew, they mean no harm. They want the family to enjoy the tree and look after it. They would like local indigenous people to be able to come here too."

That part could be a challenge with city folk, I think, but undertake to pass their requests on.

"Are they happy to be at peace with the family if they carry out these requests?"

"No problem. They thank us for talking with them and honour our path as shaman: so few they say; so few."

We take our leave of the indigenous spirits and ensure that the area is clear, then brief the family. They are surprisingly cool with everything and promise to contact the local tribal elders. They offer us refreshments and payment. Studying the young girl's aura I take the liberty of making a suggestion to her parents.

"By the way, might I suggest you keep an eye on your youngest and nurture her abilities. Please don't stifle or deny them. She has great potential."

They are surprised and look at the child, who is slightly embarrassed. I feel they might take that on board too.

After enjoying tea and cakes on their verandah overlooking the river, we take our leave of the family and head off back to the city. I am driving.

Disco Inferno

This other worldly space we are in is so real we could almost be there; our consciousness is, but our bodies are not. I am with my client Dave and we are in a disco. It is a hot, steamy, tropical setting and everyone is partying hard. It is one of those places that cater for your overseas Aussie tourist who just likes to drink, pick up a partner and dance the night away.

It has a vaguely seedy feel, but everyone seems to be happily inebriated so it doesn't really matter to them. Apart from sweat, cheap perfume and beer, I can smell the all pervading underlying odour of two stroke, kero and clove cigarettes. I notice the locals observing the scene, some involved with the party, some tolerant, others less so.

We are in the middle of our shamanic journey together. We have travelled across time and space to this location spontaneously. The thing is, we don't seem to have travelled very far at all.

Dave, does this place feel familiar? I telepath.

He is relaxed, I have already told him that as time travellers we will be invisible to the locals.

No mate. I can guess where we are, but I've never been here. He is soaking up the atmosphere like he is on a fairground ride.

Oh I inadvertently respond, *Right. Are you drawn to anyone in particular?* I am fishing.

I feel a pending dread deep in my gut. Part of me senses what may be about to happen but it does not make sense. I am perplexed because what I fear should just not be possible.

That girl over there, she could be my sister, if I had one.

OK. Go over and step into her body and tell me how it feels.

He steps into the body of a young, attractive but rather shy girl, out for the night with her friends.

Weird man! Like soft and sensitive, she's got no muscles. What's going on inside of her? So emotional. She feels vulnerable, She's thinking about how she looks and what people think of her. I want to look after her. Is she, like, my sister or something?

Sort of. I respond; I am still figuring this one out.

Normally when we travel through time and space there is a good and obvious reason. We do not just arrive on the other side of the world to participate in a drunken party. Usually we find ourselves in a past life, or even on another planet, but this is a new one. We are obviously on Earth in the recent past, within Dave's lifetime but he has never been here and he is not a girl. Something is wrong.

While my client gets up close and personal with his new found girly-ness. I survey the nightclub. Really we could be in any one of hundreds of cheap bars or nightclubs anywhere in the East, I start to relax a little. We could even be in a parallel reality. It is confusing for clients but occasionally this trans-reality trip can happen. But no, Dave would still be here, much as he is now, he would not be experiencing life as a young woman.

What concerns me is that without fail with this type of regression (or whatever we are experiencing) it is trauma that shows up first. Usually I have a handle on it, today I don't - another reason why I am feeling apprehensive.

The drunken Aussie boofhead next to me lifts his overflowing beer from the bar and his mates laugh raucously as he raises it to his lips. The cardboard coaster has stuck to the bottom of the glass and he looks an idiot as he slurps the clear, icy liquid. Playing to the gallery he allows the frothy lager to spill all over his shirt as he knocks it back with gusto. He is choking with laughter and having a fine old time, as the coaster catches the light, I catch my breath. The name of the club is familiar. It is time for us to get out. Now.

Dave its time to step out of her body now. You have experienced enough. We need to move on.

Aw mate! I was just gettin...

His sentence is cut short as the room fills with swirling fireball; beautiful in its own perverse way, it takes on a life of its own and becomes, for a moment, the fiery aspect of Shiva. It is a terrible scene to be in, and I am just a silent witness, Dave is experiencing it as if he was there in person.

He is about to be consumed by the wall of fire racing across the room. He starts sobbing as he realises what is happening to him/her. He experiences fear, anger, extreme physical pain but above all else acute emotional anguish as he comprehends exactly what he is experiencing.

Why me? How could anyone do this to me? I have never hurt anyone, what did I do to deserve this? I am not ready to die here, so far from home!

My worst fears for him are realised. We are in the Sari club in Bali, on October 12, 2002 and I have to get him out before he is scarred for life. This life...

Dave is a new student, a big bull of a guy with a square jaw, big chest and a soft heart. He is a good old fashioned Aussie bloke. He has his mates, he likes a beer, he loves his motorbike and a good laugh. He wasn't taking life too seriously until he was diagnosed with cancer a few years back. Then everything changed.

Having seen his mum go down a rocky, painful and unsuccessful road with chemotherapy, he wasn't too keen on the conventional treatments, so he sought alternatives and found me.

I am always very clear with people who are desperate or have a life threatening health condition. All I can promise is that I will do my best. My aim is to help them get to the root cause of the life threatening condition and understand why it is happening and the choices that led to it.

I would be a fool and a charlatan to promise anything more; I am not in the business of giving people false hope. What I never tell them is that when we do find the original trauma, which is often emotional and not in this lifetime, then we may be able to change things; although sometimes the reasons for a life threatening illness may be deep seated and unchangeable, relating to karma or pre-birth agreements.

Dave had been through this process and he was getting better. Many other people could be doing the same thing but they do not realise that it is possible. The challenge with our present culture is that our medical system just does not recognise this avenue as even a remote possibility.

A person may present to their doctor with repeated physical trauma in the same part of their body, a classic case, from my perspective, of a deeper challenge calling out to be released. It is not too hard to release it with appropriate guidance. Once the original trauma is released the body no longer holds it and therefore it has no need to repeat itself. As a consequence the illness or life threatening disease to which it was connected, also permanently disappears.

In another culture and another time, the shaman would be the first port of call for a sick person. A shamanic journey would be one of the tools used to diagnose, locate and release the cause of the health challenge.

Dave's illness related to a past life incident where a close friend's betrayal led directly to Dave's torture and death. It is not possible to change his experience, but it is possible to change how he feels about it. In one session we were able to remove this past emotional pain and naturally the present illness went with it.

Now in his follow up session, which I thought would be a breeze, we spontaneously find ourselves in Bali experiencing an illogical and painful death in a terrorist attack, not quite the calm session I was expecting. There is obviously another trauma to be dealt with before he can relax and I need to get Dave out of the girl's body before he experiences much more of her pain...

Dave step out of her body now, you don't need to experience any more of this pain.

No response from Dave who is totally there, in agony, in Bali.

Dave now, mate. Step out of her body. Now!

He hears me, realises he can, then steps out of her body and stands next to the dying girl looking down at her. She cannot see him.

Oh mate that was intense. What's going on. Why am I here? He is dazed.

I wish I knew. Keeping that thought to myself I take Dave into no time-space and call on the spirit of the girl from Bali.

She arrives looking fresh and well and I get straight to the point.

Why did you call Dave to the Sari club to experience your death in Bali? What is your relationship?

We are members of the same soul family. Dave and I have agreed on the highest level that he can release the trauma on my behalf during this session. If he agrees to do so now.

So are we, like brother and sister? Dave cuts in.

We are much more than that. On the deepest level Dave, you and I are one. We are part of the same consciousness, having simultaneous incarnations.

Of course. Why didn't I get that? I think to myself. I teach it often enough. I have just never seen a trauma release played out so immediately before.

What, you mean there are more of me running around?

Yes, we are presently also a little boy in Africa and an old woman in Greece. She responds.

Are you cool with releasing the trauma for her and for yourself?

Absolutely.

I take them both through the release process and we part company; the young woman and Dave embrace and she thanks him. She explains that in any future incarnation they will not need to deal with her experience in Bali and the physical illnesses that would come with it.

When Dave returns to his body he sobbing, Bryony comforts him and we debrief. In due course he is escorted out and Bryony returns.

"That was pretty special," Bryony observes, with just a hint of irony.

"That was a classic case of multiple, simultaneous incarnation and trauma release, which I was planning to discuss with you after this session."

I catch Bryony's sharp, dark, hawk-like eyes and they sparkle as she smiles at me, knowing that was not my plan at all.

Templar Knight

It takes me a while to realise where - or perhaps what is more important, when - we are.

I sense immediately that we are in a hot part of southern or eastern Europe, I have been there and it feels right. I stand next to my client Madeleine, we are in a sparsely vegetated area on a rough dirt track. I can tell that she is poor by the stinking rags she wears for clothes. She is now a man, walking beside me in his sweat-stained work clothes, which I suspect are the only clothes he possesses.

He is returning from a day's hard labour and from the way he walks, he is exhausted. He carries in his hand a primitive but well honed sickle, its curved blade swings by his side. It is strange but despite this desolate poverty I sense he somehow loves this place. It is very far removed from the comfortable city life my client experiences now.

We have embarked on a shamanic journey together. Our bodies lie comfortably inside a mandala of crystals in the session room, above my crystal shop, as we explore other realities together.

I look around for clues as to when we might be and I see none. We are returning to this man's home as the sun approaches the end of its slow downward arc towards the horizon. Because my client has stepped spontaneously into this full-body, past-life recall I know that it is likely to be a profound and possibly traumatic experience.

I make no attempt to contact the man who is Madeleine as he cannot see me. Normally Madeleine would be standing next to me witnessing the scene as I am. I would be in telepathic communication with her by now, guiding her through her journey, making suggestions about what she might do next.

Today Madeleine is a man and she is oblivious to my presence and totally involved with her experience in this distant country, probably in the distant past. As a time traveller visiting this time and place, I am invisible to her as I am to anyone in this reality. I have no idea what is coming next.

I hear a disturbance as we approach a small settlement. My disheveled companion's pace quickens as he realises something is amiss. We also smell burning and mixed with the coarse, brutish shouts of men, I hear the cries of a child and the sobbing of a woman.

As we round a small hillock the scene unfolds before us. Still some distance away I see a group of soldiers, some are on horseback. They wear an emblem I recognise and I know the time I am in. The soldiers on foot are involved in the timeless war crimes that seem to accompany undisciplined soldiers wherever they go, whatever century they are in.

I feel my own gut tighten as we approach the scene; the soldiers are so involved with their malicious destruction they do not notice the peasant farmer approach. He is enraged. Without hesitation he races into the thick of it, leaping on the back of a soldier trying to rape his wife. He pulls the rapist's head back and slits his throat with one fluid pass of his razor sharp sickle, which has become an extension of his sinewy body.

Before the soldier even realises what has happened, he is falling to the ground with a surprised and vacant look in his face. Immediately the farmer who is Madeleine turns to another nearby soldier who is about to harm a child and completely decapitates him with one explosive strike of his sickle. The peasant farmer, has become a whirling dervish, a wailing, wiry banshee. He is screaming with rage as he hacks into and drops another, then another of the invading infidels, who are randomly destroying everything he holds dear.

I know this cannot last, he is totally outnumbered and out equipped. In a moment there is space around him as those on foot allow the skilled and well practiced armoured knights on horseback to surround him. It takes a few skilful turns of the knights' horses and he is impaled on their long lances, which pin him to the dirt. They overcome him easily, his rage and sickle are no match for their training and equipment.

The man in charge dismounts. He stands surprisingly short, once he is off his horse and he walks with a pronounced limp. I can see he is a young man, who in our culture might be a fresh university student. He has an intelligence and experience in his eyes that belie his callow looks. I see as he pulls back his chain mail hood that has a broken nose and a deep and livid scar that crosses his forehead and cheek. He is thin but muscular and looks better fed than the peasant he is confronting. He looks at the farmer as if he is the foulest vermin imaginable.

"You! Non believer! Prepare to meet your heathen god." Turning to the soldiers he shouts, "Set fire to that hovel and bring the woman and child over here. This pile of filth can watch them die, before I kill him."

A leering soldier calls out, protesting, in a thickly accented dialect, that the fun was just beginning. His mates laugh at his impudence.

"Enough! Or you will follow him," the knight interrupts.

And so my client watches, as the wife and child of the man she is in this past life are put to the sword, whilst he remains pinned to the ground. I see the look of sadness and love pass between them. Her eyes tell him that this quick death is far better than the lifelong humiliation and defilement by these infidels.

I see the spirits of their dead relatives come for them as they are taken home to light, returning to unity consciousness. Tears well up in the peasant's eyes as he chokes back his emotions. Emotions which I know are being locked into every cell of his being as he approaches his immanent death.

With lances passing through his body pinning him to the ground, he feels his life force slowly ebbing away as he looks up to see this so called knight standing over him.

This knight's soiled, once white surcoat with the symmetrical curved red cross in its centre flaps in the early evening breeze as he straddles my client. He lifts his heavy broadsword above his head and brings it down with one almighty blow, plunging it to the centre of the peasant's chest.

"Die, pagan scum."

The knight takes pleasure in the kill as the soldiers turn their backs on the execution, rummaging through the meagre possessions of the farmer, looking for booty and finding nothing worth keeping.

I am ready as Madeleine leaves the peasant's body. She will be confused. I know she may still be feeling the intense physical pain of the past few minutes' action, but it is the emotional pain which will have scarred her etheric body. Scars which will have been affecting her behaviour every lifetime since this event, around 800 years ago.

I must catch her attention and find out exactly what she is feeling, as this will be the key to the lifelong issue she came to explore with me in this shamanic journey. We are about to discover what it is and how it relates to her life as a conservative primary schoolteacher in the twenty-first century. But first I have to counsel her.

As the peasant's last gasp eases its way out of his aching lungs I see his spirit rise from his body.

Madeleine here! It is me, Raym. I am here, I have been waiting for you. I telepath her.

Madeleine's confusion is apparent as she stares at me blankly.

Wha... Who am I. What am I doing here?

Your name is Madeleine Petra you came to me for a shamanic journey. Your body is in the twenty-first century. You have just experienced your death in the eleventh century. Everything is OK I am here to help you.

My wife, my child! She starts sobbing.

They are OK, they have gone home to light. It is you I am concerned about. How do you feel?

I know this sounds like a silly question but I must get to her core issue while it is still raw and present.

A novice healer or a member of the general public might expect her to be feeling intense fear or even to be totally absorbed by the physical pain she has just experienced, but I have been through this process many times and I know that there is more to it. She is still sobbing.

Madeleine it's OK, everything is OK. Tell me how you feel.

A pause.

That big bloke just killed me! The sobs are subsiding.

I realise from her perspective, pinned to the ground, the short disabled knight would have appeared much larger than he was.

What did I do to deserve that? Jeez, it was a hard life back then, but we were happy. I wasn't harming anyone, what was that all about? I had no idea his kind were even close. I had heard stories but just stories, you know.

You are a school teacher you should know.

Yes of course, the Crusades, but I had no idea they were so brutal to ordinary people.

This is part of the Crusades they do not teach at school. They were allowed raids away from the eyes of the Lords who controlled them. They were taught that their pagan idolatrous enemy were non-Christian scum and sub-human. They could do whatever they liked, out of sight of their superiors. Some things never change.

Madeleine was calmer now.

I want you to get in touch with your feelings at the moment of your death, describe them to me. Remorse? Sadness?

There is a pause

Nope. Intense anger. Rage. How dare they do that to me and my family!? She responds as her present life Greek feistiness comes to the fore.

Now I see clearly the connection with her present life challenge and it is not without irony. She is a devout Christian and a pillar of the local Greek Orthodox church. She has dedicated herself to good local community work and over the past few years has devoted her energies to raising funds for survivors from the wars in Iraq and Afghanistan, with the emphasis on helping women and children.

She had sought help from other therapists and was referred to me. Her challenge as a primary school teacher was her intense and uncontrollable outbursts of anger which erupted in her classroom, terrifying the children she loved to teach. As she aged these outbursts were becoming more intense, a sure sign, from my point of view, that the original issue was ready to be released.

From my perspective releasing this anger is simple, but I suspect from where she is now it may not be quite that easy.

Do you see how this trauma is affecting your life now?

Another pause. I know she knows, but is reluctant to admit it.

Are you ready to be free of this trauma and lead a happy, balanced life?

Absolutely.

OK. I want you to call on the spirits of the knight who killed you and the soldiers who abused and killed your wife and child, say out loud after me... "Across time and space I call on the spirits of the people who killed me and my family, please stand before me now." Repeat it three times out loud.

She does so and I know the assistant in my shop will be relieved to hear it.

The knights and soldiers step forward materialising out of the mists of time. They stand before us looking both humbled and remorseful, their heads are bowed.

Are you ready to do this?

If it stops me screaming at the kids I love, yes I am.

Then repeat after me. Across time and space, of my own free will, in full consciousness, as the universe is my witness, I freely forgive you. Say it out loud please.

She starts this very powerful affirmation but slows down as she gets to the crucial statement.

"*...I freely... fff..., fff... I freely fff... Faaark! YOU FUCKING BASTARDS!*" she shouts out loud.

For a Christian school teacher, this lady's language is getting pretty rich. I hope that there are not too many customers in the crystal shop beneath my session room.

You realise that the only way you can be free of this trauma is to forgive the perpetrators with all your heart?

As I say this the knight and his companions kneel before us.

Are you sure?

I know it's hard, but yes I am sure.

She tries several more times but each time the rage it brings up in her is so intense it prevents her from completing the affirmation.

I am patient, because I know she is on the threshold of a life-transforming breakthrough. I give her the rest of the affirmation so that she really understands where I am leading her:

I forgive you, I forgive you, I forgive you. In forgiving you I release you, as I release myself from this trauma, to find joy peace and freedom. Go in peace. I leave this trauma in the past where it belongs, It no longer affects me, I am free from it, now. So be it.

Finally she summons up the courage to complete the affirmation and she is crying when the final release takes place. The knight and his companions are grateful. They dissolve into unity consciousness bowing, thanking her for their release and honouring her bravery as they do so.

I take Madeleine through the cleansing and healing processes that complete the session and bring her back into her body. We open our eyes, stretch and I pass her a tissue.

"Wow, that was intense," she smiles, still crying, knowing full well that her anger management issues have been completely resolved in this one session.

"I don't know where that language came from, it's not like me at all." She looks a little sheepish.

"Of course not. It was just the intensity of the experience," I respond, taking what she has just told me with just a pinch of Greek sea salt.

Miracle Man

I am taking a breath of fresh air in the quiet and breezy street outside my crystal shop, waiting for my next client. My assistant Bryony had taken the call and booked Shelley in, I have yet to meet her.

Bryony joins me on the pavement, resplendent in her blonde dreads and glad rags. I wonder how my two assistants always manage to look like they are about to have a great night out.

"Sounds like you'll have your hands full with this one" she says grinning. "If she is not too attached to her pain, this could be one of those miracle healing jobs."

"What? The ones we don't tell the authorities about?" I smile back.

Then I see the person who must be Shelley approaching. I know as she walks towards my shop that I am up for a long and interesting session. I see a woman approaching in early middle age, a woman who should be in her prime and full of beans. Instead she shuffles down the street towards me like an ancient and totally decrepit bag-lady. I know from my briefing with Bryony that she dodders along like this because she is in constant and unrelenting pain.

I try not to make sweeping assessments of my clients when we first meet. I prefer to allow the unfolding of their own realisations without even the slightest contamination from my thought forms, but with this woman I just cannot help myself. I see clearly by the way she holds herself that there are several key points in her energy field that are causing her extreme pain. I admire her stoicism, a meeker soul would resort to pain killers, but as Bryony has briefed me, not this lady.

Bryony has told me some of Shelley's story. Believing that the source of these pains is not physical and will therefore not respond to conventional medicine she has tried many alternative therapies to get to the bottom of the issue, with little success. She is at her wits' end and so now has turned to me, her last resort, the twenty-first century shaman.

I read her like an open book and promise myself I will not lead her during our session. A session where we will access altered states of consciousness together, on a journey to discover the truth behind the worsening pain that is slowly destroying her life.

"Have fun!" Bryony disappears into the shop leaving me to greet my client. I know she can read Shelley and what is coming in the session, just as well as I can.

As we slowly climb the stairs to my session room, she tells me her story.

"This started out of the blue a few years ago and its been getting steadily worse. I am so over this pain. Do you really think you can help me?"

I pause, I am mindful not to give desperate people false hope, "My aim is to take you to the source, to discover the moment where it all started. That way I can help you understand why it's happening. After that it's up to you."

"So you don't think it's physical?"

"Well, I bet it certainly feels that way to you right now, but I know that it isn't. That's why you came to see me, isn't it?"

She looks relieved and I can feel she may be about to cry.

"Lets see how we go; I will do my best to help you." I open the door to my compact sacred space, my small inner city temple.

She gasps at the beauty of the complex mandala of crystals laid on the floor around the futon we will occupy for the next few hours. I try to display the stones at their best; I like to honour the beautiful crystals that are my allies.

"I feel light headed," she says swaying over the crystals.

"That's normal, they have already started the process." I help her lie down and quickly take my place next to her.

I must make haste, or she will move ahead of me without my guidance, a potentially dangerous situation. I love ceremony and have become a master of it, but for this client there is no time. The space is already cleared and primed, ready to go. I make a brief invocation and suggest she close her eyes, advice I see is redundant as I glance at her before closing my own.

Floating above her body we scan it together and she sees exactly what I saw when we met. She holds five major energy blockages, each where the pain is most intense. I ask her what she sees, she telepaths me as we work our way down her body.

I see a deep wound in my shoulder and it is bleeding. I see a golden chalice floating in front of my chest. I feel pain in my back and I am pinned to the floor by something very heavy across my knees.

Is that all?

Isn't that enough?

OK let's start at the top and work down. Say out loud after me: "Body I command you, release the cellular memory I am holding in my shoulder, into full consciousness. Now."

Immediately we are in the thick of a bloody and chaotic battle some time in the distant past. She is in the body of a big strapping Native American man who is dealing out death and destruction with a large tomahawk. I wouldn't say he enjoyed what he was doing but this bloke can certainly handle himself. He is a proud and fearless young warrior. It is hot, sweaty, breathless and dirty work, but he is doing well and he has the upper hand. I can see the battle is going in his tribe's favour and it will be over soon.

Spirit World

I have witnessed many skirmishes like this, but the ferocity of these life or death struggles takes your breath away. Ancient warfare was fast, messy, viscous and very personal: Hollywood does not get the half of it.

Shelley is so into the experience of being the warrior that she does not see what is about to happen. In the subsiding melee an older, more muscular man, of the same clan, works his way towards Shelley. In a moment when everyone's focus is elsewhere he plunges a long knife deep into Shelley's back, on the left side, aiming for his heart. He twists it with a warped grin as his pushes the beautiful bone dagger home.

The young warrior is is taken completely by surprise thinking his back was covered by the man who has just stabbed him.

We understand the thought forms that come with the ancient language.

You will never take my position. I am the lead warrior here and I will be for a long time now. Die, upstart!

Shelley is in utter shock and disbelief. The young man that she is, is speechless as his heart falters and his breath comes in gasps. He just looks wide eyed at the older man, his face like a Kabuki mask, a mixture of horror confusion and deep, deep sadness.

I catch her attention as she leaves his body. She is surprisingly coherent.

Oh man, that was such a mean thing to do. I had a lovely wife and baby. I had lots going for me, and boy was I strong. That mean selfish old bastard.

OK, stay calm.

This back left shoulder is exactly where the pain is. What do we do now?

You need to forgive him.

Say what?

You are tied to the trauma through the feelings you experienced then. They are locked into your cellular memory. They have travelled across time and space and are still with you now. They will stay in your body as pain, or even disease, unless you release them by forgiving the old man.

Shit.

Are you up for it?

Well, if it stops this pain, then yes I am.

We call on the old warrior and I take her through the forgiveness process, his murderer is relieved and grateful that he has finally been forgiven, as he was tied to the trauma too.

Unbelievable. I can feel the pain just easing away. What's next?

Keep scanning your body, what did you notice next?

Oh yes that lovely gold chalice, what's that all about? It looks like a gift.

I know better, but I will let her discover this one for herself.

Commanding her body to release the cellular memory she finds herself in the body of a mature and elegant woman of high status. We could be in the time of King Arthur, it looks so mythical; her headgear and the long dress she wears are beautifully made. We both take a moment to admire the intricate embroidery on her gown. Her surrounds are Spartan in some ways, being in a stone building, but they are also spotlessly clean and the furniture is comfortable.

She is lounging on a day bed and it is dusk. A young woman enters, she is dressed in simpler gown, and is very respectful towards Shelley.

"My Lady, I have brought you a glass of wine before supper, if it pleases you."

"Thank you, so thoughtful, my child. Of all the neophytes I have taught, you take most care, you are my best pupil, my finest achievement. You know you just might find yourself being put forward to take my place as high priestess, one day."

The young girl blushes and bows her head. However I see her look up intently as Shelley brings the golden chalice to her lips. Every muscle in the neophyte's body relaxes as the high priestess takes a deep draft of the sweet red wine. She smiles.

"I am ready now, to take the role of high priestess in this order."

Shelley laughs. "Oh my child you must learn patience. Haven't I tau..."

"Tongue feeling heavy?"

An inhuman sound comes from Shelley's slobbering mouth as she tries to speak.

"It is time for fresh blood in this order now. It is rancid with your fetid, outdated rituals and ceremonies. I have direct access to the Goddess and she works through me. Your time is finished."

The pain of betrayal in Shelley's eyes speaks volumes.

"The poison I have prepared is painless, in thanks for your teaching. The paralysis is spreading through your body, from your mouth to your lungs and heart. You will be asleep soon and will never wake up."

The neophyte walks close to the now wide-eyed and panicked high priestess. She lifts up her heavy limbs and rests them in repose, as if the high priestess was having a nap.

"This is how they will find you tomorrow, passed peacefully in your sleep. Thank you for telling others that you saw me as your successor, it has made things so much easier for me. I will be sure nobody disturbs your nap," she smiles and kisses the priestess's forehead. "It's all for the best."

I am ready when Shelley leaves her body, she is a quick learner and is looking for me; she is breathless.

The bitch! What an absolute fu...

No need for that. I interrupt. *What part of your body are you feeling it in?*

My heart. Oh dear me yes. That really hurts.

She does not take too much persuading to go through the forgiveness process. The trauma, and the pain clears immediately.

What's the next thing you noticed?

There is something else, a weight on my stomach or my back.

We command the body to release the cellular memory and immediately Shelley is on a beach. She is a gentleman sailor, in olden days, a military man and an officer, in tight breeches and an open shirt. He lies relaxing, in a warm climate with a young islander boy's head on his chest.

Shelley the sailor runs his fingers through the boy's hair, they are obviously lovers and she talks to him asking him questions.

The sailor is trying to get information from the boy, and has misled the boy into thinking he loves him, so the boy will tell him all he needs to know. Once he has what he needs he cruelly discards the boy, mocking and humiliating him. The boy is totally devastated and runs back to his village.

That evening the boy's extended family visit the sailor and club him to death for the insult to their family's honour. I wait for Shelley and again she is coherent.

Well, that sleaze-bag deserved everything he got. She telepaths.

Where are you feeling the pain?

My back, they broke it.

Releasing this trauma involves Shelley begging for forgiveness from the boy and his family. It is easily given. One last trauma left, and the five traumas I saw will be clear, then we will see how Shelley feels after that. We command she release the memory held in weight that is pressing into on her knees.

Oh this is nice!

I catch her thought forms as she steps into the body of a plump and happy woman in beautiful, sumptuous, colourful clothing. It could be ancient Greece, certainly feels like an island in a warm climate. This woman just loves her family and entertaining, she is having a ball. People come and go, there is happiness, good food and laughter. It's hard to imagine what could spoil such a perfect day.

And then without warning its starts, the terrible rumbling, and it is over just as quickly.

A huge earthquake shakes the structures around them to pieces. Her little boy runs screaming from the building and she heads after him, but she does not get out. A heavy beam falls on her and pins her down as the building disintegrates around her, almost smothering her with rubble. But it does not kill her. She stays alive and conscious for days, pining for her son, wondering when people will come for her.

She shouts till she is hoarse and dehydrated, and then after a couple of days, the rats come.

They nibble away at her living flesh and she is helpless to stop them. She dies screaming for the rats to stop, calling for her husband and son who never came because they too, are dead.

I catch her as she leaves her body still screaming.

Oh that was awful. Poor woman, what a terrible way to die. They were all so happy. It's so sad. She starts sobbing.

Where do you feel the pain?

My knees, for sure, They were shattered.

To release the pain we go through a process of forgiving the rats, the people who did not come to her aid and ask her lovely boy to forgive her for not saving him. As we do so the pain subsides, dissolving completely as the last pain left to clear gently fades away.

I return Shelley to this here and now and after cleansing and protection exercises she opens her eyes.

"How about that?' Shelley breathes blinking and stretching.

"How's your body feeling?"

"Sensational!"

"Any aches and pains?"

"None."

"Try standing up."

She stands and for the first time in many years realises she is totally pain free.

"How did you do that?"

"You did most of the work. You realise that we were releasing emotional, not physical trauma?"

"I got that, yes."

She pays me and thanks me. I follow her as she glides effortlessly down the stairs and through the shop, hugging Bryony, who smiles after her as she literally skips off down the street.

Bryony turns me with a twinkle in her eye, "So miracles do happen then?"

"I am just waiting for someone to declare me a saint."

"Could be a long wait, 'cos nobody's going to be sharing that story with anyone real soon...

Cup of tea?"

Zero Point

I am spinning, traveling at high speed through a wormhole traversing the Time-Space continuum with my client Brad. We travel through a matrix of light, colour and sound. I see lines, patterns and blurred Galaxies whizzing past me, I feel the music of the spheres in every cell of my being. It is an extraordinary adventure, but I am hoping this does not last too much longer as I am beginning to experience motion sickness. The young man next to me appears to be unusually free of fear. We have just embarked on our shamanic journey together and he is having a ball.

Whoah...yee-har!

He telepaths as we spiral down a tube of light, leading god only knows where, because I do not have the faintest idea.

Man this is SOOO cool. His American accent twangs through my mind. *Is this, like, normal? No wonder you're so popular. I had no idea, man.*

Me neither but I keep the thought to myself as I try to figure out what is happening to us and where we are going.

Brad was referred to me by some turned-on friends who sensed he had potential and would respond well to my Crystal Dreaming technique. He is an international student, here to study technology and to enjoy all that this beautiful country has to offer. He had recently started to attend meditation classes and it was there that others noticed his potential and referred him to me. Apart from looking like your all-American, clean cut kid, he does have a light in his eyes which shines a tad brighter than most college kids his age.

Oh dude, this is so much fun. Where are we going?

We are traveling through time and space to an unknown destination.

I respond honestly. I am surprised by how authoritative I sound.

I sense our journey is nearing its end, we are slowing down and the zone outside the wormhole is becoming more stable, even recognisable. Solar systems, planets and stars, all become clearer as we slow to a stop and the hole spits us out into a void.

I have dealt with Demons, misguided ETs and angry entities of all shapes and sizes and so far this session has not gone to any kind of plan, so I am ready for anything. What happens next takes me completely by surprise...

With any client we begin a session by interacting with the spirit world and I act as a bridge for that, so in the truest sense of the word I am a Shaman. We also deal with good and bad spirits, although a more accurate description would be that we interact with love or fear-based non physical beings. There are many to deal with on this and other planes of existence and I have met them all.

However, in my practice there is more than simply dealing with good and evil. What I hope to do is to create the space for a profound expansion of consciousness from this limited reality into the infinite reality of the superconscious. Experiencing this first hand is life changing, it breaks the trance induced by our predominantly fear based reality. When you have experienced the energy that unifies everything, everywhere, you realise on the deepest level that everything else is a temporal illusion. The energy I refer to is unconditional love.

The most aggressive, confused, fear based beings can have no purchase or tenure on, in or around any other being that has woken up to the fact that they and their reality are love based. This realisation may be a challenge for many people living in the twenty-first century, experiencing life in a society that is participating in the powerful illusion of fear. An illusion which is deliberately pumped up, out and into our hearts and minds through the forms of media most are addicted to.

Understanding our limitless being remains a profound concept for many spiritual seekers, theologians and intellectuals. For some this is something to be considered, debated, dissected and theorised. I feel for those people who have yet to be touched by the intense joy of knowing that we are everything and everything is us.

My aim in any session is to reunite my clients with this experience in a tangible, personal and physical way, so that there can be no doubt in their mind ever again that they are never alone, they are loved unconditionally and they are infinitely powerful beings of light, creators of the reality they choose.

However, there is usually a block to this powerful realisation. Some fear based thing, somewhere gets a hold on the client and does its best to prevent this opening to love. As we exit the wormhole I am expecting to find just such a thing and I am not sure what form it will take.

I am wrong.

As we exit the wormhole we are greeted by cheers, laughter and applause, as if we have just completed a marathon. The sense of joy and unconditional love so is overwhelming, we both spontaneously burst into tears.

I have been in this space many times, frequently alone and often with clients but its power always takes me by surprise. Particularly in this case when there have been no obstacles to overcome, no entities to be released and no trauma to be forgiven. I can spend several sessions bringing a client to this point of clarity and self realisation. Accessing this level of bliss can only happen when my client is free of all fear based attachments and free of fear itself, the one thing that keeps us feeling separated from each other and from the Divine.

With so much trauma and pain to be dealt with, blessed and released before my clients reach their final goal of utter and complete bliss, I sometimes lose track of my primary motivation for doing this work. You may think you know what bliss is, the joy of newborn, a lover's kiss, the recognition of workmates or if you are a star, the adulation of your fans. These are all wonderful fragments of the absolute bliss that is open to us all, now.

The level of ecstasy we can reach in an altered state of consciousness when we become one with All There Is, is beyond words. Paling into lesser significance are the three dimensional expressions of the joy we experience as humans. Incidents that become memories that remain as book marks in our life's journey. When we access the all encompassing love that holds the fabric of our Universe together then everything in our reality changes, permanently.

Brad and I are in that place right now and Brad is sobbing with joy. I know my assistant Brianna will be looking in on us at this point, checking on me as she hears the sobs emanating from my tranced and supine body, back in my crystal shop on Earth. Brianna is large, loving and a top class martial artist, it is great to have her around when the going gets weird. I know she will be smiling down at us and will close the door quietly when she leaves.

OK, so we have arrived somewhere and it is safe, there is no doubt about the level of love that surrounds us; it cannot be faked.

Please show yourselves to us and tell us what you want. I am trying to pull myself together.

Namaste dear Raym, thank you so much for bringing him here, we have been waiting.

The light-beings around us form into humanoid shapes out of consideration for our sensibilities. They can appear as anything they wish but they know it will put Brad at ease if they appear human.

My pleasure. I respond. *What is your relationship with Brad?*

We love him dearly and eternally, of course. We are what you might call his family, we are here to remind him why he came to Earth.

I realise my usual questions about whether these beings love Brad unconditionally are redundant. I don't normally speak for my client this much but I sense Brad is still overwhelmed and so I take the lead on his behalf.

Please show or tell us why he incarnated, I think he may have forgotten.

Indeed he has!

The warmth of their laughter caresses us both and it feels like being massaged in a warm steam room, with choice essential oils, by the finest therapists on the planet.

Earth is a complex and intriguing paradigm for the love based non-physical beings who observe our journey here, from other planes of existence. The idea and experience of living in a fear based reality is alien to them. It seems to them that we, its inhabitants, are less than a hair's breadth from experiencing infinite and total bliss. It is both fascinating and a little perplexing to them that we cannot see or feel our proximity to the truth of the Universal unconditional love that surrounds us.

They observe, they do their best to help without interfering too much. Their ethos is that help may be given when it is asked for. And help was asked for, some time ago by the planet herself. Many beings, whose only experience was to hold the vibration of unconditional love, boldly stepped forward to offer themselves as volunteers to incarnate in Earth and share their love, at a time she needed love most.

This group of volunteers arrived in large numbers a few years back, bless them. However, shining your light here on Earth is not quite as easy as it seems from the outside. The vibration of fear here can be intense and it is amplified and manipulated by those who enjoy power over others, for their own temporal and shortsighted purposes.

Some of these naive volunteers find this fear based energy too much and become distressed. They escape into drugs and other ways of not being here and now, as a way of dealing with the pain that surrounds them. Others just escape, full stop. Many of these young people are suiciding now because the level of fear here is so overwhelming for them, that they just can't stand it. When they leave their bodies they discover that there is no sense of failure in abandoning their plans. They tried hard and they are welcomed home to light with much joy. It was a big ask and a big learning curve, I thank you all for trying, your intentions were pure.

Occasionally I come across volunteers who have not succumbed to fear and who, whether they know it or not, are blessed. They are able to access bliss and unity consciousness with ease because they are totally free of fear. Brad falls into this category.

I step back and watch and listen as his team brief him. He is composed now and has a more serious demeanour.

They tell him that he has enrolled in most of the right courses for his mission but they ask him to change streams and options slightly so that he can re-learn what he already knows. His mission here is to quietly bring through new technology that will benefit all of humanity. They tell him he must be careful, the military industrial complex would love to get their hands on the technology he is being downloaded with now.

I watch as streams of hieroglyphic like symbols pour into his body from above. I have seen these light codes before, I have received them myself. They lay dormant on every cell of our being until circumstances initiate the release of the knowledge that they hold. They are triggered by states of bliss and they will not activate or open for fear based technologies.

I hope he takes their advice seriously; I can see that right now he is being given priceless information that could be abused in the wrong hands. He is given a starting project, diagrams, three dimensional developments for a zero point, free energy device he is to build in his spare time as a practice for his abilities.

What is interesting to me as a non-scientist is that I can see from their schematics and explanations that the free energy that the machine utilises is from a nearby dimension. It appears to be limitless and totally pollution free and the components for the device are easy to find. Its mass production and application would totally change the way we live. It would doubtless remove the cause of many conflicts.

Jeez, I could make a mint with that device.

The thought escapes me before I have time to contain it. His team turn towards me.

Sorry just a passing thought. I smile pathetically.

We know you are honourable Raym, but take care. They laugh.

They finish briefing him and thank me again for bringing him.

Not a problem.

I respond, as if I had navigated the journey consciously.

May we ask a favour?

Sure.

We would like you to "keep an eye" on Brad please, teach him and guide him...

Of course, my pleasure.

They smile and the love goes up a notch.

We understand you may need a little assistance with some numbers you have been considering. We suggest you memorise this sequence. Use it wisely.

They give a sequence of seven numbers, which I commit to memory.

OK. Time to return Brad, I think we are all done here.

We say our goodbyes and they escort us back to this Solar system by a smoother and easier route than the one we took to get to them.

I take Brad through my usual post session processes and we return to our bodies.

"Far out! Totally mind-blowing. I can still see, hear and feel them. Will that go on for long?"

"As long as you wish, keep your vibration high. Ease off on the partying."

I am not sure I like the fact that I already sound like his dad. We discuss the session and I reinforce the need for secrecy. I am not totally sure he gets it.

"Hey. I built a machine like the one they showed me at high school. I chased up some Tesla diagrams on the net."

"Did it work?"

"I had to switch it off after six days it was annoying me."

I realise Brad will have few challenges fulfilling his mission and I wish him well.

"Dude, what were the numbers they gave you all about?"

"Oh, nothing special, just some sequences I have been working on."

I escort Brad downstairs and we say goodbye.

"Another bliss session?" Brianna smiles.

"Thanks for looking in on us," I say pulling on my jacket.

"Where are you off to? You have another session in a few minutes."

"Just popping over to the newsagents, won't be long."

Brianna looks at me, contemplating what she sees.

"Got some numbers floating around here. Feeling lucky? It's the jackpot this week, you know." She smiles broadly, opening the door for me.

Sometimes I tire of working with psychics.

Cursed

I sense my client approaching my crystal shop. Scanning the street I notice a young woman who looks like she has just walked out of a Stieg Larsen novel. Her jet black, yellow tipped hair is combed vertically like a coxcomb and matches perfectly her matt black leather jacket, jeans and boots. She has stainless steel studs in her nose, her bottom lip and through her eyebrow. At first glance she does not look the type to be on a spiritual quest, many of my regular clients waft along wearing crystals and long shimmering white dresses, but in my business I have learned it is best not to judge by appearances.

My assistants, resplendent in their blonde dreadlocks, glad rags and glitter, greet her like a long lost sister and are soon totally at home together. They have a knack of making anyone feel welcome and at ease, something I could learn from. They introduce me to our visitor, her name is Nicki.

Upstairs in the peace of my crystal therapy room, we discuss the reasons for her visit. She tells me that she feels her life is stuck. She had a successful business as a fashion designer until her estranged father passed away. From the moment he died everything seemed to go pear shaped. Her business went downhill, she lost clients and she lost her creative drive. She is seeing me out of desperation, she thinks she has been cursed.

"Why would you think that?"

"The old bastard treated his Aboriginal labourers like shit, cheating them out of their pay, giving them squalid little humpies to live in, working them hard and polluting the environment. He didn't give a toss. He had no respect for their culture or their sacred sites.

He was a piece of work. He was a miserable, abusive alcoholic, that's why I got out as soon as I could. None of the locals liked him."

It did not seem fair or logical that this young woman should be cursed for her father's shortcomings but it was the only conclusion she could come to, having tried everything else to fix the chaos that now surrounded her. In desperation she decided to see me, hoping a modern shaman could unravel an old curse.

After briefing her that we would travel together, we lie in the crystal mandala I have prepared, close our eyes and embark on our shamanic journey.

Immediately we find ourselves in the outback, in intense dry heat. The smell of dry gum leaves mixed with clean air permeates our pores. We look for shade and under a nearby tree I notice two aboriginal men. They are in a classic stance, on one leg, spear in one hand supporting them as they stand, one leg lifted and bent, foot resting against the knee of the standing leg. They look cool, calm, collected and as if they are on a mission.

Rather than walk towards them I suggest we walk away from them and see what happens. I know they can only be there if they are attached to Nicki, but I want her to figure that out for herself. Sure enough they follow us at a distance. We allow this for a while until we reach another shady spot when I suggest we stop and wait for them to catch up.

They pause about twenty feet away and wait for us. I suggest that Nicki go over to them and ask them why they're here.

What the fuck do you want? she telepaths.

Too late, I realise I should have briefed her to be more respectful. They do not appreciate being addressed in this manner and take an aggressive stance. Reluctantly I intercede before things get out of hand. I move over quickly and stand next to Nicki. An absurd thought runs through my mind, I should have brought a sunhat.

We are honoured to have your company. But I feel your business here may be complete. You realise you should not be here?

They look bemused.

You have no quarrel with this girl. She respects and honours your culture, she has never damaged any of your sacred places nor would she. You can leave now, you are not bound to her in any way.

A pause.

Who sent you?

Without thinking they respond by sending an image of a very black old man with a snowy white beard and curly white hair.

We have no argument with you, go in peace, return to your ancestors, your service is complete. I will speak with the man who sent you.

They look at each other and decide to leave. So far so good, that part was relatively easy.

Sorry about the language, I was out of line. Nicki telepaths.

Just take a breath before you speak, it's appropriate to be respectful, even if you don't like what's happening. It always buys us time, which is useful.

OK is that it? Are we done?

Not quite... I respond as I notice a willy-willy heading towards us across the dry scrub.

We are about to meet the man who sent them.

Stand behind me.

The wind comes to a stop in front of us; as the dust clears, in its centre is the old, white-haired man we saw earlier. He is not happy.

You fellas, what you doing here? In this place? You not supposed to be here. How come you here? Interfering with my work.

We are here to make peace, this has gone on long enough, this woman is not responsible for her father's actions.

I make this curse, it last a long, long time. It goes father, daughter, grandson. This man, her father, was a bad man. He deserves this.

Maybe HE does. But he's dead now. His offspring do not deserve to be cursed for his actions.

What do you know white fella? Why are you putting your nose in here?

I'm here to help.

I realise from this man's attitude that he is dead but he has not gone home to his ancestors or as we would say "home to light". He is stuck, he is an earthbound spirit, held here by his righteous anger at the way he and his relatives were treated by Nicki's father.

What year is it? I ask knowing that he will be stuck in the year he died.

1982.

Do you realise you're dead?

Pause.

Don't try any tricky white fella stuff with me.

Okay, you think you are in a trance, where is your body? Try to go back to it now. It is dust, it is long gone.

The old man pauses and sits on the ground cross-legged closing his eyes. He is still for a while, then he opens them.

This don't change anything. That white fella, bad man. He deserves all he get.

This anger is holding you in a stuck place. Wouldn't you like to go home? And join your ancestors?

The old mans cogitates.

Nicky, call your father three times invite him to join us.

She does so and her father appears next to us, it is an emotional reunion that takes Nicki completely by surprise.

Dad, where have you been?

It's okay darlin', the relatives were waiting for me when I passed. I know I did a lot of bad things in my life and I'm happy to come back and experience them all when the time is right. It's time for me to sort this out with this old bloke. And with you too. I am sorry, I was not the best father.

They embrace and there are lots of tears. I can see that despite his failings she still loves him very much. Her father then kneels in front of the old aboriginal man and begs for his forgiveness. It is not easily given, they have a long dialogue, but eventually it comes.

Spirit World

I ask the old man to take back the curse and he obliges. In his ancient language with an archaic ritual he undoes the curse he placed on Nicki's father and his lineage. When that is done I call three times on the ancestors of the place we are in. It is a happy reunion; as they depart one of them turns to me. Standing still he makes eye contact with me and nods, respectfully.

You, kadaitcha man. Lawman, you.

He smiles, perfect white teeth and sparkling eyes set off against dark, dark skin.

Nicky looks at me perplexed as he leaves.

Are those tears in your eyes?

No, It's just the sun and the wind.

This old man has just paid me the greatest compliment I could imagine from one of his culture. Most non-Aboriginals might know the kadaitcha man as the bone pointing sorcerer, but there is more to it than that. He has described me as a healer and spiritual lawman in its purest sense, one who upholds justice with humility.

It is such an honour I am moved to tears.

Talisman

It is a bright cool day in the city I have come to love, I stand in the fresh air outside my little crystal shop and enjoy the busyness of the city. The sunshine dazzles as the crisp air bites into my cheeks.

I sense my client walking up the street. To say that he emanates tension would be an understatement, he is wound up tight. While I occupy myself tidying crystals inside the shop, Bryony, the leaner and sharper of my two assistants, welcomes him.

I notice something unusual. Her bright and easy-going demeanour has given way to something different, she is cold and aloof. Although she has done her job well, I sense there is something about this man she does not like.

She sends him upstairs to my session room and once out of earshot I turn to her.

"What's with you this morning?"

"I'm not too partial to priests. They give me the creeps."

His occupation explains his tension. He is concerned that one of his congregation may spot him entering my shop, a forbidden zone in his subculture. But not for him, not today.

I catch up with him at the top of the stairs and as we enter my small session room his eyes widen as he looks at the crystal mandala on the floor, which we will both lie in. His discomfort is apparent, he must need to see me badly.

A bead of sweat runs down his temple as tells me he senses there is some energy present that he can't put his finger on that is preventing him moving forward in life. The colleagues he has confided in cannot help him and lately he has been experiencing chest pains that are mystifying his doctor. He has been referred to me by a friend.

When he is a bit more relaxed, we lie in the beautiful mandala that will trigger our expanded state of consciousness. We close our eyes and unusually we find ourselves in utter nothingness. Often my client will naturally take us to the key issue that affects their lives. Today we find ourselves in the void and I sense he is feeling apprehensive.

It is okay this is quite normal. I telepath, stretching the truth. *In this place we can find out exactly what the challenge is. You have x-ray vision, scan your body tell me if you notice anything unusual or uncomfortable.*

He looks down at his body and sure enough he sees immediately what I have been seeing since he entered my shop.

Holy Mary... Oh, no! Do you see what I'm seeing?

Tell me exactly what you see. I do not want to lead him.

In my chest next to my heart I see something, it is shaped like a mummy and has hieroglyphics on it. Why do I feel so afraid?

I know why.

Say out loud after me, "Body I command you show me the moment this came to be here, show me NOW."

As our movement accelerates, the nothing we are in changes to a blur of images and feelings that could be stars and constellations or lifetimes full of joy and sadness. We are time traveling.

We approach a large stepped pyramid from above and pass easily through the huge stone slabs into a central, beautifully decorated, "burial" chamber, which is so much more than that. It is humid, well lit by oil lamps and I can smell sesame oil. There are two men waiting for us, they look lean and stern. They are totally shaved and appear very clean, each is wearing a white linen robe with a gold embroidered sash.

Rather than travel to a graphic recall generated by the client, we have travelled through time and space, where these men are waiting for us in their current time. They are not spirits, they are not memories, they are alive and they are expecting us.

They speak in an ancient dialect, simultaneously telepathing us the reason for their cold rage. My client is standing next to me, his mouth gaping, he is way out of his depth.

I decide to speak on his behalf, telepathing our ancient hosts.

Please show us when, how and why you placed this talisman inside my friend.

They look at each other, shrug their shoulders and take us to the time and place where this all started.

We see my client as a high priest, a member of their order, respected, powerful, arrogant and flawed. He is a good-looking man, years of focused study in the esoteric arts, combined with an austere but well nourished lifestyle have left him looking quite handsome. He knows it and he cannot resist flirting with the virgin, novice priestesses that also serve in their order.

The inevitable happens and he consummates a relationship with a shy, impressionable young woman. At this point he ruins not only her life, but his life at that time and every other subsequent incarnation up until our present.

Her teachers notice a change in their behaviour and she spills the beans. They are angry with her but surprisingly compassionate. Her punishment is to be expelled from temple in disgrace, her family dishonoured, her life destroyed.

For him, nobody has any compassion whatsoever. He watches in horror and shame his own past life trial and slow, painful ritual execution.

They cut open his chest, moving his still beating heart, pushing the cursed talisman into his chest cavity, while chanting. His screams are not just about the agony he dies in. He is utterly terrified because he knows this talisman will affect every incarnation from now on. Traveling with him in his etheric body forever, destroying any chance of future happiness or fulfilment.

They sew his chest back together and leave him to die alone. The priests are happy with their work, they have rectified an imbalance and everything in their world returns to normal. My client has been cursed.

These Ancient Egyptian priests were really smart. They knew at some stage he would return with a priest or shaman like myself, trying to undo what was done in their time. So they have placed themselves in a trance, entered no time-space and waited patiently for his return.

I have to use all my negotiating skills, learned growing up in a tough neighbourhood where everyone seemed to be bigger, stronger and meaner than me. At one stage I even raise a smile from them. It takes an age to persuade them that his penance is complete. Reluctantly they remove the etheric Talisman from my sobbing client and we depart returning to our present time.

There is some irony in the fact that his present order has recently been exposed in the media for doing exactly what he did so long ago. He assures me he is passionate about ensuring those responsible are brought to justice and punished. The Universe has a dry sense of humour.

He takes his leave and as the shop door closes Bryony turns to me, one eyebrow arched.

"So, did you sort the philanderer out?"

"He has suffered enough."

"Five thousand years was barely enough." She smiles.

Waif and Strays

Occasionally I take on an apprentice, often to the amusement of my two mature assistants, who have seen it all. Today I have invited Jo, a gifted and enthusiastic young rebel to travel with me.

She looks the part, wearing black, with studs through her lip, tongue and eyebrows, her hair is cropped short like a gooseberry. She walks with a pronounced limp, her smile although beguiling, reveals crooked and chipped teeth.

I arrive at my practice and Jo is already there, looking a little out of place amongst the elf and fairy paraphernalia. My Earth Mother assistant Brianna is in the shop today with her nurturing vibe which is good, as Jo will have nothing to rub up against. She smiles as I enter the shop, nodding towards my young apprentice.

"I found this waif in the doorway when I opened up this morning. Do you know what it is doing here?"

She refers to Jo's androgynous appearance, there is a soft irony to her question. I sense she has noticed the self inflicted scars on the young woman's arms.

"Ah yes, I forgot to mention her, my new apprentice. She has potential."

Brianna's eyebrow arches as studies Jo who is shuffling through the goddess guidance cards with an air of barely concealed contempt.

"I am sure she will make your clients feel at ease." she smiles.

"It's good to get them used to expecting the unexpected."

I respond, immediately having second thoughts about Jo's appearance. I send her upstairs to wait in my session room.

"Don't tell me, not only is she angry and disabled, she is a transgender anarchist and aboriginal rights activist who is into wild conspiracy theories and believes Elvis never left the room." Brianna rolls her eyes.

"Three out of five, not bad for a psychic." I grin as my client enters the shop.

I interview my client upstairs, after explaining my apprentice will be traveling with us.

Mary is the editor of a high circulation woman's magazine. She is looking for answers as to why she is experiencing so much irrational fear, which is affecting her work. I ask about any recent trauma, her answers reveal a great deal.

The three of us lie in my crystal mandala and close our eyes. I invoke and immediately we are transported into another time-space.

It is cold, snowflakes are falling softly on my nose and cheeks and the air is full of the padded silence that comes with a recent heavy snowfall. We are on the edge of a pine forest, tree branches are bent under the weight of their heavy lightly frosted coating and the ground is covered in deep soft fluffy snow.

My apprentice is next to me staring wide-eyed at the tranquil beauty of our surroundings. Until today all of her shamanic experiences have been about herself often less than pleasant. Now she is experiencing someone else's journey and she is loving it.

It is beautiful, our surroundings sparkle and glisten and the cold numbs our ears. We could be standing in an idyllic scene from a children's film. Everything is pristine and appears to be just perfect. But it is not.

Our attention is drawn elsewhere by faint groans coming from a pile of snow further down the slope. We approach and there lies Mary, one leg still attached to a ski folded back under her at a sickening angle.

We have arrived at the moment of a recent accident she described to me earlier. She is regaining consciousness, becoming aware of the intense pain in her leg followed by the realisation that she is totally alone, with no one around to help her.

Her enthusiasm to be the first to ski on virgin snow has led her into a life threatening situation. She begins to feel deep fear verging on terror and her instinct for survival overrides all rational thought. She starts screaming.

She calls for help repeatedly, until she is hoarse. Jo starts towards her, to offer comfort.

I step forward and grab her arm.

Don't! I telepath. *You must not get involved. Let this play out.*

Mary lies there for some time, drifting in and out of consciousness. The sky turns grey-blue, a sure sign that more snow is imminent. She looks up at the darkening sky and understands that her situation is about to get worse.

"Will somebody please come and help me! Please help me. Help me! Take away this pain." She sobs.

Thin black shadows approach her from all points of the compass. She has just called them in, unwittingly entering into an open-ended contract with any being who is prepared to take her pain away. And there are many who will fulfil this role in exchange for a place to be.

The energies converge on her body and enter it through her broken leg. Her pain eases.

Look at the energies, look into them tell me what you see.

I telepath Jo who is drinking in the first-hand observation of theories taught in class.

Wow, lots of stray souls. Confused dead people, looking for a place to hide.

Well done, they are just along for the ride. But what is perpetuating her present fear?

She pauses scanning the situation, she is surprised at her own observation.

It is not here yet.

Good! It is arriving now. Stand back.

We feel an ancient energy approaching from beneath us, one that has been on this planet long before humans became self aware. These beings live in a dimension close to ours and see us as interlopers. They do not like our presence on their planet and given any opportunity they will attach to humans and perpetuate fear.

It emerges from the ground and stands next to Mary. I am familiar with its form, Jo is not. She does well to contain her fear. Part humanoid part reptile it stands on its hind legs, over two metres tall, it mocks Mary who is again unconscious.

I accept your contract. It telepaths, stepping into her body. Her pain ceases immediately.

As dusk approaches a ski instructor passes by and notices her body, he calls for help and she is rescued. As they lift her body onto a snowmobile I call Mary out of her body.

She is groggy.

Oh dear. I think I understand what happened.

The lost souls will be grateful for our help and are easy to handle. Let's deal with the reptoid at first. Command it to step forward. Tell it you would like to speak to it.

It confronts her. Its form is terrifying to both her and Joe, I have seen this kind many times.

Thank it for coming when you called for help and tell it that its contract is now complete.

The response is predictable, a torrent of abuse peppered with a selection of foul language. It laughs. I sense Jo is rising to the bait and becoming angry. Not the smartest of things to do, this energy will feed it. I need to intercede, I step between it and Mary.

You know you cannot stay here without my client's permission. I telepath.

All I have to do is help Mary believe that. The moment she does it will have no leverage and no choice but to release its hold on her and stop feeding off her fear.

It takes a while for Mary to step into her power, but when she does it leaves and we her return to this time and place.

We debrief the client who is shaken, amazed and very grateful. After she has left I spend a few minutes debriefing Jo. Her comments are unexpected.

"Did you realise that you make yourself look younger, leaner more muscular and better looking than you do in real life?'

"Is that possible?" I joke.

I do not mention that in the journey she was no longer disabled and had perfect teeth. She was also not wearing studs or short hair. In fact she looked a lot like the goddess on the card she was holding earlier.

Space Cadet

Johno is a big man. When he enters my shop it's like a shadow has passed over the sun, he blocks out that much light. My petite assistant Bryony gets the giggles. He is just unbelievably large, solid and muscular. Bryony looks like a little doll next to him, but their unique individuality somehow makes them a matching pair.

"I've come to see a bloke about a healing. I spoke to someone on the phone. It's about my neck."

"Ah yes your girlfriend referred you, she's a regular here." Bryony composes herself showing him upstairs.

In a recent session with his girlfriend I had noticed that there was more to his stiff neck than was apparent. I follow him into my session room. It feels a bit cramped, the big man taking up most of the space. I squeeze in next to him, lying with my feet pressed up against the door.

Johno explains to me that he has an ongoing story with his neck. He is a regional football player who stands an excellent chance of being selected to play for his country. But, the lack of mobility in his neck is proving a handicap. He has tried everything to fix it, physio, massage, heat treatment, even electronic devices. None of them have worked permanently, at best some have brought only temporary relief.

"Okay Johno this is all pretty straightforward all you have to do is lie here, close your eyes and try not to think".

"That won't be too hard for me" Johno grins sheepishly.

I can't figure out whether he is really smart and self deprecating or not very smart at all.

Lying in my crystal mandala we move into no time-space and I wait for Johno's higher-self to take us where we need to go. As we begin our journey through time and space I notice an irregularity with his Light-body, his energy field is not quite as it should be. I sense this does not relate to his neck and I hope we will have time to deal with it later. Right now it is appropriate that I just allow what needs to unfold to happen.

We find ourselves in an old cobbled square, it's been raining and rather than smelling fresh and clean this place smells rank. There are piles of putrefying rubbish around. This is not a place that is looked after or cared for by anyone. There is a feeling of despair here. There's a small crowd of rough looking, pungent misfits waiting for something to happen.

We see a wooden cart approach with a half starved, filthy man chained to it. I try not to lead Johno in his understanding of what is happening and how this relates to him.

Do you recognise anyone here? I telepath Johno.

What?

I can see he is having a little difficulty comprehending that we are in another time and place witnessing something relevant to him.

Feel into the energy of the people here, does anyone feel familiar.

The bloke on the cart, that's me!

You are right, go over and step into his body, tell me how he's feeling.

Well he feels like a skinny little bloke, not very strong.

No. How is he feeling emotionally, tell me what he is feeling now.

Oh. Well he's not frightened. He's angry. And he's really really sad.

The grubby petty officials waiting near the rickety wooden structure in the centre of the square unchain him and lead him up the rotting steps onto the platform, where his fate awaits him.

As they put the thick rough rope around his neck he scans the crowd and sees what he has been hoping both to see and not to see.

There at the back of the crowd are his wife and child, they look totally destitute and utterly despairing. His eyes meet theirs and he starts sobbing.

What is he feeling now? I ask.

Johno is sobbing. He feels like shit. He feels like he is abandoning his wife and child. All he did was steal one loaf of bread to feed them. And now he's getting hung for it.

I watch as with little ceremony or speeches they place the noose around his neck read out his name and offence and open the trapdoor beneath him. The sound of his neck cracking echoes across the square as his wife covers and their son's eyes.

I catch him as he leaves his body and we move into no time-space.

My neck!

What are you holding there?

Despair, anger, a feeling of utter helplessness. He starts crying. *I let them down! They will die without me. I left them. I did not mean to.*

Can you see how this relates to your neck pain now?

Yes.

Would you like to release it?

Too bloody right.

I call on his wife and child from that time and suggest he begs their forgiveness, which is given freely and received emotionally. He sees the energy he was holding in his neck evaporate as he accepts their unconditional love. As he says goodbye to his loved ones, he moves his neck freely.

He has cheered up. *Brilliant mate. Are we done?*

Not quite, I think there is something else, if you don't mind?

In for a penny...

Please say out loud after me. "Body I command you take me to the moment my Light-body was traumatised."

Not really fully grasping its implications he repeats the affirmation and we find ourselves in the middle of a pitched battle in outer space.

Johno has the hang of it now. *Thats me, the bloke in that jet thing.*

He has already stepped into the pilots body.

Cool. This bloke, me… I am, he is… highly skilled. I am flying this thing by thought! How does he do this?

He is happy to be here in service to the light on this mission. He is beyond fear. He has been trained for this and he is good at it.

Alarms are going off in my head. I need to evade...

Behind him I see an enormous black hole of a mothership. Utterly black, the lack of stars are what defines its presence. It is totally featureless, approaching fast and very, very big.

The opposing forces in the skirmish disappear. He and his companions are alone in space in their tiny craft. They form a holding pattern and wait for orders which they will never hear.

The mother ship belches a cloud of nothingness towards them. It destroys their craft and the brave beings inside them, in a way that is beyond comprehension.

The physicality of their beings is destroyed, disintegrated, but there is more going on. Their very essence, their souls, their Light-bodies are deliberately fragmented into billions of pieces and scattered throughout time and space. Very nasty.

I am so utterly fascinated by this unfolding drama I almost forget to call Johno out of his traumatised and rapidly dispersing Light-body.

Oooh. Not good.

It is okay Johno you got fixed, but lets look at how. Give yourself permission to remember.

We witness the endless separation of his being into minute particles, randomly scattered, absorbed by a vastness that is beyond comprehension. A long time passes, then we see other light beings of many types gathering his soul together, volunteers, carrying out soul retrieval on a grand scale.

We call on them and thank them. They are happy to see he has reincarnated on Earth and advise it will take time for his being to become completely whole again, but he is doing well.

We return to our present time and space and I debrief him.

He sits up and moves his head neck and shoulders freely.

"Mate, that was sensational! It's fixed."

"So you will be referring your team mates then?" I give him a cheeky smile.

"I doubt it. Too weird" He rolls his eyes in disbelief of his own recent experience.

I escort him downstairs, accept payment and advise him not to drive.

As he leaves Bryony comments quietly on totally spaced out look on his face.

He turns around at the door.

"Hey, I heard that. I'm no space cadet. I graduated!" He chuckles to himself as he leaves shaking his head.

Braided

It is a clear, warm, fresh morning; the pink blossom on the almond trees emits a subtle, sweet and exquisite aroma. I am time traveling in the distant past, walking next to my client Fran, who is one of a group walking through an ancient town. Which one she is, unusually, is not clear to me yet. I watch, invisible to the crowd, as a lean man, near exhaustion, struggles up a dry, stone street dragging a heavy burden surrounded by spectators.

The yelling crowd around him embodies the weirdest mixture of emotions; hysterical anger, incandescent rage mixed with deep grief, profound sadness and despair. Amongst the locals are a few Greeks moving with a small group who are in a state of shock and desolation.

He is almost naked, parts of his beard have been pulled out and he is drenched in sweat and blood. In fact he actually seems to be sweating blood, a phenomena I have heard of but never actually seen. The cruel headgear he wears cuts deeper into his flesh with each painful step he takes towards the outskirts of the city. Yet behind the intense pain there is a surreal inner calm.

Men in uniform follow the victim as he struggles resolutely on; one brute, their leader carries a whip with fragments of bone braided into the end of each strand. Instantly recognisable in any time or culture as a pathological sadist, he enjoys making his prisoner suffer.

> "Where is your father now? He's left you well and truly in the shit hasn't he?" the brute hisses, as he viscously smashes the butt end of the whip into the staggering man's spiky headgear.

The throng witnessing the spectacle pushes through narrow streets past people trying to carry out their daily business. Some bystanders care little for the drama unfolding before them, for some the whole spectacle is an annoyance. The procession passes a place of worship festively decorated with flowers and greenery, which creates a bizarrely gay backdrop to the theatrical tragedy rolling by. I am in the crowd now, heading up a stony slope towards a small hill which in the soft morning light looks eerily like a skull.

As we reach the top of the hill I feel an unexpected coolness in the air; what was a typically warm spring day has become atypically cool. The prisoner drops his heavy load on the ground and falls to his knees next to it. He is laid face up on top of it, arms spread wide, as large nails are driven by the sadist in command, through his wrists into the large timber crucifix he has been dragging through the town.

A few look away, most give a hearty cheer. The man on the cross is not well loved.

> "Heretic! Blasphemer!"

Men with thick, long, black beards are working themselves into a frenzy of hatred for the young rebel who has challenged their dominant paradigm. This is going to be a tough one for Fran to deal with, once I figure out which person she is.

Spirit World

The cross is lifted vertically, slotted into a hole and the man wearing the crown of thorns has his feet nailed in place. Dark grey thunder clouds are forming above us. The cool damp air that they propel towards me is refreshing. I feel an occasional large heavy spot of rain.

There are now three crosses in place with two other men being executed either side of the man with the thorny crown. The dying takes some time, each man resists the inevitable asphyxiation as the lungs fatigue by lifting themselves for a moment, using their legs. Over the next few hours most of the crowd lose interest and melt away, knowing that no one can possibly survive.

Eventually all that remain are some angry old rabbis determined to see the young subversive take his last breath, a handful of bored soldiers and a dozen or so shamefaced friends. Three women kneel quietly before the central cross. He remains very still, the two others groan in agony as the afternoon wears on.

"Break their legs!," the Brute orders yawning, he has had enough. An act of mercy rather than cruelty it hastens the inevitable suffocation as the legs can no longer be used to bring relief. Soldiers break the legs of the two man either side of the crowned one. Approaching the central cross one calls out,

"This idiot is dead already."

The man in charge is disgruntled. He stands up grabbing a spear and pushes it into the rebel's side, to see if he lives.

The crucified one opens his eyes and gazes down at the three women before him. Although in agony he tries to smile at them. As tears well up in his eyes he whispers.

"Forgive them."

This insolence is too much for the Brute who immediately pushes his spear deep into the left side of the rebel on the cross.

"Eli, Eli, lama sabachthani?" the dying one moans as pain tears through every part of his being.

Blood splashes down on the neat red tunic of his Roman tormentor as the spear is removed. There is an explosion of thunder with lightning and the ground shakes as wind and rain tear through the small crowd scattering everyone, apart from the women who remain, still, crying.

I must intercede now, I understand what is happening. It is time to collect Fran before she becomes very confused.

As the spirit of the dying man on the central cross leaves his body and becomes one with everything I collect the part of Fran's consciousness that is there and pull it to one side.

She is bewildered and crying.

It's OK I am here. I telepath.

What the f...

Remember we are on a shamanic journey together, you wanted to find out more about who you were in a past life.

This cannot be true, I can't be HIM. I can't walk on water and perform miracles... I work in an office! I can't possibly be who I think I was. I'm making this all up. This is bullshit.

It is true. But it is not that simple. I call on the Master Yodheshinwa, who we call Jesus, please come close to us now.

We are immediately enveloped by complete and utter unconditional love and we both start crying. I ask the Master to explain what has happened and why we were called here. He does so far more eloquently than I, using holographic diagrams and soft words.

Fran, along with thousands of other souls, entered a pre-birth agreement with this Master that providing all her Karma was cleared during this lifetime they would soul braid. Their consciousness would be braided together but remain separate, enabling the Master to incarnate (incognito) in many thousands of places simultaneously, continuing his service to the planet, without any interruption. This revelation creates the opportunity for her to achieve great things, she could be come a great teacher herself, a guru, a global peace worker or healer.

It is all a bit much for Fran but I can see the level of ecstasy she is experiencing is overriding logical thought.

The Master departs, explaining that Fran has free will and that she might like to take some time to consider her future. Together they may be of great service to humanity, it is entirely up to her. I have witnessed this revelation before, it can change peoples lives profoundly, if they allow it. Some do, some don't.

We accept his blessing and return to this time and place. I am gentle with her, it's a lot to take on board. We chat for a while as she slowly comes down to earth.

"The three women in front - one was his mother, Mary, right?"

"Yes, in fact they were all called Mary".

A thoughtful pause.

"Who was the beautiful pregnant woman with long red hair? What was his relationship with her?"

I smile at the totally perplexed look on her face. "I'll leave you to figure that one out."

Karma

Isabella is in a state. To my eyes she is an attractive intelligent young woman with everything going for her. She has come to see me in order to understand why she has such low self esteem. Even her close friends don't get it; great career, fit and active lifestyle, bright easygoing personality but terrible self worth. She has tried various forms of emotional therapy and counselling but nothing changes.

My assistant Bryony, ever intuitive and observant, has already tuned in to the reason for her appointment.

"You might be appearing in court today." She whispers as Isabella enters.

I take longer with my pre-journey interview than normal, with Bryony's insight I know I will need more backstory than usual.

Isabella shares her life story with me. She knows she has a good life but lately her feelings of lack of worthiness have become more acute. They have been compounded by a recent abusive relationship. She was attracted to a handsome young European who had little difficulty seducing her with his charm and quick wit. However once it was clear she had fallen for him and their relationship was consummated, he started to treat her badly.

His quick wit turned to cruel sarcasm with relentless put downs about her looks, her figure and her weight, which are of course just fine.

And yet she is still irresistibly attracted to him.

She was unable to leave him. Their separation was caused when he was called back to Europe on family business. She confides that she is pining for him.

I have heard enough. We lay in my crystal mandala, I invoke for guidance and protection and we close our eyes. At my suggestion Isabella says, "Body take me to the moment this all started."

Immediately we are in ancient Rome. The enticing, rich and complex smell of good cooking permeates the air and there is order in the busy streets around us. A glance at nearby buildings, the opulence of their architecture and the well kept soldiers uniforms confirm my knowing, as Isabella also realises where and when we are.

It's OK no one can see us. Soak it up and explore. I telepath.

I allow myself a moment of indulgence as I look at the personalities going about their daily business, oblivious to our presence. I play a game with myself of seeing people not in their smart suits and modern work gear but in clothes of another time period. Everyone seems to fit in somehow, doing similar meaningful things to their present day activities.

A first experience in another time period can be overwhelming for a client but I just am enjoying just being here again. I follow Isabella into an imposing civic hall as she leads me into a meeting room. There are plans on a large marble table and important looking men in fine togas are discussing improvements to the city.

Suddenly, a man in green rushes in and stabs one of the men to death. It all happens very quickly and there is chaos as he dashes out, dropping the bloodied knife on the floor.

I understand what is happening but I need to help Isabella get it without telling her.

> *Do you recognise anyone here?*
>
> *The guy who got stabbed, I think that is my boyfriend now.*
>
> *Anyone else?*
>
> *No.*
>
> *Are sure? Ask your body to show you again, this drama will replay itself for you.*

She does and second time around she gets it.

> *The assassin, that is not me, but I am connected to him somehow...*
>
> *Oh no! I hired him.*

I can almost see cogs in her brain moving slowly into gear as she tracks her and her boyfriends dance together through time and space. Many opportunities to resolve this incident, none fulfilled. The magnitude of her actions cuts deeply into her psyche and she collapses into grief.

> *It is OK, we can fix this today. I reassure her, a tad optimistically, but I need her to get a grip on herself.*
>
> *Really?*

I call on the man she had assassinated and help with their reconciliation.

I ask her boyfriend if everything is now settled. His response is just what I do not need to hear.

> *Unfortunately not. This is a karmic issue and is out if my hands.*

What does that mean? Isabella asks perplexed.

> *Your boyfriend has forgiven you but we need to appeal to a higher authority to finally clear this up. Otherwise this dysfunctional relationship will continue, in fact things could get worse.*

She nods.

> *We have the right to appeal the judgement of the karmic court and as they sit in no time-space will can have a hearing immediately. Are you OK with that?*
>
> *Who?*

I sense things are moving a little too quickly for Isabella.

> *Compose yourself and please be restrained and respectful.*

I connect with my inner barrister as I plead Isabella's case, standing in an empty courtroom, in front of a dais where several Masters listen patiently to my appeal for clemency.

To sum up, I respectfully request that the karma attached to this relationship now be declared clear, for the Divine highest good of all.

The court has a brief discussion.

We declare the karma not to be cleared.

In every other case I have pleaded for clients successfully and I lose my cool for a moment.

Why not? She has been forgiven. There must be a way out of this... Then remembering were I am. *Your Lordships.*

Further discussion.

Providing she apologises to him in person, in your time-space the karma will be considered clear. She must kneel before him and beg his forgiveness.

But he lives in Crete! And he is the one who has been abusing me! He will think I have totally lost the plot. Isabella cannot restrain herself.

The courts decision is final.

We must accept their decision. I counsel Isabella as I respectfully take our leave of the court and bring us back to our present time.

"They must be bloody well joking!" She sits up, a picture of runny mascara and mixed emotions.

"It is your decision, I know what I would do".

We chat for a while until I am certain she grasps the importance her choices, however I can see she is unable to accept the logic of the court. She will not be apologising to her boyfriend in person, in the near future. I usher her out.

"How was your day in court?" Bryony looks up from her crystal polishing.

"Not good. She has a great opportunity to step off the wheel of karma but she won't take it". I am crestfallen.

"Oh well, you did your best. Win some - lose some. Coffee?"

Boy

I am time traveling with my client Marie, a nursery nurse who also works long hours as a volunteer for a variety of children's charities. She is with me to understand why she overcommits and burns herself out.

We are standing next to a small boy, he has an unruly mop of dark hair and large brown eyes which conceal a quick intelligence. He is busy polishing a large slab of stone by hand and he seems happy in his work. It is hot and dry but lush, we can sense in the distance the beginnings of a desert. We stand close to high majestic buildings, beautifully built with tall entrances.

Where are we, and why are we here?

Marie telepaths squinting at her surroundings, breathing in the atmosphere of a time long gone. She does not yet understand that she she is observing herself as a boy in a past life.

You will see, I respond. *Remember why you came to see me.*

Although the boy is relaxed, those around him are not, they have a harsh taskmaster. A beefy man wearing a golden circlet walks around with a small whip which he uses freely, encouraging his labourers to work harder and faster. He is not a cruel brute, rather a man on a mission, using the tools of his time. He must have a soft spot for the boy, or perhaps he appreciates the care that he takes in his work, either way the child is left unmolested.

Invisible, we explore, observing that this intense activity is part of a massive project. Stones are being prepared and taken away to a huge structure nearby. The air around us pulses with sweat and fear, but there is more, there is also an undercurrent of awe. We are in an ancient time when things were very different but something is going on here that we are not yet aware of.

The foreman walks over to the boy and barks instructions at him. The boy retorts with a cheeky grin and moves off quickly. The response of the child initially annoys the foreman but then he smiles and shakes his head. He looks reflectively at the young slave as he carries out his new task with enthusiasm and care, exactly as instructed.

The foreman delegates responsibility and disappears into the shadows of a nearby building, when he returns he calls the boy over.

Without any prompting from me Marie gasps, recognising herself in the energy field of this cheeky boy, who is now following the foreman into the dark high entrance of a tall stone building. Other slaves exchange concerned glances as the boy dutifully walks behind the man with the whip. In their eyes this excursion is not good and will not end well for the child. Some shiver and make a sign to dispel evil. We follow.

As we enter the magnificent building our skin is caressed by cooler, damp air which smells of moist earth. It takes some time for our vision to adjust to the gloom inside. When we do we see that it is a beautifully kept building. The murals are fresh and vibrant, the people inside well-dressed and very clean. We walk towards a central chamber.

I can see that the young boy is putting on a brave face trying to conceal his growing apprehension. The arrogant, bossy demeanour of his supervisor changes to deference and humility as we approach a majestic being sitting on large stone throne in the central chamber.

The child is doing mental arithmetic as he looks at the strange hybrid-being sitting there. Seated it is already taller than the nearby priests that serve it.

"Six cubits" the boy mouths to himself.

The foreman kneels before the creature in front of them and the boy follows suit. We can see that even with his head bowed, the boy is fascinated and intrigued by what he sees.

Sitting on a throne is a large humanoid. Dressed in the clothes of the period he appears normal and human, if not exceptionally tall and well built, but he does not have a human head. From the shoulders up his form changes into the head of a large bird. This is not a huge man wearing a headdress, it is a blended being, part human, part bird.

This being does not need to use any words to communicate with those kneeling before him. He scans the child reading his thoughts, feelings and intentions. Then he addresses the supervisor.

Well chosen, he telepaths, *this child is perfect. His insolence indicates a quick wit. He has an intelligence and integrity that we need. You did well not to punish him, he will be reliable, he has a pure heart.*

He turns to the clean shaven, bald headed priests nearby.

Give the boy the package and tell him what to do with it. Turning to the boy, *This is to remain a secret.*

A priest steps forward carrying a small basket which they hand over to the child. His eyes widen as he sees what is in it.

Reward the child, we may use him again.

The creature on the throne focuses his attention again on the boy, this time I sense that he is opening the boy's heart. The child sheds a tear as he smiles at the bizarre half human creature before him.

The child is ushered out carrying the basket, now covered to hide it's unusual and precious contents. We follow and as we leave we realise we are not invisible to the being on the throne. It scans us.

You know you cannot change anything here. It telepaths probing me.

Spirit World

This is not our intention. I state clearly and quickly.

Then bear witness to my greatness and the truth of my being. I know in your time you have forgotten my kind. Share this with the others from your time... I and my brothers and sisters will walk again on this earth.

I turn and bow, truly understanding that ancient hieroglyphics were not symbolic drawings but accurate depictions of the beings who once walked amongst us.

The child is smart enough to obey his instructions to the letter. But he is anxious.

He walks through the building site and finds a quiet place on the banks of the broad muddy river that dominates the environment. He wades out as deep as he can. Removing the cover, he looks down at the gurgling happy child in the basket, a well fed and joyful little boy. Doing as he was told, he releases the basket into the current and it floats slowly away downstream, buoyant. He returns to his work but he is deeply troubled, not knowing what will happen to the baby in the basket.

Marie is sobbing quietly.

So this is where my guilt started, she telepaths.

Yes, the boy carried this for the rest of his life and you have experienced it in every subsequent incarnation. It has affected your actions ever since. Are you ready to release it?

Absolutely.

Then come with me.

I take her hand and we leave the sprawling construction site, flying over the great river, following the basket downstream. It travels downstream, occasionally spinning but always righting itself. The baby is exposed to the sun and becomes sunburnt; it begins to dehydrate and starts crying. Whoever made the basket knew something about buoyancy, because although the reeds are absorbing water it is not sinking and the baby, who now has a wet back, is still above water.

The basket washes into reeds at the side of the river as the sky turns blue-pink with the setting sun. The baby is now exercising its lungs to the fullest. An elegant, well-dressed woman wearing the signs of a priestess is walking by. She hears the child and instructs her acolytes to retrieve the basket and feed the child.

She does not seem terribly surprised to find it and it is obvious she will care for it.

Marie is sobbing again, but now it is with relief.

It's time for you to forgive yourself and stop feeling guilty about this incident. Once you do so everything will change. You will no longer be driven to exhaustion trying to save children, your life will come into balance.

You can be at peace now, the child is safe.

Hive Mind

I remember being human but the memory is fading. I vaguely remember love, something that propelled me onward, now I sense it as a rapidly dispersing jet-stream. My love-based momentum is fading and slowing.

I try to recall why and how I came to be what I am now but it is difficult. I am being absorbed by the hive mind, a oneness that is warm, comforting and has purpose. Perhaps this is what love felt like. I no longer know. I must remember why I am here, I am not one of this species although I like this simple existence. There was an important reason why I ceased to be human, I must try to remember what happened to me...

The pain in my human body is excruciating. I sense that limbs are broken and missing. My fresh wounds have been cauterised by the intense heat of the lasers that have terminally damaged my undernourished female form. The battle playing out around me is chaotic and terrifying to watch, but my priority right now is just experiencing my next precious breath. Comrades lift me and carry me from the heat of battle to a wagon and then into a dimly lit underground place with rough but clean bench-tops, a field surgery. I am placed next to one of those repulsive creatures we fight, it too is barely alive and restrained. Its soft, six tentacled, aquatic form looks vulnerable outside of its armour.

Now I remember the oath I took and feel sick to the core at the realisation of what will happen to me next, maybe I actually vomit, I am way past caring. Other women look down at my broken body. I see such love and compassion in their eyes, I feel hot tears roll across my face.

Be strong little sparrow. They telepath.

Your time with us is over, you were never meant for battlefield duty but our need was great and you were brave. We love you and honour your choice to continue to fight for freedom in the resistance. Remember your training, remember us, remember how much you are loved. We love you.

This small group of battle-hardened women weep as they wait for my final approval to attempt the unthinkable. My throat is dry and my consciousness weak but I am able to nod, blink my eyes and attempt a crooked smile as they commence a process which has already cost many lives and which may not succeed. But we are in desperate times, overwhelmed and close to extinction. Our men are long gone, women now are all that is left of our once dominant and careless species.

Nobody had any inkling of what SETI's Aricebo message would invite onto our lush green Earth with its simple broadcasts about our planet and species. Nobody thought that other distant species would have the all too human trait of resource plundering, enslavement, domination and destruction...

I was a child playing in the fields near my home when it started. Without any warning on a clear bright Autumn afternoon they came in their thousands, fast and merciless. Puncturing our sleepy reality from that clear blue sky, in their weirdly organic, gravity defying ships. Contradicting our known laws of aerodynamics and physics they moved left-right, up-down at ridiculous speed. Before our armed forces and governments grasped what was happening all military infrastructure and communications networks were trashed and modern weaponry rendered totally useless. Planes fell out of the sky, rockets exploded on their launchpads, submarines sank - never to resurface.

Electronic equipment, engines and weapons involving bullets, shells, rockets or lasers ceased to function in an instant. Crossbows, arrows and simple explosive devices were all that was left to the those who fought back. A few tried gamely to form themselves into something cohesive. In the weeks that followed the initial attack, we naively thought we had a chance.

Then the wholesale slaughter of men began. Ignoring all females they targeted the alpha males in the military and government through direct attack then later through their creepy, insidious male killer virus. That horrible bug that took my sweet baby brother and disfigured my dying father. It was awful and things did not get better.

From baby boy to grandfather they died rapidly and in their millions. The intention was to create a slave race of the apparently more passive females, who would work for food, water and shelter. There was no concern about reproduction or regeneration of the dominant Earth species as their project would be complete before they ran out of able bodied slaves.

Ma, me and my aunties fended for ourselves. It was harsh but not as bad as in the cities, we heard tales that made your flesh creep. At least we had clean water and food. Life was not as brutal and violent as any similar survival situation might be with men, but it stole my girlhood and after Ma was killed, turned me into as fierce a resistance fighter that any woman could hope to be.

No attempt was made by the invaders to dialogue or treaty. As human colonists have done on countless occasions, their aim was to subjugate, enslave, exterminate the uncooperative and take what they wanted. In this case fresh water, a resource so abundant that most people, apart from desert dwellers, took it totally for granted.

Everyone knew this steady, massive depletion spelled inevitable disaster for the planet and all beings living on it. The resistance grew slowly. Although its weapons were primitive, like all insurgent groups it relied on fast surgical strikes to inflict damage and disruption. Its actions were more symbolic of a resolute and resilient human spirit than a threat to the invaders. However the invaders became irritated and took reprisals.

They would completely destroy any hamlet they suspected harboured the resistance. Those who were killed had no idea what was about to happen. It was as if a the hand of God appeared out of the sky, razing everything in an instant. This meant that the resistance was not welcome anywhere; most people thought we were wasting our time anyway.

I joined the sisters when I was a still a girl. Joined, well I was more adopted really. Ma dead and aunties half crazy, I was a stinky little sewer rat, barely surviving on scraps and the patchy goodwill of others on the edge of survival themselves.

We travelled in small groups scavenging as we went. By the time I was bleeding I knew how to rig a lethal explosive device, break down, clean or repair any weapon in our small arsenal, as well as make a good feed from, rat, rabbit, cat or dog, as long as it was not too long dead. We were expected to fend for ourselves. Theory was that the big sisters could be killed at any time so we best know how to manage on our own. So I became a huntress, small and as lean as a leopard.

Our faded hope, and there were cults based on this hope, was that the aliens would only take some of our water and leave us. It was obvious to most sensible people after 20 years of occupation that this was a foolish dream.

Now as a grown woman I know nothing of men, they are a fairy story in my life. I remember my father's smile but as a woman I have never known a man's touch. The old ones talk of a man's love as being overpowering, they talk of the sensuality of having a heavy man lie on top and push himself hard inside that sacred place of the goddess.

The love of a man is beyond my comprehension, only the crones give it time and share their moist memories. I know the love of the sisters and it is good, we share soft love, passion and delicious sex. What I don't know I don't miss. I will never be touched by a man.

The senior sisters worship the Goddess and some are able to communicate in the way that our ancestors once did. They do not use this thing called wireless electricity they use their minds and their hearts. They use trances and herbs and we rely on them for news from across the planet.

The world I knew as a child has changed forever, most of humanity is a subspecies of obedient workers. A few do well as stewards and go-betweens, living a life of comparative luxury. Others live on the fringes surviving on their wits, supporting the resistance.

The invaders care nothing about the way humans organise themselves, only that the harvesting of fresh water continues. No one knows what they do with it or get from it, only that their appetite for it seems to be insatiable and continues 24/7.

Parts of the globe away from fresh water are left relatively untouched, save for an absence of men and boys of all ages, a scarcity of consumables, lack of TV and formal schooling.

Indigenous communities have thrived and a subculture based on ancient beliefs and healing arts has grown. Goddess worship has become commonplace and old mainstream religions have floundered. None had an answer for the ubiquitous devastation which was obviously manifested by ETs.

There are no schools, hospitals are ruthless triage centres for those injured at work, the elderly are discarded when they are no longer productive and the young are prepared for work early.

The invaders have proved to be unstoppable, resistant to every kind of attack.

Over time desperation has led to a bizarre and far fetched idea being germinated, nurtured and haltingly hatched, through the resurrection of long forgotten esoteric techniques, this do-or-die plan is our last hope.

Terminally injured freedom fighters can, having given prior agreement, have their consciousness transplanted into the body of an injured ET. Theoretically enabling total immersion and acceptance on the Mother ship, creating the opportunity for sabotage.

Desperate times lead to desperate measures...

I take my last breath as a human being, struggling to control the fear of becoming one of the hated ones. No one has any idea how the transition of consciousness affects us as none have ever come back or communicated from the other side. To date no mission has succeeded and we have only the vaguest notion that the transfer works at all.

I enter the consciousness of the six limbed one, I breathe through my skin, the air is repellant, unnatural but acceptable. It is nitrogen rich and lacks the sulphur and carbon dioxide I prefer. I sense humans nearby, I am far from the hive and I fear. But the humans are not aggressive and do not harm me.

The dead human female next to me looks familiar. I remember what I must do next.

I lift each of my limbs separately slowly, familiar but new and very strange. I repeat the pattern remembering my training.

> One of the women speaks "It looks like this transfer has worked, she is in there, bless her. God only knows what she must be going through. Bless you little sparrow, be swift and remember us. We promise to bear your boy child when you succeed. Remember us, we love you."
>
> "Leave her on the battlefield and be sure they discover her, there is hope if we act quickly; she will be subsumed into the hive cloud and her individuated consciousness will fade."
>
> *Be strong little one...*

Years have past and I am at peace in the hive, there is comfort in serving our one purpose. I felt different once. A long time ago I had more feeling, but now I am hive and I serve.

Spirit World

I am nearing the end of my eight year lifecycle and will soon cease to be. I help now in the control room of the mother ship. It feels right that I am here. There is some thing I must do here but I have forgotten. Our domination of humans has been slower than expected. We exterminated the males expecting the females to be passive slaves but some are not. Why do they resist the inevitable?

Resist. That word is special. It means something I must remember. I like being hive, it is comfortable.

I brush against another of my species, it feels different, like me.

Sister, you have found me.

A human voice startles me, it speaks inside my being.

Sister, do you remember why we came here?

I have a sense of being human. I was human once, before now. I remember a battle, intense pain, sadness and my own death. I was little sparrow, nicknamed after the commonest of species most resistant to extinction. I remember my purpose. In turn I help my sister remember, I do not know her, only her purpose. Together we help each other recall why we inhabit these alien bodies and why we are here.

The hive is sleepy. It will take a while before they realise our purpose.

Move slowly but with purpose. I am senior here and understand how to break this thing we serve.

I follow instructions carefully and slowly so as not to draw attention to our actions. However the hive mind notices our separation and purpose and is concerned. There is no failsafe, the hive mind is the failsafe and it is disturbed.

Now little one, together we must do this at exactly the same time, copy me.

For freedom!

For my unborn son!

A flash of intense brilliance as I and everything around me for many, many miles is vaporised. All species within a huge radius are terminated, including humans. I feel sadness for the Earth species I have killed but I know that those that remain will be free.

I experience the exquisite trauma and bliss of my own death.

I draw air into my aching chest. "Light. I am the light. I am light, I am one with everything. I am! Alpha and Omega..."

I feel a hand gently shaking my shoulder.

"Raym, come back into your body, you are too loud, you are frightening customers in the shop downstairs." My assistant Bryony's concerned face looks down on my convulsing body as I open my eyes, drawing deep irregular breaths.

Seeing I am OK her tone changes "You tell your students never to lie in the crystal matrix alone, you should take your own advice".

"Just finishing some parallel reality business." I gasp breathlessly, enjoying the intensely physical sensations in my aching body, the fresh clean air in my lungs and my freedom.

The Tower

"So what would you have done when the entity dragged the client's body across the room and out of the crystal mandala?"

"Same as you. Carry on with the process, the client could still breathe, they were just frightened. Just because some entity calls itself Beelzebub, does not mean..."

Our conversation is interrupted by the soft chirruping of the shop landline.

We are having an unusually quiet afternoon in my little crystal shop. My assistant Brianna has grabbed the opportunity to pick my brains. The shop is warm and cosy, it is grey and drizzling outside with few potential customers passing by. My appointment book has empty spaces and we pass the time chatting about some of the shamanic journeys she has facilitated. There are always questions, even from the most experienced of my students about their technique and the unusual things they discover. Answering leads me into reflection and deepens their understanding of my own uniquely modern form of an archaic and arcane healing art.

"Inner journeys, crystal emporium and shamanic healing centre..." Brianna answers the phone, making my little shop sound much grander than it is.

I can hear an excited male voice raving on about something important. She rolls her eyes handing me the phone with her hand over the microphone.

"It's that crazy used car salesman. He says he is calling from the south of France, something about a sea chest, a book and an old man. Seems to think you might be interested."

"Its true, all true!" A breathless tinny voice breathes into my ear from the other side of the world. "In the chest there was a book, in the book there was a note, folded in right next to a page with an illustration of the tower and the old guy we met. Unbelievable! I quit my job and came here to to France. According to the message and the code left by my uncle, I am..."

"Best not to talk about these things over the phone". I interrupt. "Thanks for letting me know, I am not at all surprised."

"But what the fuck do I do now? With all this information? I sell cars on the Parramatta road for christ's sake!"

"Not any more you don't. Your brothers in the order will help, seek them out, but be careful who you share this with, yours was and still is not a popular group in some quarters. Gotta go, I have an appointment, good luck!"

I hang up not wanting to get into a lengthy conversation, both for his safety and my sanity.

Brianna arches an eyebrow, she knows that I have no appointments scheduled until tomorrow. I sense her probing me. "Its rude to probe anyone, especially your teacher".

Spirit World

She blushes. "Sorry I couldn't help myself, wouldn't you like to share? We have all afternoon...".

How did this all start? I remember just two weeks ago Brian came to see me with absolutely no idea what was in store for him...

I am with Brian, standing on a desolate plain, we are at the start of our shamanic journey together. He has come to me to find his life's purpose, feeling limited and bored by his job as a car salesman.

He is excited - I am troubled. For the first time in his life he is having a visceral, first hand experience, in full consciousness of another reality and it is blowing his mind. I am trying to place the the time-space we are in, so as to navigate our journey safely and I can't. Something about this place is not quite right. I have not visited this space before, for the first time in a long while I feel quite lost.

What do we do now? He telepaths.

Let's explore. I respond with far more confidence than I feel.

We wander around aimlessly for a while, I suggest he listen to his heart and trust his guidance.

Over there, a tower! He squints into the hazy distance.

Barely discernible, a pimple on the horizon extends its invitation to us. It takes an age to walk there. I prefer clients to figure out for themselves that they are not limited by gravity so I do not usually tell them they can fly. By the time we reach this place I am beginning to wish I had.

This tower is like no other I have ever seen, majestic and spiralling upwards to a point, it seems ribbed like a seashell from a distance. It becomes clear to us both as we get closer that it is not constructed using conventional building materials, made of neither bricks nor stone, this tower is constructed entirely of books. It looks weatherbeaten and very old.

We walk around its broad base looking for an opening and find the remains of a crumbling stairway on the outside, leading to a narrow arched entrance which reveals a fusty, dim interior.

Inside the tower has a more solid feel. There is only one way to go, so up the spiral staircase we tread. Brian is beside himself with excitement. I find myself totally perplexed.

I have spent many years drumming into my students that nothing is ever symbolic in a shamanic journey, everything is real. Right now I am in a psychologists dream environment, full of symbols, a desolate plane with a mysterious tower, made entirely of old books. All I need next is some wizened old character in a room at the top and I have a complete set of set of symbols to analyse over a period of weeks. Not my style at all.

Brian who has shot up the stairs ahead of me telepaths excitedly.

You are not going to believe this, there is an old guy up here, who says he has been waiting for me.

Just as I expected. Ask him if he loves you.

I reach the room at the top and sure enough Brian is there with an ancient man, who looks harmless enough.

I know this is not symbolic, it can't be, we must be in another reality somewhere, perhaps one created and maintained by a powerful group. The ancient one addresses me:

Greetings my friend, thank you for bringing him. I thought he would never get here.

It is an honour, you have something for him?

Indeed! Some information that may be to his advantage. The old man turns to Brian.

My child you really have no idea who you are, do you?

Brian is speechless.

Your great uncle who died some time ago by your reckoning, left something for you. You will find a sea-chest in your grandmother's attic, in it there is a book. You came on this journey to find out more about yourself. You have an inheritance which is priceless, the book is yours and it has the key you seek.

Wha...

Brian has no clue where to start with his questions.

All will be revealed. In the book you will find clues to who you are and you will recognise this place. This is how you will know the truth of your experience.

Thank you for visiting. I can be at peace now. He folds his arms and slowly closes his eyes.

It's obvious that he will say no more. We take our leave and depart the tower walking back across the plain in silence.

I know that Brian will find all that he needs in the sea-chest and I sense it will change his life forever. Power flows down the male lineage with old brotherhoods. Brian lost his father when he was a child so he was never formally initiated into his ancestral order.

I wonder how he will integrate into his present life his new found position in the Order of Knights Templar.

Old Soldiers Never Die

I am in a chaotic and filthy place. The stench of death overwhelms me, it penetrates my being to the core, I try to get a grip on the time and place I am in, but right now I am in overload. Nothing could have prepared me for the pandemonium I am experiencing.

The noise is unbearable, I already have a headache and I have been here for just a few moments. The mud around is a mush of earth, excrement and decomposing organic matter. I just cannot believe how foul this place is - yet, there are human beings here. And some are smiling.

I am in the middle of a fierce battle involving relatively modern weaponry. The soldiers around me use heavy rifles with wooden butts. They are wearing green steel helmets and their clothes are coarse and look uncomfortable. They are half-starved, small men, their skin grey and filthy. For some reason there is a lull in the fighting, the irregular explosions and rapid gunfire subside and I get the chance to take stock.

My ears are ringing and my eyes watering from the acrid residue of cordite in the air. My surroundings are smothered in dust and mist, it softens the muddy colours around me into a sepia monotone. The artist in me wants to take a photograph, but my memory will have to suffice. I won't be forgetting this experience in a hurry.

In the trench next to me I see two soldiers, they squat with their backs against the timber and sandbags that shore up its sides. They share a cigarette and take a breather in the unexpected and surreal stillness. I overhear their conversation.

"Jerry is laying it on thick this morning... Wouldn't say no to a nice hot cuppa cha."

"Wouldn't say no to a nice lie down, in a dry, clean bed... with my girl."

They sit in silence for while drawing in the poisonous smoke and nicotine from their army-issue cigarettes.

"Do you reckon we'll ever make it out of here?"

"Sure Jack, sure. Look!" Pointing into the clouds. "A flock of flying pigs." They both laugh.

"Tell you what, we've made it this far, you and me. Why don't we promise to really stick together and look out for each others from now on? We will be real muckers!"

"Corker! We might make even it back to dear old Blighty in one piece."

Their rough, soiled hands engage in a firm handshake and they smile as the last mortar of the day finds its target, exploding immediately behind the man farthest from me. His back ripped to shreds by shrapnel, he dies instantly. His body protects his mate who collapses, concussed and wounded, but alive.

At last I recognise which of these men is my client. She is not, as I first expected the man who died, but rather the man who survived. Traumatised, injured and scarred for life, emotionally and physically he lies groaning in the mud calling for a medic.

As he slips in an out of consciousness and I invite my present day client to step out of his body to ease the confusion she is experiencing.

That was intense. She telepaths, crying.

So much pointless destruction and death, they were so young and such good mates, what a waste of life. Am I going to die now?

No, you live to a ripe old age. Honouring the memory of your fallen mates every year, without fail.

So why are we here?

In my session room, surrounded by crystals in our present time-space I have instructed my client to command her body to take her to the moment when the communication and relationship challenges in her present life began.

I don't get it. What is messing up my life now, this war trauma?

Not quite, in your own way you deal with it. By the time you die you are at peace with it.

What then? I can't see anything here that is screwing up my present life.

Think about what just happened...

Escaping death by a hair's breadth?

What was happening before that?

I was talking with my mate.

About what?

We made a promise to look out for each other.

How do you feel remembering that promise?

Emotional. She tears up.

You made a real heartfelt commitment to each other?

Of course.

Do you remember it?

No, that was a long time ago and you told me I lived a long life. I probably forgot it then.

The promise faded into a mass of uncomfortable memories for you, but not for him. For him it is still fresh.

What do you mean?

He is still bound by it. His promise to you was very clear and heartfelt at the moment of his death so he is still keeping to it. In fact he does not realise he is dead. Your mate from the trenches has been with you ever since, looking out for you, just as he promised. He does not understand that you are now incarnated as a woman. He sees you as you were in the trenches in World War One. He is here with your permission and his presence, although loving is conditional. It creates a barrier between you and the beings who love you unconditionally,. Why don't you call on him now and explain things, release him from his commitment to you?

I sense my client is confused but she plays along with me, hesitantly…

Jack! Where are you mate? We need to talk.

Out of the mess around us the form of her dead mate appears.

Jesus this has gone on for a long time. And they're still hammering us. Good job we stuck together.

I've got some bad news…

What? Run out of bully beef? No more fags? I feel like I have been living on thin air for bloomin' eternity. How can things get any worse than this god-awful cock-up?

Sorry Jack, but you were blown to smithereens a second after we made our promise to look after each other. And you've been stuck to me, looking out for me, ever since. Jack I am sorry but you are dead, your body is long gone.

Bull mate. You can't bounce me with that crack. Shell shocked you are! Give over…

He looks concerned.

It is now 2016 and I am a woman. I really appreciate your help but your presence in my life is creating problems for me in my relationships. It is time to release each other from our promises. I now release you from your promise, it has served its purpose.

I intercede as Jack starts to panic.

Jack I know you can see me, and that you don't recognise me or the way I appear to you. Your mate is telling the truth, let us help you. The war is over, you can go home now.

There are tears and they embrace as we help Jack transit home to light.

As there now is nothing blocking my client's perception of unconditionally loving beings close to her I make a suggestion.

Why not call on the beings who love you unconditionally? It is time to meet your spirit guides…

Slayer of the Beast

My vision and hearing are impaired and I am hot. My body moves to a natural but non-human rhythm. Sweat trickles from my forehead into my eyes and it stings, blurring my vision; I sense vertical lines of light before me. The distorted background sounds that I can hear are strangely tinny, I might be hearing birdsong; I do not know where I am, what I am or why I am here.

I have invited my apprentice to time-travel with me on an open-ended adventure and I am reminded that the trouble with open-ended adventures is just that, their open-endedness. I have left it to my higher-self to take us to wherever we need to be.

An unearthly screech rattles my bones, triggering contradictory feelings of fear and calm. Wherever I am this is not new to me, I know what to do next. I tell myself to stop questioning and just experience.

I feel into my surroundings and gradually grasp what is going on around me. The armour and padding I am wearing are heavy and it feels like I am trapped in a slow roast croc-pot. The blokes who wore this stuff must have had ways of dealing with this claustrophobia, I am not doing so well. My body is smaller and leaner than the one I have now, which although fit and muscly might be considered overfed by my past-life self.

My vision clears and I can see greenery through the vertical slits in my visor, a gentle grassy slope dotted with daisies and European trees. It is a cool spring morning, somewhere in Britain. If it wasn't for that disturbing sound and the fact that I was sitting on an armoured horse ready for some kind of battle it would be a pleasant day.

I look around me, which is a challenge in this helmet, I have to move my whole body and my twisting unsettles my mount. I notice that he is armoured too, his crinet, peytral and shafron have been well attached by my squire.

I see also that I am pretty much alone, no armies massed to meet each other as I had expected. Just a small, rag-tag group of peasants who are watching from some distance away. I know my apprentice must be nearby and I wonder how her appearance will differ from her usual twenty-first century street chic.

Then I spot her, my squire, a young man in period dress. He stands between the locals and me, a shiny polished shield resting against his feet. Behind him our traveling ponies, supplies and the gear used to help me onto my horse.

In my right hand I become aware of a long heavy sword and in my left a shield, like the one at my squire's feet. I am ready for action, but what kind of action? I can see no enemy.

The otherworldly screech fills the air again; the villagers flee, my squire stands his ground and I feel the earth vibrating through my horse. He is stock still, ears pricked, breathing loudly through his flared nostrils. I realise he is waiting for

Spirit World

instructions from me and as I gently lean, he moves forward in the direction I am intending. We make our way slowly up the grassy knoll towards the sound. He traverses the hill sideways as if he is performing full-pass in a modern dressage competition. He is a fine beast; he presents my sword arm to the hill.

My past life self is feeling confident but my present logical mind is not, we are making our way sideways uphill towards an unknown enemy, surely we will be vulnerable to whatever crests the hill as it bears down on us?

I do not have to wait long to find out what is making that awful sound.

A large, scaly, green, reptile-like creature appears over the rise before us. To say it breathed fire would be an exaggeration, but plenty of snot and steam emanate from its nostrils into the crisp morning air.

It must be warm blooded. I catch myself thinking.

It stands three metres tall on its hind legs, both its front and rear claws flash pink and white, clogged with flesh and wool. Intestines dangle from its mouth. The villagers have deliberately disturbed its morning feast on one of their precious lambs.

My job, I quickly realise, is to curtail its eating habits, permanently.

I become an acutely aware observer as the action unfolds around me. I hear myself shouting insults at the reptile, I make bird calls, animal noises, cows, sheep, goats - you name it. I could have been a great stage performer. It is as if the creature understands me, it responds by bellowing what could be insults back at me, in its strange shrill way.

I hear myself giving it the option to retreat to its cave and leave the villagers alone. It does not care for or understand my words and makes its way down the slope towards me, ready for another snack.

I notice the shield on my left arm is smaller than I expected and I feel myself positioning it carefully before I engage with the dragon. I also know I am relying on my squire to use the highly polished shield he has to reflect the morning sun into the dragon's eyes.

Everything is in my favour, the reflected sunlight dazzles the beast and it rears up momentarily distracted. In an instant the horse changes tack, responding to my gentle, almost telepathic signals, he moves quickly and courageously right in, under the reptile, giving me a clear lunging strike with my sword.

I thrust my blade deep into the beast's underbelly and immediately retreat, so as not to be trapped beneath its shocked, staggering bulk. The kill is all over in a few, adrenalin-pumped seconds. The beast falls, writhing, wailing in agony, thrashing around with its long claws, seeking some kind of retribution. My big, brave horse gracefully backs away from the danger, eyes fixed constantly on the dying dragon.

I am totally drenched with sweat and exhausted, my squire helps me off my horse and removes my armour, I thank and embrace him.

The shepherds and local villagers are grateful, but also afraid of me. I smile inwardly; they have no need to fear me. I accept their gold as my squire packs up and readies to depart. I can see parallels to my present life as a shaman, people respect me but also fear me: there is no need for that, now, either.

"Shall we return?" I speak to my squire/apprentice using the knight's vocal chords.

This is our pre-arranged signal to return to our present time-space, s/he nods. We stretch as we feel ourselves back in our bodies in this here and now.

"Wow! Way cool. You were a really brave man."

"I was skilled at my craft."

"Unbelievable... Dragons - far out. But there was no trauma there, you did well. Why were we taken there? So you could experience what a great warrior you were?"

"No... It was so I could remember the mutual bond of total trust I had with my horse: such a fine, noble and beautiful animal." My tears surprise her.

"You could have one again now."

"No need," I smile, "the dragons I deal with now are non-physical. Anyway I have a bicycle, less space and lower maintenance."

Long lost sister

Marjory is not what you might expect to see in an alternative crystal shop. In her conservative, twin set and pearls she looks like a zipped up tight version of a mature lady who has walked straight out of some dated period drama.

My assistant Bryony has briefed me: Marjory is desperate, seeking help in a realm that she might otherwise quietly dismiss as silly nonsense. As Bryony greets her, I observe Marjory, assessing the deeper reason for her visit to my practice - it is not what she thinks it is.

Marjory is not feeling comfortable in such an alien environment and I sense my assistant Bryony's concealed contempt for someone who epitomises all she has opposed in her life. It is hard to believe that my free spirited, dreadlocked, fairy-loving assistant is probably the same age as the straight laced client she is ushering upstairs to my session room.

"Good luck with that one." She breathes as she walks past me rolling her eyes.

"She is an embodiment of the Goddess, who moves in mysterious ways."

My comment is quite serious but it totally cracks Bryony up: she doubles over stuffing a hanky in her mouth so that the client upstairs will not hear her raucous bird-like laugh. I leave her holding her stomach with tears streaming down her cheeks.

Upstairs I greet my client who is unbuttoning her cardigan.

"Do you need to examine my breasts?"

"No need. I am a Shaman, not a doctor, my assistant has briefed me."

"What about the crystals on my body?"

"Crystals can work through concrete, there is no need to disrobe as long as you are comfortable." Marjory looks relieved.

"You are concerned about the number of cysts your specialist has been finding in your breasts....?"

"Yes nobody can explain why there are so many, it's a worry."

"Our aim today is to find the cause, release it and then observe what happens after the session." I know that once we find the cause and deal with it the cysts will disappear, but I am mindful of my promises.

"Is there anything else?"

Silence. I know there is an issue but I need her permission to explore it.

"How are your relationships?" A pause.

"Well to be honest I find it hard to be close to anyone, even my husband and children."

"Would you like to change that?"

Spirit World

"I always thought it is just the way I am, is it possible to change?"

"With your permission we will look into it today, if there is time."

"OK."

Laying in my crystal mandala we start our shamanic journey together. We scan her body and notice a variety of energies in her breasts, I suggest she commands her body to show us what it is holding there.

Immediately we are overcome by the sharp smell of burning flesh as the young woman Marjory is, has the right breast removed by a hot copper knife. She stifles her screams knowing it is not appropriate to show weakness during her initiation as an Amazonian warrior.

In a perverse repetition of this trauma Marjory experiences being a beautiful Native American woman lying on the hard cold ground in a decimated and burning camp. Her family have been massacred and she is being mutilated by leery American bluecoats.

In another time we find ourselves in the fetid, close air of a dark workhouse in seventeenth century Britain. Marjory is a grubby undernourished young woman who has just given birth. She is hiding, cradling an illegitimate, suckling child which is torn from her breast and taken away.

This experience repeats itself with a mid-twentieth century variation, where Marjory re-lives being an Australian Aboriginal woman living peacefully with her extended family in humpies in the bush. She adores her little children and is breastfeeding when they are suddenly stolen by ghostly White-fella's, she is devastated.

Some incidents intertwine more than once in their similarities, anyone could see their interconnectedness. They cover a huge span of time and each experience is held in a different part of her breasts.

As we re-live each of these ten past lives I wish I had a room full of students to witness how we hold multiple traumas. Unresolved trauma can repeat itself lifetime after lifetime, until it is resolved. This is the body's way of helping us, by bringing it to our attention. Unfortunately present day society does not understand our bodies' signs, as our ancestors did. Ignoring them can be fatal.

Each trauma has its own unique resolution and it takes the whole session to release them all. As we finish I find myself hurrying as I am keen to get to what I feel is the real reason for Marjory's visit.

You wanted to look into your relationship challenges?

Oh yes, I had forgotten, let's do that.

Please repeat after me - I call on any being close to me, please join me now.

A woman appears dressed as an affluent Victorian lady, they embrace. They are both crying.

Spirit World

Sister! Where have you been? I have missed you so much, it has been a long time! Marjory sobs.

I have been here with you all the time. Remember we promised we would never leave each other?

Marjory looks perplexed, I intercede.

What year is it?

1856. Who are you and why do you ask?

I am your sister's friend. Do you realise you are dead?

Her response takes me completely by surprise.

Of course I do, I remember the day well. I keep my promises, I am staying here, looking after my sister.

How do you feel about the others in her life?

I am all she needs, I love her, she knows that.

Marjory, please allow me to help your sister. She is Earthbound and confused. Can you see how her presence is affecting your present relationships?

Before she can respond Marjory's sister interrupts.

How dare you sir! I am not confused! I am here by choice, keeping my promise.

Marjory, all you have to do is release her from her promise and I can help her go home to light and find peace.

Marjory's response is bewildering, unexpected and a first for me.

No, we love each other, I want her to stay. They embrace.

I try my best to persuade Marjory that this will impair both her and her sisters growth, but she will have none of it. Mindful of the implications for my own karma if I push too hard, I respect their free will and wrap up the session, which has run over time.

My assistant Bryony returns after escorting a still emotional client out into the fresh air.

"Breasts are looking good, no more challenges there…"

"Her next scan will be clear." I manage a wan smile.

"Pity about the sister…"

"I really wanted to help them both, maybe another time." I am doing my best to surrender to the perfection of their choices and not to sound too glum.

"Yes. Another lifetime."

Bryony's irony reveals a deep truth, Marjory has missed a great opportunity to dissolve a co-dependent relationship, be closer to her family, step into her power and truly be herself.

The Dark Lord

Linda has come to see me because she is ready to solve the mystery of the constantly repeating injuries to her arms. She rolls up her sleeves to reveal a blotchy pattern of multiple scars, old and new, that cover her flesh - a roadmap map of past pain.

I hear my apprentice Jo's sharp, wincing intake of breath. She has been through periods of self harm in her youth but she has seen nothing like this.

"How did this happen?" I ask, covering Jo's lack of tact.

"Since I was little things are always happening to my arms; burns, cuts, scalds, bruises, one thing after another. They no sooner heal than something else happens. Look at this." She indicates a purple welt on her elbow.

"Beauty!" Jo breathes involuntarily.

"Also, I live in a constant state of fear, it has been with me for as long as I can remember and it is particularly intense now. My doctor feels this stress may be contributing to my heart condition."

I catch Jo's eye to be sure she recognises a classic case of major past life trauma manifesting in the physical body. From a shamanic perspective this kind of repeated injury happening to the same part of the body over a period of time, is a clear indication of trauma begging to be released. Her body is saying 'Here, here - look here! This is where I am holding it.'

The three of us make our way up to my session room and lay in the crystal mandala. I close the door and windows having briefed my assistant downstairs to ease up the volume of the ambient music in my crystal shop, as the session progresses. I expect this could be noisy and we have had enough complaints from neighbouring businesses.

As soon as we close our eyes we are back at the source of the trauma. There is no time for any kind of triggering affirmation, Linda's body is so ready to release its cellular memory that it takes us all straight there. Her sobs start to build as she unlocks the secrets her body has been carrying since birth.

Holy shit. Jo telepaths.

Stay calm and allow. Let this play out, it is her journey.

We are in a ghetto. This place once had a semblance of order that was held together purely by willpower. Today it is chaotic, the air pulses with the sounds and smells of violence and fear. Around us people are being forced from their homes and treated brutally by armed men in dark grey-green uniforms.

Hugo Boss I catch myself pondering as I unconsciously appraise the style of the officers who stand chatting, wilfully ignoring the brutality that is happening under their command.

Jo and I are witnesses to something terrible and it is hard not to feel for the innocent men, women and children being brutalised around us.

Stay detached. I telepath to Jo as I notice her eyes blaze with anger.

We are close to our client Linda who in this time-space is a pretty, feisty young Jewess taking issue with the soldiers' harsh treatment of her grandmother.

"Sie ficken!" the senior non-commissioned brute shouts. His underlings happily obey by dragging her into an alley, beating and defiling her.

Jo is enraged; I caution her.

You can't get involved - they can't see you anyway.

This is bad but it is just the beginning. We have not yet found the emotional trauma Linda is holding in her arms.

"Ein exempel statuieren!" The sergeant commands smiling.

Linda's past life feistiness has totally evaporated, I know her cries of terror are now filling my healing space and possibly the shop below.

We, like her kin, watch helpless as the soldiers wrap her arms and shoulders with barbed wire, hitch her to the back of a dusty VW kubelwagen and drag her around the square laughing and shouting insults, until she is lifeless.

We catch her as she leaves her body, totally traumatised. This brief, brutal act will affect every lifetime from this moment onwards until it is released. Fortunately we have the opportunity now to free her from it, so it is worth re-experiencing it.

My arms. She telepaths. *They killed me!*

Jo comforts her; the first time I have seen my cool, streetwise apprentice in tears.

Are you ready to release the trauma? I ask.

Linda nods.

You must call on all those responsible and forgive them.

Even though the trauma is fresh she grasps the logic of my suggestion as we help her address her torturers in no time-space.

I forgive you, I forgive you, I forgive you. In forgiving you I release us all from this trauma, we are no longer bound by it. Go in peace, be at peace, you are completely forgiven.

Those responsible are filled with remorse, humbled and grateful to be released, from an interaction which also continues to affect them.

It looks like we are about finished. Linda is calm and Jo is looking brighter.

I prepare to return us to our present when I notice something unusual. Jo has noticed it too.

A figure is approaching us, one that Linda has not called on. I sense who may be joining us and quickly I telepath to Jo and Linda.

Spirit World

Do not say or telepath anything, under any circumstances, for the next few minutes. Be mindful of your thoughts. Understood?

Grasping from my tone that I am serious they both nod, perplexed.

The gentleman nearing us is very smartly dressed in twenty-first century clothes, he has an air of total confidence and congeniality, with an undefinable edge.

Honoured to have you visit, how may I help? I take the initiative.

This ageless, suave and handsome gent smiles, his eyes twinkle.

Your friends are quiet.

He nods towards Linda and Jo, who has turned quite white.

A little shy, I respond, *what can I do for you?*

Lots! He laughs. *Do you like my suit? It's your favourite designer, you were admiring his work earlier. It's yours if you like it.*

No thanks I'm not really a suit kind of guy, more T shirt and shorts.

Anything else you would like? Money? Fame? Women? Cars? Property? Power?... Anything you wish for can be yours, for a little exchange. Just sign here.

He unrolls a parchment scroll and offers me a pen..

I'm honoured that you take an interest in my wellbeing but I have all I need, thank you.

And your friends?

I interrupt Jo who is about to speak.

Just fine thanks, all their needs are met.

He looks into my eyes.

You know, I could use a man like you. You don't scare easily do you?

I smile and say nothing, choosing not to give him an opening. When fear has no purchase, charm is the next line of attack.

You know you should not meddle in other people affairs.

I respond.

I never meddle, I help when I am asked to do so, otherwise I mind my own business.

His tone changes.

Mmm, I am sure you do. I have my eye on you, we will meet again I am sure.

I nod my head.

It is always an honour.

He smiles at the three of us and wanders off into nothingness.

We return to this time-space and debrief a shell-shocked Linda, who I expect will have no more challenges with her arms, heart or her fear.

After escorting Linda out, Jo returns to the session room, happy to have assisted.

"Why did you stop me speaking? Was that guy who I think it was?"

Spirit World

"Lets just say he was an aspect of that consciousness."

"Man that guy was slick." She shakes her head.

"You don't know the half of it." I smile.

Fear of the dark

Helena is a mature, well dressed, aristocratic looking woman with great poise and a commanding presence. My assistant Brianna and I sense her approach before she enters our little crystal shop.

Brianna spontaneously steps forward to open the shop door for our visitor. A surprising gesture and something I have never witnessed before. Brianna is a feisty, independent woman but there is something about Helena's bearing that changes Brianna's normal demeanour.

She ushers my client upstairs with a hint of deference, leaving us in my session room with a subtle bow. I almost expect her to say, 'Will that be all ma'am?' but she does not make my day.

Helena sits, back ramrod straight but somehow also relaxed. Not knowing what to expect, she waits for me to open the conversation.

"You have come to see me about a phobia?"

"Yes, for sixty years I have lived with it and I am sick of it. I hear you may be able to help. I have tried everything."

"How does it manifest?"

"I am terrified of the dark. For as long as I can remember it scares, me; I sleep with the lights on. It limits my activities. It is beyond reason, the fear just takes over."

Phobias may relate to past-life or childhood trauma, so I ask what kind of place she grew up in. In her soft European accent she replies:

"What you would call a castle." I picture a large fancy house with turrets.

"It was on our family home in Europe, a large old place." She pauses, "too big to look after properly."

She spent her childhood there until she was sent off to boarding school. With busy parents and no siblings, she had enjoyed many happy hours playing alone in and around the big old house. That's all I need to know, we lie in my crystal mandala and Helena moves into an altered state easily.

In no time-space I telepath asking her to repeat after me *Body I command you take me to the moment this phobia started. NOW...*

It is bright and sunny, I feel the warm breeze on my face cool as we follow the little girl that is Helena into shady places as she dashes around the grounds of her family home.

It is much larger than I expected, her family must be wealthy. She runs around the huge well kept garden. She seems happy, singing, skipping and talking to herself, the way solitary children do. She plays with a misshaped ball that has an uneven bounce. She calls it her "adventure ball" because it takes her to unexpected places.

She throws it, laughing at its crazy, wayward bounce. It takes her underneath bushes, around corners and into the dark potting shed where a bulky gardener is tending his plants.

Startled, he turns quickly trowel in hand to see what has disturbed him, looming over little Helena. I catch a glint in his eye that could be malevolent. Could this be the point of trauma? Something Helena has hidden from herself for all these years?

The glint turns into a sparkle, as he reaches under his bench and pulls out the crazy ball, throwing it on for Helena to chase, away from his workspace. He laughs to himself shaking his head as he continues to tend to his green children.

The ball bounces on, tumbling over a shallow river bank and into a fast flowing stream. It wedges itself under a large rotting tree limb. Helena follows; recklessly jumping after it, she slides down the muddy bank straight into the creek feet first. The speed of her descent wedges her calves under the dark rotten timber. It is heavy and it rocks, crumbling away from its foothold on the bank, ready to tumble forward and pin her under the shallow water.

But today she is lucky, she gets away with wet underwear and muddy skirt as she retrieves her ball, wriggles out and races on, oblivious to her condition.

The shadows are lengthening and the air is cooling. I sense she is some distance from her home and like a homing pigeon, without any conscious effort, she turns in that direction, kicking her crazy ball head of her.

Then I see it. What she described as a castle and I envisioned as a large home actually is a castle. A real one, with turrets spires and ancient stonework, it is an impressive and foreboding sight to me. But to her it is home.

She enters though a simple side entrance some distance from the imposing grandeur of the main building. Inside she bounces her ball hard against the floor and walls, knowing there are no adults around, she is totally carefree, forever fascinated by its unpredictability.

She does not notice the coolness of the air or the damp smell of the neglected corridors she plays in, her young eyes adjusting easily to the rapidly fading light. After a particularly hard throw the ball takes off on its own self-willed way, bouncing erratically down some stairs at the end of the corridor. This area was never well maintained and is now crumbling. We follow her downstairs. I sense my client's mounting apprehension as she relives an incident that impacted on her life from this day forward.

I don't want to see... She telepaths *It is not nice down here.*

You wanted to be free of your phobia? We are close to where it starts, please bear with me.

Intent on following her little bouncing friend the child is oblivious to the gloomy, oppressive atmosphere. She pays no attention to the unkempt nature of the place she is in or the dank air seeping into her little lungs, as she continues her descent into darkness.

Now deep beneath the castle she finds her ball in a particularly musty mildewed corner. When she picks it up and turns around her carefree expression changes. She has lost her bearings in the gloom, but more than that she senses a presence nearby that is not benign.

We can see it clearly: standing close to her in the shadows, is an emaciated man in rags. His hollow cheeks and bulging eyes speak of malnutrition and deprivation, his appearance terrifies the young Helena. She screams and calls out for help. Only the stone walls hear her as the man obliges by moving closer to her, amplifying her fear.

Please someone help me. She trembles, the wetness of her clinging underwear chilling her to the bone.

This plea gives the Earthbound spirit permission to help her by attaching himself to her energy body, temporarily calming her but forever amplifying his and her fear of the darkness that he died in centuries before. Left to starve to death after days of torture, the trauma of his slow and solitary death had kept him stuck in the castle dungeons, until today.

I invite Helena into no time-space and he joins us, following her. Counselling him is straightforward and he journeys home to light with ease.

His disappearance allows a reunion with Helena's own spirit guides, who had been unable to communicate clearly with her because of his presence. They take her to a place of such exquisite beauty and love that Helena becomes ecstatic. Not since she had been in an accident years previously, and been clinically dead for a short period, had she experienced such bliss.

She has no doubt whatsoever that her phobia has completely vanished.

Ceremony

A ceremony is commencing. It is dark, yet people wear masks and hooded capes. They stand in a circle, heads bowed, illuminated by thirteen thick, greasy, spluttering candles. My apprentice, Jo and I have travelled through time and space with my wealthy client, Sandra. She has just triggered a recall of the source of the uncontrollable promiscuity, that is ruining her relationships.

I can see she is totally taken aback by what she is witnessing. I have seen this before; what IS disturbing for me is the contemporary nature of the surroundings. Although at first glance we could be anywhere, any time, I pick up subtle clues as to the closeness to our present time. Sandra has not yet noticed.

Jo catches my eye, the nausea we are feeling is deep seated and irrational. It is as if our stomachs are gripped in a hot vice, our chests are constricted and saliva oozes into our mouths.

Why is this happening? My panicked apprentice telepaths.

I know but I am not sure how to break it to her without causing further irrational fear, which could exacerbate the situation.

Well, you know how it is for beings not totally aligned with unconditional love, when they enter a sacred space that we create?

I pause, swallowing the hot pre-vomit stream of spittle that involuntarily fills my mouth.

Yes, they feel nauseous and want to get out.

We are in a so-called sacred space now and it is having that effect on us.

But we are aligned with love and light, how can a sacred space affect us that way?

I said so-called for a good reason, this space is aligned with the opposite - hence our reaction to it.

Oh shit.

Try and take your focus off the nausea, if you throw up your physical body, lying in my session room, may choke.

I feel for Jo who has volunteered to travel with me to learn more about shamanism. If I am not mistaken the grossness of what she is about to witness will change her perceptions of what human beings are capable of irrevocably.

Sandra came to see me because she wanted to get to the bottom of her self-sabotaging behaviour. Not only is she prone to wild outbursts, her licentiousness has led to the break up of several promising, stable relationships. Just when things are looking good she subverts her own joy by sleeping around.

She suspects this might be due to past life trauma and I am more than happy to help her discover the root cause of it, through our shamanic journey together.

However as we witness this twisted ritual unfold, I sense she still feels it is in the distant past, when in fact it is much closer to home.

Jo has her hand in her mouth and is dry retching.

You can return to our present time-space if you wish.

This is all she needs to hear to activate her resolve.

No way, I want to learn how to do this stuff.

OK then be still and observe. Some of these people are in a trance and your agitation might betray our presence.

And so we observe. A girl is brought into the circle, she is terrified and is not there of her own free will. The horror on Sandra's face tells all I need to know about her realisation of what might be happening.

Oh NO! That's me, in this life. How can this be? I thought we were in ancient time, I recognise my dress and shoes... I don't remember this. Who ARE these people?

I know, but I prefer that her realisation be complete and unaided by me.

Please, if you can, just observe. This may not be pleasant but you wanted to understand where and how your behaviour started? We are here now.

The pre-pubescent girl is led to an altar where incantations and offerings are made to entities who feed off the energy released here. A man comes forward dressed as the most common and feared manifestation of evil our culture knows, he appears to be in a trance.

They go through a pseudo wedding ceremony and with everybody watching he rapes the traumatised girl. I feel sick to the core and my feminist apprentice is enraged. I have to restrain Jo to stop her from interacting, exposing our presence and placing us all in grave danger.

This is too much. ENOUGH! Sandra is close to collapsing.

I am sorry, there may be more. Do you recognise anyone here?

They are all masked or hiding under hoods...

I know, but in the state you are in you can read their energy. Tune into them.

I can't believe this is true, why don't I remember it?

We will come to that later. Who is in this circle you know?

There are close members of my family here.

You know who they are?

Yes.

Then we know enough.

I decide she has seen enough when a black obsidian knife is placed in the girl's small hands and they drag a young boy, a street kid "gone missing," into the centre of the circle close to the altar.

I take Sandra to the time and place her memory was erased and she witnesses the process. After that time she was treated as a normal teenager by everyone around her, those who knew and those who did not. Naturally any reference to the secret society and their repeated rituals did not happen when she was around.

This misguided group was confident that this brain washing was permanent. However it is not. One session can unlock it all, totally involuntarily. The challenge now is helping Sandra come to terms with it.

In no time-space I take her through processes that release all vows and agreements that she may have made under duress or that may have been made on her behalf. By the end of the session she is clear energetically and spiritually, although there is much emotional healing still to come.

We return to our present time and my session room. My pale, uber-punk apprentice excuses herself and we hear the muffled sounds of her throwing up in the toilet next door. She returns wiping her mouth as I debrief Sandra.

"You have a complete understanding of what you have just witnessed?"

"I find it hard to believe, but yes I do."

"Did I suggest anything to you in any way prior to, or during our session?"

"No, you did not."

"You are well on the way to changing your behaviour, there is nothing now holding it in place. I recommend further emotional healing, but this is not my area of expertise."

"I understand." Sandra is still in shock.

Jo who has is now flushed and agitated cannot help herself, regardless of my instruction for her not to say anything to my clients she blurts out.

"I hope you are going to dob those bastards in."

Sandra reflects. Taking a deep breath she quietly exhales her response.

"Whats the point? I saw, through the other people I recognised in the circle, that this perversion pervades the highest levels of our society. An accusation would go nowhere, it could lead to me being called delusional and locked up. In fact it could even threaten my life."

My apprentice is stunned into silence as I counsel them both.

"This is entirely your choice, it is best now to focus on our own wellbeing and healing. Those confused, corrupt, sub-humans are bound by the laws of Karma whether they like it or not. They think they can avoid it by staying Earthbound, in service to their masters, after their death, but in due course they will experience everything they have perpetrated. There is no way they can avoid it."

"They deserve everything they get!" I frown at Jo's outburst, but inwardly, reluctantly, I agree.

Long-term relationship

Estelle has been a regular visitor to my little crystal shop for some time. Normally her slim, petite, elfin being is clear and bright, she walks in this morning cloudy and off-centre. Her warm, lively personality is muted; something is not quite right. I notice her mascara has run and she is sniffling as she looks through my new stock.

"Caught a cold?," I ask, hoping to create an opening for her, but realising immediately that my question sounds tactless and insensitive. She knows me well enough not to overreact.

"I need a session with you. My life is falling apart." Estelle blows her nose.

"No time like the present." It is a cold wet day outside, today will be quiet and I have no sessions booked.

"I'll put a sign on the door and close up shop. Let's go up to my session room now."

Estelle starts crying as soon as she sits down. "I have to have Chemo. They have found something bad."

"I am sorry to hear that. You know it's okay to use conventional medicine when we need to…"

"I am fine with that. They need to move quickly. I accept that. I want to understand why this is happening to me."

"How are things with your relationship. How is your partner Julie?"

More tears. "I don't deserve her. She is just so lovely."

"You two have been together for ages – the perfect long-term relationship."

"That's what everyone says and I love her dearly but…"

Her pause tells me she is reluctant to share more. I give her space and when it comes I am totally surprised by the confidence she shares.

"I have fallen in love with someone else… a man."

Wow! Estelle is the most well adjusted, committed, lesbian feminist I know; she has never expressed any interest in men. In fact I sometimes feel that to her we symbolise everything that is wrong with humanity.

"But I thought…" I stop myself mid sentence, but it's too late.

"That I was the biggest dyke you have ever met?" She smiles through her tears.

"I… well, love moves in mysterious ways," I respond lamely. I am blushing.

"I just can't get enough of him. I want to be with him all the time. It's driving me crazy. I know he feels the same way, but he has other commitments. It is just so stupid. I can't help myself."

"Have you… consummated your relationship?" I choose my words carefully.

Spirit World

"No, I would never want to hurt anyone else, but I would if we could, without a moment's hesitation. I would feel complete if only I could totally merge with him."

Estelle is a tantric sex practitioner; with practice anyone can use the bliss experienced during lovemaking to access a merging into a oneness that is sublime.

"OK, I've heard enough. Let's get into the session and see how all this connects."

We lay in my crystal mandala. Estelle is ahead of me as we enter an expanded state of consciousness. *Body I command you – show me what I am holding in this disease*, she telepaths, without any prompting from me.

As I expect, her body reveals that she is holding a build-up negative energy connected to the intense and conflicting emotions she has been experiencing over the past year. As she has been unable to process or release them, this energy has built up etherically and has now manifested in her physical body as serious illness.

Well that's not news, Estelle telepaths, with an air of disappointment.

We need to look at your long-term relationship with this man.

But I have only known him for just over a year.

I am talking really long term, cosmically. Command your body to show you how and where your relationship started.

We travel through time and space into the distant past. En route we catch glimpses of their occasional, rather than repeated, interaction. They play together in different incarnations – lovers, brothers, sisters and best friends, always in a close and loving relationship with unconditional support for each other. We move beyond and before physical incarnations, which is where things get interesting.

We approach the void.

How far back do we need to go? Estelle is sounding frustrated and a little apprehensive.

Nearly there. The profound beauty of what we witness next moves us both to tears.

Oh my God... Not known for her religious expletives, Estelle is lost for words.

We are in a garden, a cosmic garden in the far reaches of space and time. The Universe is young, very young. Floating in the barely formed reality that leads to now, we notice a solitary purple flower bud. In the soft light of young stars it opens slowly. It is an exquisite, breathtaking spectacle.

Feel the energy.

I know. I know. Sobs Estelle. *This is the birth of my soul into separate, individual consciousness... Unbelievable.*

There is more - watch.

A stamen gracefully eases its way outward, spiralling upward, then just as it looks fully extended, it splits into two strands, one heading towards future Earth to incarnate, the other to another part of the Universe.

It is us, me and him. We are one and we are separating.

And you will reunite, eventually. You understand now why you want to be together? Your mutual attraction is irresistible.

The dance of these two parts of the same whole over the aeons becomes clear to Estelle.

Twin flames, soul mates, choose a descriptor that fits. Actually no description adequately describes the oneness that you two are.

I understand but…

Let's return to our bodies and discuss this. Have you seen enough?

Yes.

In my confined session room we sit up, breathe and debrief.

"I still don't get it. Why am I having sexual feelings towards him?"

"Because we are here in gross, physical bodies, it is a natural way of expressing what feels like a passionate, true love."

"But what do I do with these feelings and our relationship? It has made me ill."

"You understand that you are one, right?"

"Well, we are all one. Aren't we?"

"Yes, in the biggest sense we are, but your relationship is different. It relates to your soul's journey. In order for this to be resolved, you must understand that the love you feel for this man is self-love. You are loving part of yourself. If you express this love on the highest level then all lower emotions become less intense; in fact less relevant."

"I am not sure if I want to stop feeling the way I do about him…"

"You are not stopping anything – just expanding it. As long as you allow your feelings to remain on a base, physical level you inhibit your growth. This isn't just any passing infatuation. You must see it as an initiation into your true power as a spiritual being of light and unconditional love. It is your chance to really step into your essence as an awakened being by expressing your love in the highest way possible.

Your expression of love for each other must move beyond, Philos and Eros and become Agape, a true expression of unconditional love for the divine beings that you both are."

Estelle contemplates. I hope that she understands. Her future well-being depends on it.

Time-Traveller

I am walking along a desolate and chaotic road; abandoned vehicles stray across pavements and verges, many are left in the middle of the thoroughfare, frozen in time. All are coated in a thin film of fine dust. The time feels close to now and I am exhausted. By my side is my assistant Brianna. She looks gaunt and tired, her clothes have seen better days, her usual vibrancy is dulled and she could do with a shower.

We approach a city, which looks deserted. We are the only ones walking towards it, everyone else is moving away from it.

I try hard to get my bearings, my body feels tired and weak, every joint aches and my usual abundant reserves of energy are non-existent. My clothes are smelly and loose, hanging off an unfamiliar form. I am a shadow of the man I am now, I have next to no muscle tone, my stomach is rumbling - but I am happy.

I notice on my left side Brianna's lovely nephew, eight years old in the present time, around twelve years old where I am now. He looks reasonably well fed and healthy and seems happy to be with us. Whatever has happened he has been protected from it. I still cannot grasp what has brought me here, where and when I am; I notice that traffic would have travelled on the right hand side of the road.

The people leaving the city look in better shape than us. There is no panic: rather an aura of relief mixed with resignation travels with them. They look timeless; they carry a few possessions, some with wheelbarrows and bicycles. We even see a horse.

Then I notice the silence, the background hum of the city is just not here. No machinery running at all, no power. What is most unusual is there are no cars or trucks, nothing moves in the air either.

As we near the centre of the city a squad of soldiers walks past us; whatever has happened, they are helping us. They wear camouflage gear and I notice their shoulder badges incorporate a black panther. I glance at their weapons and what I see surprises me.

They do not carry conventional rifles or advanced laser gear, instead each man carries a compact high-powered crossbow. Apart from the man in front all have their bows pointing towards ground, they looked relaxed and confident. As they pass we nod to them and smile. A few return our smiles and I feel comfortable; their energy is good and my heart opens to them.

We arrive at our destination, an old industrial area on the edge of the city. We stand in front of a crumbling mid 20th Century warehouse with tall windows comprised of many small dirty panes. Holding Brianna's hand I place my arm around her nephew's shoulder.

> "This is where they kept us for doing no more than sharing knowledge and love. Remember this, remember that as long as you stay focussed on unconditional love nothing can harm you."

Am I experiencing a possible future? Or parallel reality? I know my young apprentice is traveling with me but I cannot see her. Because I am aware that I am in my own shamanic journey I trigger my body to tell me more, she will witness the results although they will make more sense to me.

I telepath clearly:

Body I command you, show me what led to this. Take me there now.

I move through a tunnel composed of images from my recent past, present and possible future. I stop at the point where things start to move along the path towards this reality and consider how my present actions could affect this possible future.

I see how, in the next few short years, mass consciousness expands exponentially and becomes a global movement. Through processes like mine people become totally free and empowered, not controlled by anyone or anything, they live joy filled lives, free of all limitations. In Unity Consciousness everything around them becomes transparent; peers, corporations or governments can no longer deceive them. The level of social change this triggers is surprising, even to me.

That's a good part of how things may unfold and my heart fills when I witness humanities potential realised.

But I also see how this creates challenges for those who wish to control and subjugate humanity. Some beings do not want us to be empowered. Attempts are made to discredit methods that expand consciousness, eventually some of us are taken into "protective custody," our methods investigated and feeble efforts made to use them, not for the greater good.

How anyone could feel that a process based on unconditional love is a threat to the dominant paradigm is beyond me, or it was - until today

The weeks passed and outside of our "accommodation" we heard the civil unrest building. Human beings are generally placid easy-going creatures, but it reaches a point where people do stand up for themselves. It just seemed to take a long time, from my confined perspective on the grimy upper level of a disused warehouse.

The great irony of this future repression is that the underground movement that the state was so afraid of did not really exist until they tried to suppress it.

In our internment we used our shamanic techniques to communicate with beings who love humanity unconditionally and we asked for their help.

Beloveds, you know we may not interfere in your affairs, be patient and focus on love. All will be well. Change is coming and it will bring more than you expect.

Being patient in that space was a challenge.

Then it came, weeks later, when the pole shift happened it took out more than electronics. Whether some inter-dimensional friends were involved is not clear to me, but conventional weapons also ceased to operate and for a while there was confusion, then because of the level of mass Unity Consciousness, peace.

As I return to this time-space I see clearly my small part in this drama and how the choices I make now may ease the upcoming shift.

My apprentice is speechless, her spiky hair, black make up and wide eyes create a comical picture as I stare vaguely through her. It is so nice to be back in my strong well nourished body. I realise how much I love everything about my small esoteric practice, tucked away, in a back lane.

"Mind-blowing! What happened? Why no electrical or mechanical devices? What time-space were we in anyway?"

"It is my probable future and it is close. Ironic that our future takes a small step backwards as mankind takes a giant leap forward into expansion and freedom."

"But wasn't this was just a parallel reality? A possible future?"

I smile vaguely and sigh. "I love this little place."

My assistant Brianna gently taps on the session room door and interrupts our conversation, her Earth-mother form and blonde dreads fill the doorway.

My apprentice can't help herself. "Hey, we were just dreaming about you. You looked different, thinner" What she lacks in tact she makes up for with enthusiasm.

"I know you were..." Brianna looks at me. "That guy from the States is on the phone again; remember I mentioned he has called before? He wants to promote your work over there, he sounds keen."

"Thanks, I'll be right there."

I know what I must do.

Contact

I have returned from the States and things are much simpler, I have sold my shop and my two lovely assistants have moved on. I now work from a studio in the bush with one enthusiastic young apprentice. Clients come to me from far and wide.

Today, I am travelling through time and space with my client Jess, who is observing her near future self and is intrigued. We are here because she has requested guidance about career choices she is making now.

I look so much more confident, she telepaths, *fuller figure too, I think I like future myself. It looks like I am organising some special event, a retreat in a beautiful bush setting, lovely.*

We follow her future-self around, she and the other future people are oblivious to our inter-dimensional presence.

This is so weird. No one can see us, not even me, but I know I am here, right?

You will remember this moment. Fortunately we cannot affect the outcome from here, only observe.

"Welcome to the club," my new, young apprentice chips in. Her brief is to take notes, learn and not get involved. She does all three, occasionally.

There is excitement and anticipation in the air, the feeling is celebratory but it is tinged with apprehension. We witness workshops that are based on grounding unconditional love. It is beautiful and moving to see people sharing with such open hearts.

Things are building towards a ceremony of some sort; my guess is that the usual Earth honouring will take place around an equinox or solstice. But I am wrong.

By late afternoon people are gathering outdoors leaving a large open space in the centre of their sacred circle. They hold hands, they sit, they chant and they wait.

The air begins to throb with a deep resonant vibration, it is otherworldly, unpleasant and disturbing. The light in the centre of the circle becomes distorted as if a source of great heat was bending the view from the other side. Things become noticeably darker and vaguer. Some people slip into fear, forgetting their focus from the entire weekend; holding their ears, they back away and the circle disintegrates.

Whatever is arriving feels much bigger and more powerful than anticipated and its presence is pushing people outwards into nearby shrubs and trees.

Look, you are here too!

She points at an older, larger me who is walking around trying to calm people down, without a great deal of success. As the vibration gets more intense, people scatter, acting from some base survival instinct.

Jess and I seem calm and we move further away to observe.

The air settles and light returns to normal. but things are different, the light over a large part of the central space is distorted and there is an almost imperceptible low, throbbing hum in the air. The kind of subtle background noise you only really notice when it stops.

From our present time vantage point we perceive beings exiting the cloaked craft that has materialised in a dimension close to ours, our future-selves sense their presence.

"They can tune into us, they know we are opting out of a fear based reality. We called them here, let's walk back to my cabin holding hands, it has a clear line of site to the landing zone." I reach for Jess' hand.

She trusts my intuition she walks away with me. We stand in the doorway facing each other but also turned slightly towards the landing zone. "Now express your deep unconditional love for me, open your heart to me. Eye to eye, heart to heart."

I feel the energy leaving her heart.

"Good connection, now lets send this outwards, they are watching us, let them feel it. Send it towards them as well."

I am not sure what to expect, then something really strange happens.

"Where did he come from? What a cute little dog!" Jess' future-self looks down to her feet.

We see a small sausage type dog with a stumpy tail, he rubs against our legs like a cat

"Lets go inside with him." Jess has no hesitation.

"He's a playful little thing." Tickling his tummy as he rolls around on the floor we both notice that he is like no dog we have ever seen before: perfectly formed but his fur is not quite right, fur-like but not fur.

He looks up at us and wags his stumpy tail, then races over to centre of the room, sits and waits for us to follow.

We sit on the floor and stroke him, he settles and stares straight into Jess' eyes. They roll back into her head as she enters a light trance.

"Oh my God, so much information…" She gasps, catching her breath.

I think what we are witnessing is the beginning of the first sharing of ET technology directly with us, rather than our governments. It is something that we have been praying for. I telepath Jess.

But why the silly dog?

It is a non-threatening interaction. He is cute and loveable. We extended love and they responded. We are dealing with the good guys here. We have seen enough, lets return to our present time.

Jess opens her eyes. "Well, it's clear to me now where my focus should be. The corporate ladder has just lost all of its appeal, I will be moving sideways. Looks like you and I will be working together. Thanks so much, all my questions have been answered." She is escorted out by my apprentice who returns fizzing with questions.

"You are obviously going to be involved in that retreat, but you don't do retreats…"

"I…"

"There are multiple possible futures, right? And we just saw one of them? Maybe the most probable?"

"Y…"

"So that means that this could happen? With you being involved in our first planned, public ET interaction?"

"C…"

"I know there are many probable-possibles, what does it all mean? What can we be sure of?"

"Based on what I saw today, I am absolutely sure… that I need to modify my diet."

The ramifications of unconditional love

My client Jenny is exhausted, she is a mature and compassionate therapist who has hit a major block to her growth as a Master healer. Skilled in a variety of modalities and with a great reputation for getting to the root of things and helping others find their place of power and peace, her own healing journey is not so smooth. In fact it is in limbo.

She has been referred to me by a string of therapists who have all been unable to make any progress with her case. As she approaches my studio I sense feelings of despair and frustration, tinged with fear. My young apprentice speaks her mind without editing her thoughts.

"She looks wiped out. I thought she was one of the best healers around."

"She is - for others, but right now she has her own challenges, that's why she is here. Now greet her and think before you speak."

Jenny sighs as she takes a seat. "I have been told you may be able to help me, I seem to be encountering a never ending stream of past life traumas. Once one is cleared it is immediately replaced by another, there is no logic to it. No-one should have this much stuff to clear." She starts to cry and my apprentice passes her a tissue.

I explain several reasons why this could be happening, lack of spiritual evolution and healing in previous lives, Karma and the many layered nature of trauma release. None of them ring true to me in her case, there is more going on here than meets the eye.

"Thats enough talking, let's get straight into the session, the process should reveal everything."

Lying in a mandala of crystals we enter no time-space and begin the process of locating and releasing trauma by scanning her energy body. While she is scanning and dictating a long list of things she perceives to my apprentice, I look deeper into the complex web of past life experiences that surrounds her. My apprentice is doing the same.

There really does seem to be no end to this. She telepaths.

It's not quite infinite, but it's more than we can deal with in one session. The thing is I am not sure that it is all hers…

My apprentice commences the clearing process while I observe. Jenny experiences each trauma, usually a death, firsthand as if she was there. It is a visceral and intense experience. Underlying the physicality of her recall is the core of the trauma, how she felt and most importantly how this imprinted feeling affects her now. The effect that each trauma has on her now is not apparent, at all, which is very unusual.

Then I get it: I interrupt the process between releases.

Jenny please call three times on the beings who love you unconditionally, your soul family. Invite them to join you now.

As she does so my apprentice makes an observation. *Surely the fear contained in the unresolved trauma surrounding her will prevent her from perceiving them?* She would be right if this was a normal case, but it is not.

Jenny is overwhelmed by the feelings of deep, expanded unconditional love that fill the space.

I see them clearly, they are here. Ask them what is happening? Why are you carrying trauma that is not yours?

They embrace her. They are telling me they preferred that I did not undertake this mission but that I insisted.

I observe their interaction.

Beloved Jenny, before you came to Earth you begged us to allow you to carry and release our trauma as a soul group, you could see your own future as a Master healer on Earth. You wanted to help us avoid releasing it when we came here. We love you so much we agreed, but reluctantly. Please stop this now it is not good for you, you have done so much for us already.

Yes, yes, yes! I agree to release us all from our agreement. She sobs breathless.

So be it and so it is! We witness the matrix of fear based experiences around her dissolve instantly, leaving clarity.

That simple!? My apprentice telepaths, as Jenny and her non-physical friends have a party.

What about ego? I thought we did not have ego when we are spirits?

I'll explain later, right now let's just let her enjoy the party.

There is little need to debrief after the session; Jenny understands what has happened and why, she feels fantastic. She knows now that she is trauma free, in fact she was clear of personal trauma some time ago. She leaves relieved and happy.

My apprentice is eager for answers. "It sounds arrogant and egotistical to offer to clear your whole extended soul family's trauma before birth, in one incarnation. How can that happen?"

"It is possible, and you have witnessed isolated incidents of clearing another soul family member's trauma. Remember, after the twin towers in the States?

We cleared several traumatic deaths that were not the client's, but members of their soul family.

Her offer to clear a whole group appears to be egocentric because you are looking at it from an earthly perspective. It was a profound act of unconditional love. One that was bound to fail."

"So why did they allow it, knowing that it would fail?"

"Because she wanted it and because they love her unconditionally, silly."

"But…"

I leave my apprentice to ponder on the profound ramifications of unconditional love as I head to the kitchen.

A hidden cause of chronic fatigue

"So… chronic fatigue can relate to people not following their life's calling, correct?" My apprentice is reviewing her notes prior to the next session.

"Often people stray so far from their life path that their higher selves step in to attract attention to the situation - but not always. The challenge is that our culture does not understand how these things work and people do not look for answers in the right places. We will see when Barbara arrives."

Barbara has tried to treat her ailments with little success, they re-present repeatedly, in slightly different forms time and time again. Off the record one of her therapists told me that she suspected Barbara was "…just plain miserable" and no amount of conventional or alternative healing could remedy the situation

When Barbara arrives we can see it has taken a great deal of willpower to make the journey to us. It brings out a nurturing side in my apprentice, usually well hidden by her bright and breezy persona. She helps Barbara into our studio and we lay her in the crystal mandala immediately. She has already briefed me on the phone and I prefer to tackle challenges in a shamanic journey rather than through talking, so after a brief introduction we enter an expanded state of consciousness together.

Scanning her body she repeats after me "Body I command you show me the moment this started."

I sense my apprentice's surprise when we are shown neither life choices nor work environment but her early childhood.

Thats me, as a little girl! Barbara telepaths as we observe a child playing with her dolls while her mother lies in bed, ill. Whatever doll she plays with there is always another with her. Her dolls play in pairs.

Look I am praying! Barbara is caught up in the veracity of her time travel experience. *I prayed to the angels when I was lonely.*

We witness her begging the angels for company, we also witness the arrival of her "sister" another very affectionate and loving little girl her age, invisible to everyone but Barbara.

She was like a sister to me. A sudden upsurge of emotion chokes her words. This was the twin sister Barbara wanted, needed and expected in this life. *She protected and guided me.*

Call on her now and ask what your relationship is.

The "sister" steps forward. Now the same age as Barbara. They look uncannily alike.

She says she is my twin. Is that possible?

Is it? Chips in my 'silently observing' apprentice.

Ask her to show you what happened to her.

Her sister takes us to a clinic that has a fresh 80's feel to it. Following the advice of her doctor, we see her unwell, pregnant mother attending for a termination, which was successful, for one of the twins. She had no idea that she was carrying twins and much later found out that she was still pregnant and went ahead with the birth even though it almost cost her her life.

The sister that Barbara played with was indeed the spirit of her own aborted twin, who was so keen to experience life with her twin sister that she refused invitations to return home to light. Naturally when Barbara called for help she responded, not just for that time but for the next 35 years to the present day.

Realising that her twin sister was still with her now was an extremely emotional experience. This earthbound spirit was, with the most loving intention, preventing her from fulfilling her life's purpose by blocking her access to her own intuition or higher self.

Barbara, can you see how her presence has affected your life?

Absolutely, but I love her. She is a lovely person and she loves me.

I know she does, but she has also taken you well away from your chosen path. Call on whoever is responsible for your recent illnesses and fatigue. Ask them to step forward.

It is best that she gets this explanation firsthand, not from me. A beautiful radiant goddess-like being joins us, it is Barbara's higher self.

Please ask her to explain what is happening and why.

In order to resolve this situation Barbara's higher self has created these mysterious illnesses so that she would seek the services of a shamanic healer and discover the truth. It took longer than expected but now the cause of the imbalance is revealed and may be addressed. Barbara has a few decisions to make.

After a lengthy and emotional discussion we agree that it would be best if her twin sister returns home to light. Then in due course she may reincarnate and experience life on this plane in her own right. We also affirm that, if possible, Barbara would love to nurture and help her twin when she was born again on this plane, possibly as her own child or close relative.

The two sisters part, it is a heart rending experience.

We return Barbara to her body and she sits up wiping her eyes.

"I feel drained but I feel well, really well."

"You will be tired tonight, take it easy for the next few days. All the symptoms that you have been experiencing for the past few years should disappear, completely and permanently as of now. Let me know if they don't."

"I know, I feel that they have already gone, thank you." She stands and leaves the studio without assistance.

"It's a shame more people do not understand the indicators of a spiritual issue." My apprentice returns shaking her head.

"It's the twenty-first century. Some things were easier in the past," I respond gazing at my crystals.

Home visit

I sense my client Eve is traveling deep into alien territory, another galaxy far, far away. I decide not to travel with her as my presence will be detected.

We maintain a telepathic connection; my apprentice is observing, intrigued.

"Why aren't you going with her?" she enquires.

"You perceive that she is becoming one with an alien spaceship in real time? This is not a past life recall, she is traveling through space now, to another place, in another dimension. It is happening now and my presence could be detected at her destination. Indeed our telepathic connection could be picked up, this could be dangerous for her."

"But if they are not in our reality..."

"Yes but they are connected to it through her. A large part of her consciousness is incarnated in this here and now. But the rest of her is elsewhere, be patient and observe."

She grimaces; her almost perfect teeth appear very white next to her dusky skin. Her innate mistrust of white-fellas is temporarily suspended when she works as my apprentice.

We are both now tracking Eve's journey through remote viewing. To the uninitiated what we see would be beyond belief. Eve's form is more humanoid than human, still feminine but lean, fluid, resolute and strong.

Do you see what is happening to me? I am not human and parts of me have merged with this spaceship thing. That's bad enough, but where we are going feels worse. I hate this, I feel like I have done it before, many times.

You came to me to find out why you have always felt so separate from other people. Well here we are... Go with it.

We sense her reluctance, but she knows I am right and allows her journey to continue. She travels through space at an incomprehensible speed arriving at an alien destination. It could be a planet or a vast spaceship, it is not clear. But it is huge and its organic nature embraces her tiny incoming spaceship like a mother would a small child.

I really do not like doing this, I know now I have been doing this regularly for some time and each time it gets harder.

My apprentice cannot contain her awe, her eyes closed and flickering in a light trance. "Way cool," she whispers, "Un-be-liev-able!"

We both feel our client's nausea build as she leaves her ship. Passing through a cleansing chamber she walks down a long, living, organic corridor which opens to a large chamber. She is greeted as a team member and treated with respect.

He is waiting. They telepath her.

She enters a smaller space where a male figure of some authority greets her.

Your report?

Eve transmits her research sharing all she knows about areas of conflict, fear and despair on planet Earth, information her colleagues will use in some awful way.

I am so over this bullshit. Eve telepaths me

You have a choice... Tell your superior you have had enough, that you resign your commission. Do not be afraid, be bold. Say that you are a sovereign being of light with free will.

She does so and his response is predictably apoplectic.

"Man, is he pissed off!" My apprentice verbalises her thoughts.

Tell him as a sovereign being of light you now choose to place your entire focus on being human, you no longer serve him or the species you were once a part of.

Do not be afraid. he can't and he won't kill you. Most of your consciousness is here with us. Be strong and clear let him feel that you have made your choice. Be courteous, then return to your ship and travel back to us.

She does so and as we feel her re-enter her body I bring myself out of trance early and advise my apprentice to grab a bowl as our client is about to throw up.

She swiftly obliges - in the nick of time, as our client becomes fully present, vomiting into the receptacle provided.

"Holy shit, was that for real?" Her eyes are watering.

"What do you think?"

"So thats why I felt like I never ever fitted in, anywhere?"

"You tell me."

"Is that it? I don't have to go back to that awful place, ever again?"

"You are a sovereign being of light and you have made your decision."

"So I can be 100% human now?"

"Welcome to the species," I smile.

We hug as she sobs with joy and relief.

My apprentice rolls her eyes. "Party on!" she mumbles to herself.

Postscript. Nine weeks have passed and it is one of those crisp, clear blue-sky days. I have seen Eve in passing a few times and she seems to have adjusted to her new reality just fine. I have left my apprentice to run a small, morning meditation group that Eve attends while I enjoy the perfection of the morning with an organic, fair trade latte.

Contemplating the health benefits of my double shot and the simple pleasures of life, my moment of total earthly bliss is interrupted by a rhythmic vibration in my pocket. I know by its pattern that it is a call from my apprentice. I answer, knowing there must be a good reason for her to call.

"They tried to take her back!" My usually uber-cool apprentice sounds breathless, panicked.

"Who, what…?"

"That ET client Eve, she just nearly died, right in the middle of the group meditation…"

"Take a breath. Tell me exactly what happened."

"Happened? It is still happening! She went very deep, then after some twitching, she just stopped breathing. Her whole body shut down. Like totally… lips went blue - gone.

But I got her back, I did like you told me, I went into a trance and called her back. I remembered my nursing training too, that helped. Those creepy critters were taking her away and they were not happy with me interrupting them and reminding them that she has free will."

"How is she now?"

"Totally confused. She's all over the place, like a newborn foal, uncoordinated, she doesn't know who I am or where she is. I think she is having trouble being in a human body, its like she doesn't know how to work it. The rest of the group is freaking. Should I call an ambulance?"

I close my eyes and scan the situation, my apprentice has done all the right things and the situation is under control. I underestimated the tenacity of the beings we were dealing with, it all felt a bit too easy at the time, but sometimes it is. There is no point in giving myself a hard time I need to get down there now and ensure Eve returns to her body completely.

"We do not need them, I doubt they would understand what has happened and it could get complicated. Reassure her, get her into a private session room and dismiss the group. I will be right there…"

I leave my untouched gluten free brownie and head off wondering if this is the last we will hear from her ex-species.

A wolf in wolf's clothing

Elizabeth is a mature, poised, witty and attractive woman who has had great difficulty attracting and keeping a male partner who truly values all she has to offer. She has come to me to find out the deeper reason behind her present situation.

My apprentice sits close to us, her curly black hair framing a mischievous grin, that makes her barefaced cheek tolerable. She will track and observe the session both in and out of an expanded state of consciousness.

The mandala of crystals around us does its work and we are soon in no time-space. We scan Elizabeth's etheric body and it immediately becomes apparent to me where the challenge lies. I wait for her to become aware of its location.

After releasing traumatic past life deaths and the minor attachments that go with them, she becomes aware of a major blockage in her heart. It has been there for a very long time.

Oh, that is not nice. Even when telepathing her enunciation is perfect. *There is something hidden in my heart!*

I observe as it presents itself as every fear based trigger that could induce fear in her. A personalised invitation to collapse into panic and helplessness, thus slipping further under its control. It appears a mixture of hybrid scary things in an attempt to frighten her, with little effect. Finally it reveals itself as a tall sinister man in a dark cape.

"A shape-shifter!" my apprentice's excitement is uncontainable.

I see these images when I am trying to sleep, they keep me awake. Horrible. Elizabeth telepaths.

Don't be afraid.

I am OK, I remember your advice to stay calm - but this is not pleasant.

Tell him you love him and you can help him.

But…

Try it.

She does so and this calms things down a bit.

He can only be here with your consent. Ask him to show you the moment you gave him permission to be here…

At this point things get really interesting. We travel into a distant past. She sees herself as a wealthy, refined and well educated woman with time on her hands. Her husband is a man of striking good looks and charm, and they are deeply in love. Bored, they decide together to embark on a deep study of the occult. They become aware of the power of magic and their ability to harness it.

Spirit World

It looks like I may have abused my power. Elizabeth is mortified and stunned at both the clarity of the recall and the implications of her actions.

We witness playfulness turning into the serious manipulation of innocents as they both flex their magical muscles. Then Elizabeth comes to her senses and decides she will work only for the greater good. Her partner chooses the opposite path and their relationship quickly disintegrates.

Separation is painful, neither understanding the choice of the other. Elizabeth dies an honoured member of her community, to reincarnate many times, with a clear focus on service to humanity.

Her partner, feeling betrayed and abandoned, dies alone and angry, locked into despair. Fearing punishment for his actions, he remains Earthbound, refusing to return home to light.

Elizabeth realises that he can be with her now as she has never dissolved the agreements she freely entered into with him, when they were alive. He has her ongoing permission to stay with her, indefinitely. In every subsequent incarnation, he has found her and attached himself to her, his jealousy and possessiveness creating a barrier to deep intimacy with every possible partner in all of her lives since then.

Rising above her initial revulsion, Elizabeth feels compassion for this sad man who she once loved so deeply. Releasing him from all contracts and agreements, it takes a great deal of persuasion for him to truly understand that he can find peace, without fear of retribution.

Elizabeth is very emotional as we call on the beings who love him unconditionally, they include his mother and ancestors. Just as he is finally ready to leave, Elizabeth notices something else holding him back.

Oh my, she telepaths, *are you seeing what I am? He has something attached to him!*

"An entity, feeding off another entity. Wow!" my apprentice mutters to herself.

"He is ready to leave and when he does Elisabeth's life will change forever. It is time for you to put what I have been teaching you into practice. You can deal with this situation and finish the session." I hand over to my apprentice.

"Elizabeth, my apprentice will help you with this, it won't take long. You are about to become totally free…

"I will be making a cup of tea, let me know when you have finished."

I open my eyes and sit up observing my normally relaxed apprentice with a look of total concentration on her young face.

"No pressure." I smile to myself as I head to the kitchen.

The mystery of repeated traumas

I arrive at my client Maria's shambolic cabin which appears deserted. Tapping at the front door, my apprentice jumps out of her skin when it quietly eases open to reveal a pasty and disheveled young lady who looks as pale as a ghost.

"Oh, you came. I don't think I am well enough to do this," she whispers using the door as a support. "I have a splitting headache, I feel sick and weak, could you come another time?"

My young apprentice turns to me rolling her eyes, she knows how rare it is for me to even consider a home visit. She also knows that I have little patience for minor distractions, such as pain or nausea.

"I am here now, let's talk." I step forward.

The door opens to reveal the chaos of her stuffy, gloomy living room, complete with mattress, discarded clothes, hot water bottles and an array of dishes decorated by random, unfinished meals. Maria shuffles across the floor looking thirty years older than her twenty four years.

My apprentice, reading my mind, opens doors and windows and rearranges the mattress in a north south direction, unpacking the crystals for our layout with a focussed, practiced ease. I sense she is wondering if this is going to be one of the rare cases that I refer to a psychiatrist.

Maria has been in this state for over a year and her sister has diligently attended to her every need despite verbal abuse from Maria. She has tried everything she can think of to snap her out of her torpor and is now at her wits end. Maria has not left her home for a long time and has experienced several minor concussions. Both her GP and sister have requested I see her.

Since childhood, Maria has suffered a series minor head injuries, which she believes are causing her headaches now. However her GP has advised me that there is no physical or psychological reason for her ongoing pain and lack of ability to be with other people, particularly her sister.

We talk as my apprentice tidies up and shares her winning smile. I explain that all nausea and pain are temporary illusions and persuade Maria to lie in the mandala of crystals laid out around her mattress. We enter an expanded state of consciousness together and my apprentice observes.

I feel intense pain in my head. She telepaths as we scan her body.

Command your body to take you to the moment it started...

Maria writhes in pain. *Why are they doing this to me?*

She is being pinned down with electrodes held to her temples in preparation for electric shock treatment. She is a woman being treated in a cold, clinical and loveless lunatic asylum in the early to mid twentieth century.

I never hurt anyone! I just see and hear things they don't! I am harmless, this is awful.

I talk through the process of release and forgiveness that will stop the need for her body to hold on to the trauma and the pain eases. We scan her body again.

Now there is a man standing next to me, he is raving at me.

Ask him to show you when you were friends.

He was with me in the asylum, he had the same treatment as me. We became friends but he lost his mind, we promised to look out for each other and he is still here keeping his promise, but he is totally mad.

"A mad earthbound spirit, that's a new one.," my apprentice whispers to herself.

It takes some time to reassure him and release him into the care of his loved ones, but in the end he leaves in peace.

How is your head now?

Better, but it still hurts, there is something else....

As she focusses on the pain in her head, her body takes her to an ancient time where her large non human form triggers deep fear in people. She is a dragon.

I know I am big and scary looking to them, but I would never hurt them, why do they hate me? They are spearing me, my head! Oh… I am dying, I am lost, where is my family?

I call on her family from that time to help. The reunion with her loved ones, the other large creatures of her kind, is beautiful and many thousands of years overdue. For the first time since she was a small child she totally relaxes and she experiences her body free of pain.

I have missed them SO much. The are telling me that I can be a bridge between them and humans, their descendants are here now. They are the big cetaceans, I can communicate with them.

She starts crying, a mixture of joy, relief, sadness and grief.

As my apprentice packs up Maria stands next to us erect, her eyes clear and bright, a new woman.

We leave the cabin and out of earshot my apprentice releases the thought bubble I can see has been bothering her.

"I understand that the body will draw attention to the area in which emotional traumas are held by triggering repeated physical dramas in the same place, but this feels incomplete. I sense there is more to be done".

"You are right, she had a co-dependant relationship with her past life friend with the same trauma, she will miss him, even though his presence was causing her pain. There is a chance that her feeling of loss may open the door to another attachment. I want you to visit her again, reassure her and teach her some psychic self protection."

"Sure, so that's it?"

"Not quite, this has been going on for some time and she and her sister have also built up a co-dependant relationship, I will refer them both to a counsellor."

"So we didn't get to fix everything?"

"Our shamanic work is complete, we are shamans not counsellors. Now we hand over to other modalities to finish the job, they all have their place. Today we have removed all blocks to their success."

Past Life skills

I sense my clients confusion as she moves spontaneously into a visceral past life experience. It is dark and very cold. Her body hurts as it is hit repeatedly; left hip, head, right elbow - all bear the brunt of what feels like a hard blunt object covered in something soft. She hears a rhythmic dull thumping and wonders if she is being beaten as part of some primitive ritual...

Tammy is faced with a major, lucrative, career decision but she is unsure about her choices. She feels that understanding her past life skills could bring clarity to her present life purpose. Our interview is brief and as soon as she lays in the crystal grid she moves into a deep trance without any assistance from me. A sure sign that she has done this before, in other lives.

Rather than a gentle process of gradual recall she has moved immediately into a situation she does not understand. She is in a bone chilling space with even more frigid air outside. It feels like she is moving. Whatever she is in, it is creaking as it lurches violently from side to side. Beyond her immediate space, she hears the regular deep breathing of large animals working hard. Then she realises where she is.

She is bouncing around inside a horse drawn carriage and we travel with great urgency into a coal black night. Her deep desire to unlock her innate abilities has brought us to this moment in time and space. It is an en era that could do with better roads and with carriages with much better suspension. The track and surrounding hedgerows ahead are barely illuminated by the feeble lamps at the front of the carriage. The driver must know this route well, even so, he is barely driving on the right side of reckless.

The child, we must get to the child. Her thoughts spill into the night air.

What's the hurry? Why are you here?

I am a healer, they have sent this carriage for me, the child is close to death.

This ride becomes less harsh as we approach a grand house with tall windows, barely visible in the thick, crisp darkness that touches everything.

A retainer illuminated by his lamp greets Tammy and guides her into the manor house, her long dress catching on the spikes of frozen mud around the carriage. I notice the smell of the soapy foam emanating from steaming horses, who have worked so hard to bring us here. We enter a grand lobby, walk swiftly past imposing paintings and up a sweeping staircase into a bedroom where a little boy, attended by his parents, moans and sweats with a high fever.

The child is very sick and I watch as Tammy moves quickly lighting a bunch of dried herbs bound with cotton, waving them above the child, smudging the the air around him. Next she pulls a bottle out of her bag and splashes its contents over him, repeatedly reciting a prayer and affirmations. She is very focused and I can see what the parents do not. She is summoning all her energy to project an intense burst of unconditional love and light into the chest of the child, whose breathing has become irregular and weak. She has arrived in the nick of time.

The child's back arches and he discharges a chilling croaking groan, releasing a dark energy that only Tammy and myself can see. It drifts out of the window. The crisis has passed and the child's breathing returns to normal as his fever subsides. Tammy sits with him for the remainder of the night.

A sparkling winter dawn illuminates the room, its soft pink light caresses the peacefully sleeping child. Tammy is invited to breakfast with the family who are joyful and grateful for her work. The meal is a pleasant extended celebration in front of a big warming fire. Accepting their thanks Tammy is paid in gold coin, she refuses a carriage choosing instead to enjoy the frosty morning air. Walking across the beautiful English countryside she stops at a stream and refreshes herself, happy and content.

Wow, I did that!

Yes and you can do it again if you choose. You retain the cellular memory, it's part of your DNA, all you have to do is activate it. However, there is something to clear first. Command your body to release any fear based trauma that you still hold, that prevents you from accessing your power.

Immediately Tammy recalls being a teenager in this life, experiencing a sexual assault. She is pinned down, physically overwhelmed and utterly repulsed, all she can do is wait for it to finish. As I guide her through the release process I notice something unexpected, her assailant is not acting alone. He is being influenced by something attached to him.

Across time and space, command the energy driving your rapist to step forward, now.

It appears as a raven, angry and bitter. I sense Tammy's fear.

Do you recognise this energy?

I… Could it be the energy that I removed from the child, all that time ago, in another life?

It is. Ask it to show itself in its true form.

A wizened and vengeful old man with ragged clothes and shackles around his feet morphs out of the crow and abuses Tammy. It takes some time to calm him but eventually Tammy is able to forgive him, then gently removing him from his present life host, we help this tortured earthbound spirit find peace.

Now you can reclaim your past live skills.

Her reunion with her innate knowing of the healing powers of all things herbal and plant related is very moving. She sits up and finishes the session as abruptly as it started.

"This is crazy and beautiful, I can talk to the plants! I can hear them now. They tell me how we can work together, I can do this again! I can be a healer…"

A hidden cause of anger

Dave is a young man with large bright staring eyes. His arms and shoulders are inked with images and texts sacred to the spiritual movement that he was once a part of. He has come to see me about the anger that is preventing him from having a meaningful relationship with his partner, who is paying for the session.

At first skeptical and restless he warms to the process, helped by my cheeky, street-wise assistant. She puts him at ease by admiring his ink, before we embark on our shamanic journey together. I can tell that she feels he is a kindred spirit, where he has opted for tattoos she has chosen piercing. They are both part of the same "hard core" (zero drugs and alcohol) spiritual crew..

Based on descriptions of his behaviour I am expecting to encounter an angry entity or earthbound spirit and have prepared my apprentice for some intense action. She is focussed and ready for anything.

Rather than revealing an entity our shamanic journey takes us back to his childhood where Dave re-experiences his pain as an adolescent, dealing with his parents' divorce and his mother's subsequent remarriage. We observe that Dave is not dealing with living with his new younger siblings or his stepfather at all well. He is obnoxious and resentful and a total pain to be around. His stepbrother and sister are lovely children and his stepfather is trying hard not to have a knee jerk reaction to Dave's irrational outbursts, but it is not a pleasant time for the family.

We see his mother's distress. She is at her wits' end, totally overwhelmed with the merging of two families which she hoped would run smoothly. Eventually Dave's behaviour becomes intolerable and he is shipped off to the other side of the world to live with his father.

Dave feels angry and betrayed, even though his selfish behaviour warranted her decision. He says he has forgiven her but when I call on the spirit of his mother and take him through the process of truly forgiving, in the sacred space we are in, he finds it hard to say out loud that he truly forgives and understands her decision to send him away. It is an emotional experience when after begging forgiveness himself, he finally truly forgives her from the bottom of his heart.

As a man I can feel it could have been good to spend time with his father, at that time, but it did not work out that way. When he arrives his father is distant and totally consumed in his work as a senior organiser of the global spiritual movement that they are part of. He keeps they boy on the outer, discouraging him from deep study and participation in their religion, which further confuses and angers Dave. This is the confusion and anger that still affect the man who is with me today.

I thought he loved me, but he didn't really give a shit. Dave telepaths.

His distress is raw and he observes his younger self hanging round at a loose end, while his father spends his time and energy elsewhere. I sense there is more going on here than Dave realises. As we have travelled back in time we can observe the whole situation, not just Dave's memories of it.

Dave, have a look at what else was going on then. What else your father was dealing with… My silently observing apprentice chips in.

Lots of stuff, none of it about me. Dave's mind is made up.

Thats what you remember. Today you have the opportunity to be present and observe things that you were not aware of then. Things you could not know at the time. As time travellers we can see everything that was going on then. Have a look.

I allow my apprentice to guide him. It is good practice for her and he responds well to her. I know, because of my age and demeanour, that I remind him of his father.

Dave takes the time to really look at what was going on at that time and it is fascinating. He sees his father as the beautiful, caring organiser that he was. He is totally focussed on the wellbeing of the community he runs. Others are not.

Within that community Dave observes as his fathers suspicions grow about the practices of a few senior teachers in their group. We see that he suspects them of being pedophiles but he cannot prove anything. His dilemma is to risk accusing innocent teachers and create turmoil in a stable organisation, doing good work, or to be quiet and gather more information.

To ensure the safety of his own child he discourages him from any study with these teachers at all, shutting him out of the organisation that he really wants to be part of.

Oh. I get it… He was actually trying to protect me. He really did love me, very much. Dave's realisation is profound, moving and long overdue. His anger dissolves.

For the first time since he was a child Dave reaches a state of peace by truly forgiving and understanding both his mother's and his estranged father's actions. In that state of surrender he opens to the peaceful state of oneness with the Divine that he has been yearning for since then.

Over years of study and practice; reciting mantras, visualising yantras and holding mudras he had not been able to truly experience the unity consciousness that he expected, because of his anger. Now, free of anger, he experiences a profound connection with the Divine. As he does so a deity steps forward to greet him.

Dave is totally overwhelmed, so I encourage him to talk and take advantage of the special moment he is experiencing. He was not expecting to be able to dialogue with such an elevated being, but after reassurance from me he starts asking questions. Naturally the being responds warmly and we feel the expansive energy of unconditional love wash through our small healing space as we observe and listen to the answers Dave is receiving.

Dave is brought to the realisation that now he is totally free of anger he may truly be of service to humanity by fully embodying aspects of the deity he admires and wishes to serve.

After the session my apprentice escorts a stunned and becalmed Dave from our studio and returns bright eyed.

> "So all that was preventing him from total conscious connection with the Divine, bliss and unity consciousness was his own anger?"

> "Correct."

> "Can I have a session now?"

A dancer's dilemma

Joanne is a young woman of striking good looks. In her mid 30's, she is a dance teacher who takes pride in her lean athleticism and fitness. She has been referred to me by several therapists who have been unable to release a frozen shoulder that has become a hindrance in her practice as teacher. She is frustrated because she is in tune with her body and so far, has not found any lasting solution to a very painful physical challenge. She has tried every physical therapy she can think of and I sense her skepticism around seeing a shaman for something that she considers to be purely physical. I know I am her last resort.

"This one should be interesting." I brief my apprentice as Joanne parks her car.

"You mean she will block the process through negative thought forms?"

"No, not necessarily, she can if she wants to of course, but seeing me is an investment. I think she will allow the process to unfold."

"What then?"

"I am not sure how she will cope, when she discovers where it all started. Have you scanned her?"

"Yes."

"And..."

"Africa? It's not what she is expecting, thats for sure."

Joanne describes her healing journey and frustration before we start. We do not need to talk much as the process will reveal all that she needs to know.

Even though Joanne has a busy mind, once she is lying in the crystal mandala it does its work and she moves into an expanded state of consciousness easily. When we command her body to take us to the moment the pain in her shoulder started, it obliges immediately. Joanne is transported into another time and place. For her it is an intense and palpable experience that touches all her senses.

The smells! Woodsmoke, cooking, the vegetation, so different!. This is so real!

Thats because it is real. We are time travelling - observe. Do you recognise anyone?

I wait for her to pick herself out in this past life. We are in a simple shelter, in a bush setting, amongst dark-skinned people. It takes few moments but then she notices herself. A happy young woman, heavily pregnant, going about her daily routine, surrounded by an extended family and tribe. Conditions are primitive to our eyes, but it is a stress free, abundant life. People have time to laugh, play and snooze as they wish. It seems to be a very contented little community.

Then it happens. The labour pains begin, they are powerful and because she has already borne several children, it looks like it might be a quick labour.

Joanna slips into the body of her past life self and experiences the acute agony of labour in her present physical body.

Oh my! What women have to go through! This is unbelievably painful. I am glad I haven't done this in this life.

It will be over soon. My assistant telepaths, not so reassuringly.

We witness a difficult birth, the baby is in the wrong position and the local women work hard to try and get things right. We see they are fearful that things might not go smoothly. The labour extends and the baby is eventually born alive and healthy but after the birth her exhausted African self continues to bleed, uncontrollably.

The local healers do their best to staunch the bleeding which lessens but does not stop. It becomes clear to everyone that she will die slowly and painfully and they are heartbroken.

Oh NO. I am going to die! I am so young… Joanna is sobbing. *This is so sad. But what does it have to do with my shoulder?*

Be patient. Allow this to play out.

Really, must I?

If you want to clear whatever it is you are holding in your shoulder, yes.

We witness her goodbyes to her clan and extended family. Then she says goodbye to her new baby, her children and husband, who loves her very much. He kisses her gently, looking deeply into her eyes, tears trickling down his shiny dark cheeks. They are alone. Then he steps behind her, takes her head in his hands and quickly and cleanly breaks her neck.

Joanne's African self sensed what was coming but still the emotional trauma of her death was so great that the experience is locked into her physical body as emotional trauma, manifesting in her present physical body now, ready to be released.

Joanne calls on her husband from that time and in no time space, thanks and forgives him. He is so delighted to see her again and be forgiven.

I help Joanne finally put this trauma to rest. *Please say out loud after me - I am at peace with this death, everything is perfect. I leave this trauma in the past where it belongs. I have learnt all I need to know about death in childbirth. I do not need to repeat it. I am at peace with this death, so be it.*

As Joanne repeats this affirmation her shoulder totally relaxes.

I can feel it going back to normal. Incredible, are we finished?

Not quite…

I take Joanne forward in time and we witness her baby grow into a healthy and strong man who honours the memory of his mother who died bringing him into this world. It is a beautiful completion to the session.

Joanne has some questions as the session ends. "So thats it, my shoulder is fixed?"

"Yes, your body no longer needs to hold onto the trauma, you have released it once and for all".

"And my past life husband, will I meet him again?"

"Possibly…" I respond quickly, interrupting my apprentice who is about to speak.

"Why do you think this has come up now?"

"Because you are…" my apprentice just cannot help but share what she can see.

"…Ready to release it." I interrupt my apprentice again, glaring at her.

After escorting Joanna to her car she returns looking rather sheepish.

"She's obviously pregnant, why not tell her?"

"She did not ask. Take a breath and think before you speak."

"It is due in just under seven months, its a boy and its her past life husband."

"Yes, that's obvious, but sometimes it is best that people find these things out for themselves, in their own time."

A block to intimacy

My client Mandy has come to see me because she is feeling blocked, particularly in terms of her sexuality. At 30 she has yet to experience an orgasm. When it comes to sex she feels incredibly guilty and cannot surrender herself to a full and complete release during intercourse. Mandy has experienced many therapies that have delved into her childhood looking for any kind of childhood trauma or sexual abuse but none has revealed the source of her present challenge.

My apprentice greets her with a winning smile and puts her at ease. I sense she is intrigued by what appears on the surface to be a vibrant, confident, relaxed and attractive woman. Our interview is brief and Mandy enters an expanded state of consciousness as soon as she lies in the crystal mandala. After releasing several attached Earthbound spirits and past life traumas I sense we are close to the core issue when she uncovers a dark painful energy she is holding in her cervix.

I don't like this, I feel apprehensive and scared, there is something not nice here. She telepaths.

"Just as I thought," my apprentice mutters to herself as she feels into Mandy's experience of being pinned down by more than one pair of strong male hands.

"I feel sick," Mandy says out loud.

"It's okay, this is why you came to see us. If you are ready to be free of this limitation you may release it now. It is time to give yourself permission to remember what happened to you." My apprentice softly reassures Mandy who is starting to panic.

I am with you. I telepath. *Just command your body to take you to the moment this happened.*

Mandy re-experiences herself as a bright and virtuous young woman walking through the gloomy streets of an ancient walled city. She is beautiful, carefree and innocent. She is taking a shortcut through a part of town she does not know so well and it is getting dark. She begins to feel apprehensive as the light fades and the air chills. She quickens her pace realising she is further from home than she would like.

One, two, then three pubescent boys call out to her whistling and shouting playfully. As they gather in number their comments become more suggestive, then obscene. She quickens her pace and soon there is a small group of rough looking young men at her heels. She realises her situation is dire.

Mandy feels fear and foreboding building inside of her but there is more, there's a tinge excitement pulsing through her adolescent body. As a virgin she has not yet known the touch of a man. She has overheard the older women talk about the pleasure that a man can give a woman and she has been yearning to experience this.

She has learnt to pleasure herself, but she knows that there is more to it, that a man can bring greater pleasure and a deeply hidden part of her is perversely excited by what might happen. She feels guilty about being this excited in such a dangerous situation.

The men corner her, they are rough but not terribly violent as they rip her clothes off and violate her. She is overcome by fear, gagging, repulsed by the by smell of stale sweat and filthy clothes. The first to enter her is the biggest and roughest of the group and she feels pain as something tears inside her. He is with her for a short period of time then the younger ones follow, excited by their twisted initiation into manhood.

They are less harsh and she realises that the less she resists, the less painful her experience. Although she hides it well, she begins experiencing some pleasure as her body lubricates and naturally responds to the sexual act, even though it is without her consent. Her orgasm, when it comes, is intense and confused. It is happening in the middle of an awful, horrible experience, these men may even kill her - but it is beyond her control.

Eventually it is finished and the last of the young men slink off one by one into the night, disgusted with themselves and with her. Innocent and virginal as she was they call her a whore to hide their own shame. Mandy is left in a shivering, sobbing, bleeding heap under her torn clothes. Barely able to comprehend the greater implications of what has just happened to her, she makes her way home.

Soiled, sore and bruised both inside and out she feels overpowering shame, as part of her body still aches with the residue of illogical and illicit pleasure. It is very dark when she arrives home and her family is distressed. Although her mother and sisters comfort her as they bathe and cleanse her, her brothers and fathers mutter about the dishonour she has brought to the family.

The family's deepest fears bear fruit when she is ostracised by her community and spat at by the locals who somehow believe that she was responsible for the rape she endured. Things get worse when her mother discovers that she is pregnant. Her mother quietly slips poison into her food so that the family will not bear the further humiliation of bringing up the bastard child of an unknown rapist.

We arrive at the moment where recall started - the acute pain in her cervix. The birth of the stillborn child goes badly as she bleeds to death, deeply ashamed of the disgrace she has brought on her family. Hidden deep inside her is the mortification and confusion about the small amount of pleasure she spontaneously experienced during her rape.

Her sisters help her to leave her body with some dignity but she senses that her mother, father and brothers are relieved that they will not have to be reminded of their dishonour by seeing her or her baby ever again. The process of forgiveness of both her abusers and her family is emotional but it comes easily to Mandy, who sees the power of the release and the freedom it offers. Then we connect with the beings who love her unconditionally and ask them how this session will affect her life.

> *You have carried this trauma for many lifetimes and it has prevented you from having complete and fulfilling sexual relationships. You have, ever since this time, not been able to experience sex freely, joyfully and without guilt. You are now able to attract into your life a caring, powerful, vibrant partner with whom you will have a loving and guilt free sexual relationship.*

Mandy sits up as she returns to her body, drying her eyes.

"That makes so much sense to me. Is it really possible that I can truly enjoy the physical part of lovemaking now?"

"They told you the truth, believe them. Your life changes permanently starting today, if you wish. It is that simple, the trauma is cleared."

My apprentice escorts Mandy to her car, encouraging her to walk a while before driving.

"Is it really possible to enjoy such awful abuse?" My apprentice asks.

"She did not enjoy the abuse. Part of herself could not help but respond in a natural way to the stimulation she was experiencing. It is not a bad thing, it just is."

"And this has affected her intimate relationships for hundreds of years…" She shakes her head dumbfounded.

"Not any more…"

A Pull in the fabric of Time

I am with my client Vlad, in the grey light of an early morning we are standing at a road junction in an ancient, dry place. Just outside a city's high walls we observe people going about their business before the heat of the day. They move around and through us totally unaware of our presence as we are travellers in time. Vlad merges with his past life self feeling himself inside a strong male body, he is is in charge of a group of workers, preparing for an event and he is a conscientious boss.

Vlad has come to see me to understand why people, regardless of his easy going personality, charm and striking good looks, seem to take an instant dislike to him. Laying in the crystal mandala he has moved spontaneously into a past life recall that takes us to the distant past in another part of the world.

Feeling into his past life body, he begins to understand what kind of man he was and he is surprised.

Geez, I am a hard man, fit, ruthless, totally in control and proud with it. He telepaths

Look down at your body...

I am wearing heavy sandals. I feel comfortable in my clothing, it fits me like glove, I am actually quite clean, even though the place we are in is not.

The morning warms and as the sky clears as a noisy crowd approaches spilling through a small opening in the city wall.

"Here comes the scum" He breathes to himself, disgruntled he should be given such an insignificant event to supervise. Surrounded by a ragtag mob, the prisoners drag their heavy burdens towards him. Part of their punishment for sedition and thievery is their public humiliation. And they are being abused heartily by the mob, which is becoming unruly.

"Get down there and sort this mess!" He directs his men decisively, rapidly bringing order to the chaos. His authority subdues the mob as the lawbreakers approach. His men place the criminals in their positions as the crowd jeers.

I am wearing a leather breastplate and helmet... This man is in the military.

A bit more than that, I resist the temptation to tell him more, it is his journey, not mine.

How are the others dressed? The ones you are supervising?

Like me, but I have a cape... and a short sword on my left. They carry theirs on their right. My breastplate is decorated with medallions. I carry a cudgel, I have earned it.

How do you feel, being here?

Happy to be serving my superiors but pissed off I should be doing such a menial task. My place is on the battlefield!

Spirit World

The day warms and after several hours he decides to be merciful to the moaning thieves and orders their legs broken. The hard case in the middle he leaves for a while longer. As the day becomes hotter and the shouting subsides, people start to notice their empty stomachs and drift away.

"No leg breaking for you today." Vlad stares at the gaunt young man, the one particularly reviled by thinning crowd. A young man with a faraway look in his eyes, mumbling to himself. He is a tough nut to crack.

Rebel filth, he deserves everything he gets. Vlad hears himself thinking. It slowly dawns on him where he might be and what might be happening, as the crowd slowly thins leaving just a dozen or so weepers, friends of the stubborn one still clinging to life.

After six hours of standing around in the sun listening the whiners that are left, he has had enough. The mumbling fool in the middle has settled down and is almost dead. He steps forward and finishes him off with one clean casual lunge with his spear to the left side. He hardly notices the clap of thunder, flash of lightning and the unseasonable rain that follows.

As the bodies are removed he supervises cleaning up, happy that things are drawing to a close and that he has fulfilled his duty. This whole episode was beneath him.

Wow. I really had no idea who I was dealing with did I? While Vlad sounds calm his body is shaking with such force that it has vibrated itself off the futon he lies on. Tears are flowing freely from his closed and flickering eyes.

Very few people truly did. A few more than a dozen, if you count his wife and female followers...

I can see how this has affected my relationships over many lifetimes. What should I do? I feel terrible. I was only doing my duty. He chest heaves as he releases loud remorseful sobs.

Call on the Master involved and beg his forgiveness it will be given freely.

Absolution is given joyfully and it is beautiful to behold, as some small cosmic balance is restored.

After Vlad leaves totally stunned and exhausted, my unusually quiet apprentice voices her concern.

"How has such a major trauma never been dealt with before?"

"It probably has, but not for Vlad and not in this timeline or in this body. This fragment of his consciousness, incarnated here and now, had not yet had an opportunity to clear the trauma. Opportunities like this are rare, much as we would like it to be otherwise.

Our higher self can experience multiple and simultaneous incarnations, our consciousness is also part of a group of souls soul that travel through time and space together. As you know we are all part of an infinitely larger Superconsciousness or Oneness that holds the fabric of this reality and our Universe together.

If major trauma in any one of these interconnected threads of consciousness is not dealt with it can affect everything it touches. It may subtly distort the weft on which the warp of time and space is built. if this was not addressed unreasonable and inexplicable things can happen. A person's instant dislike for Vlad could translate into something more violent and things could be pulled further out of balance. His visit today was timely."

The Goddess unveiled

My apprentice reflectively observes our client Lakshmi as she approaches our studio. She is walking up the long path from the road having been dropped off by the infrequent public transport that services this part of the bush. She does not own a car.

Lakshmi has been a committed devotee of a popular global Eastern spiritual group for many years. Running away from an unhappy home as a teenager she found a new "family" of like minded spiritual seekers whose austere practices somehow suited her aesthetic. She moved wholeheartedly into the mode of dress and worship that is the norm in her group. Abandoning her given name she was effectively reborn as Lakshmi, a new and pain-free person focussed on devotion and her own spiritual growth.

One of her challenges is that she does not have any money or savings and having recently been through a crisis of faith triggered by scandals within her organisation, she has come to us to discover more about the next step on her spiritual path. My apprentice is bemused. In her indigenous culture connection to the Divine comes easily and naturally through time spent in nature.

"Why do people need this structure? These organised spiritual groups? It is so limiting".

"For many this structure has the opposite effect. It creates a context, a safe place with known outcomes, known variables - It also creates communities. There people may express their devotion to a higher power together and in so doing feel a part of something bigger than themselves."

"But if we are all one why do people need to do this?"

"You and I have experienced a profound connection to unity consciousness through our shamanic practices, but not everyone cares to tread the shamanic path as it can feel isolated and lonely. The advantage of these groups is that people get to experience a spiritual connection as a community."

"Yes, but even for some of the most advanced theologians, this whole religious story can all just be a concept, a grand spiritual theory."

"Yes, it can, maybe that's why Lakshmi is here to see us. Invite her in."

Lakshmi shares her life story. She has spent 25 years dedicated to fundraising for her organisation and she has been a devoted disciple. Through her early morning rituals and pujas and the public chanting and dancing that is the trademark of her organisation she shares that she has truly experienced a blissful and uninterrupted connection to the Divine.

Now she wants someone not even remotely connected to her group to help her look with fresh eyes at her life's path. She has had a crisis of faith which has left her wondering just what she has been doing with the last 25 years of her life. She is contemplating leaving her group and wants to know where her energy would be best placed in future and how she might provide for herself.

As soon as Lakshmi lies in the crystal mandala she easily enters an expanded state of consciousness.

Wow this is fast! She telepaths. *No chanting, I am just here…*

"She is so pure." My apprentice breathes to herself. "Beautiful, no baggage, no attachments, total clarity. Her practices have worked."

See how far your consciousness reaches. I suggest.

Sat-cit-ananda, infinite consciousness. I have been here before, but never so quickly or effortlessly.

In this sacred space we may find the answers you are looking for. Call on your namesake the Goddess Lakshmi, she will come.

I am not worthy…

Of course you are, her love for you is never ending. Invite her to join us, now.

The meeting of devotee and ancient Hindu Goddess is profound and very beautiful to behold. My apprentice and I feel privileged to observe such an expansive and heartfelt connection based entirely on unconditional love.

Lakshmi moves into such a blissful state that she forgets why she came, I make some suggestions.

Ask the Goddess why, even though you carry her name, you are not experiencing an abundant life.

The Goddess responds. *My child, abundance is at your fingertips, if you choose to have it. The only thing preventing this are your choices and your own beliefs.*

And what are they? I take the liberty of asking.

That spirituality and abundance do not go together. That the devotional path requires abstinence and forbearance.

Is this the truth? I ask again on my clients behalf who is speechless.

Not at all, spirituality and abundance can and should go hand in hand, the Universe exists to support us. The paradigm that you have accepted is outdated. Look at the lifestyles of the senior disciples in your organisation. Do they live in poverty?

"Not too attached to the organisation then…" My apprentice thinks out loud, surprised at the Goddesses frankness.

How will I serve you? Should I stay in my organisation? My client finds her voice.

Beloved, all your choices are perfect. The question I ask you is, do you feel comfortable staying?

No in truth I do not. But what will I do? This has been my whole life…

Do you truly wish to serve me?

Always, but how can I share your wisdom with the uninitiated? With those outside of our group?

The Goddess stands erect.

Behold!

For a moment both myself and my apprentice are taken aback by the intensity of the latent power expressed in this one word. The Goddess stands in all her magnificence, awesome and in some distant way quite terrifying.

I am the Goddess Lakshmi!

Then she steps forward and changes, stepping out of Lakshmi into something else, a Goddess with horns, with the sun suspended between them.

I am the Goddess Hathor!

As if taking off a robe she steps forward again transforming into a lush green, sensual goddess with long dark hair

I am the Goddess Demeter!

Stepping forward again her robes drop to reveal a goddess of classic Greek beauty holding a wheel.

I am the Goddess Fortuna Copia!

Stepping forward once more she appears more Roman…

I am the Goddess Abundantia!

Then her changes become more rapid…

I am Pachamama!

I am Kunapipi…

I am all of these and more. All are me in various guises. You may serve me by educating people as to the truth of my infinite being. In doing so abundance will flow to you with ease and grace, as is natural.

There are a few more questions but when we close the session it is clear that our client will cease to be Lakshmi and leave the organisation that has meant so much to her, for so long.

"I will be running Goddess workshops, where do I start?" She ponders. "I am no longer Lakshmi what do I call myself?"

"What is your given name?"

"Bridget, I have never liked it."

"Bridget - the Celtic goddess of prosperity! I think it's appropriate that you honour your birth name. There are no coincidences and there is a great deal of power in a name."

"Everything IS perfect." My apprentice smiles to herself.

Running with the wolves

Jenny is a composed, mature woman who emanates grace and charm. I can see that her well spoken and clearly enunciated vowels and consonants are off-putting to my street-smart apprentice. People who speak that way in her world are usually authority figures, magistrates or head teachers, not clients seeking a shamanic journey to the core of their being.

The crystal mandala has a profound and immediate effect on Jenny. As soon as she lies down in it and closes her eyes she senses radiant beings approaching her. My apprentice and I have to move quickly to keep up with her. She telepaths us…

The love emanating from these beings is so intense. It's overwhelming. They are showing me another being, like them. I don't understand… It is magnificent.

She pauses, breathless, overcome by the power of her totally unexpected realisation. *I think I existed with them, ages ago. This is how I was…*

This is how you were then. In fact this is how you are now and always will be.

It can't be. I am so human so - fallible. This being is not like me at all, it is so perfect.

This is you and always was and will be you. Call on your your Higher Self now and merge with her.

She does so with some trepidation. *Oh my god, I am everything. This is so beautiful.*

I allow her time to integrate the enormity of her realisation, then I make a suggestion. Ask the beings close to you why they have come to meet you today.

As they dialogue I realise that something is not quite right. They are talking about her completing some work that they started together eons ago. They love her yes, but they have an agenda and they are full of sadness and remorse that their work is incomplete. They are evolved but their love is not quite as unconditional as it could be.

"Not the sweetness and light that they appear to be." My apprentice whispers having picked up on their energy. "They are still attached to outcomes, they have refused to transit to higher consciousness. They are stuck".

Mindful that Jenny believes she is speaking with beings without any agenda, who have her best interests at heart I decide to intercede. I address the radiant ones directly.

Do you realise that you are dead?

We never lived in bodies like you.

Yes, but you did exist in a lower vibration once and you are still attached to it. You are disappointed that that things did not go the way you planned here on Earth.

They talk amongst themselves.

Spirit World

You are perceptive - our work is not complete. We will work with Jenny, she is among you and she was one of us. She has great work to do, thank you for connecting us. We have been trying to get through to her for some time.

She does indeed have work to do, work of her own, not yours. It is time that you returned to the source and stopped trying to interfere with her free will. She has been brave enough to incarnate here, you can do the same. We need all the help that we can get.

Their consternation is palpable. How dare I address them in such a manner? I clarify things for them.

I know that on the highest level we are equals. Your contribution to this planet's existence was profound, however you may have to drop your vibration further to truly be of service. As it is, you are interfering and have no real power, until you incarnate as physical beings on this plane here and now. It is time to stop being disappointed and participate. Get down here and lend a hand!

Confronted and abashed they feel the truth of my words, much as they do not like it. After further discussion and parting words with Jenny they accept my offer of assistance, returning home to light.

Jenny is perplexed. Was this grand, incomplete work, the cause of her sadness or was she feeling their emotions? Rather than move into a lengthy explanation I decide to help her clear the trauma I have noticed in her heart. I am hoping that this will give her the clarity she is seeking.

Command your heart to show us what it is holding there.

Her recall starts as a joy filled experience of being part of a group mind, living as a wild animal in the distant past. She feels the freedom and joy of being part of a pack, beholden to no other beings, particularly men.

Such freedom, such love! I love my pack, we care for each other, we are totally free. We run, hunt and play together, I am so happy.

"But..." My apprentice whispers, knowing that it is trauma we are releasing.

How does this life end?

Jenny starts to cry, *Oh so sad, I have an infection and a fever from a wound I got protecting cubs from a bear. I am going to die. I will miss my pack.*

I suggest she calls on them across time and space and thank them, telling them she hopes to be with them again soon either in spirit or as human beings. Their reunion is touching as they express their profound gratitude for her sacrifice. The deep sadness she has been holding in every cell of her being dissipates and her whole body relaxes. She opens her eyes and smiles.

"I don't feel sad any more! I can see a way of connecting with that love again and being of service to my community. I will help out with my local animal shelter. That will bring me and the animals lots of joy. It's a small thing but at my age its much simpler than trying to save the world."

"Every loving interaction, no matter how small, affects those around us. All actions based on unconditional love shape our reality, their positive effect is incalculable and their value is priceless. Your choice of community service is ideal."

Open heart surgery

Jamie approaches our healing studio and my young assistant surprises me with her soft reflective sigh as she gazes at him. Standing close, I unintentionally read her unguarded thoughts, *He could put his shoes under my bed any day.* I can't decide whether she is being absent minded or trying to tease me by being deliberately inappropriate.

Jamie is a mature handsome man with an air of confidence befitting movie star, you might think from appearances has everything going for him. But he has come to see me today because he has never been able to have any kind of warn, affectionate relationship with anyone and he wants to find out why.

As she is so taken with Jamie I suggest Jo interview him and I smile inwardly as her usual confident, cheeky self is flustered by my request. In a moment however she is the professional I have trained, asking all the right questions and listening.

I study Jamie's responses as he tells us that he is a high achiever in his work and people like him and even though he feels ready, he just can't seem to let anyone into his life. In response to our standard question he confidently declares that he has not experienced any major trauma in his life. Then he pauses…

> "Unless you count this." He unbuttons his shirt to reveal disturbingly deep indentation in the centre of his chest. Jo releases an involuntary gasp.
>
> He looks up at Jo's wide eyes, "It doesn't hurt, I was born this way. They used to call me 'heartless' at school, which was a bit mean." It is the first time I have seen this natural birth defect. The hollow is big enough to put a child's fist into. It's unusual because it appears to be square rather than round. Jamie is an expert at hiding it.
>
> "Thanks for showing us, please lie down." We lay next to him in the crystal mandala and journey together entering no time-space ready to discover the reason for his aloneness. I suggest he command his body to take us to the moment his chest trauma started.

He is spreadeagled, tied securely on some kind of cold slab, in a stone chamber lit by oil lamps. The walls are painted with symbols I recognise and I promise myself not to lead Jamie.

> *How do you feel?* I telepath.
>
> *Cold and terrified. Something awful is about to happen to me and I can't get away!*

A totally bald man with smooth shiny skin steps forward, he is dressed like Jamie and he realises that they are both priests in Ancient Egypt. He leans over Jamie holding a sharp knife. Without a word he expertly opens Jamie's chest as he writhes in agony.

> *Holy shit, do I have to go through this?* He pleads.
>
> *To discover why you feel seperate? Yes, you do.*

It does not take long for his tormentor to extract Jamie's still beating heart and place it in a small square box covered in hieroglyphics, which he locks. Before Jamie leaves his body the priest looks down at him with a sad and twisted smile.

"There, I have it. See how that feels, you will never feel anything for anyone. Ever again!."

Jamie sighs as his body expires. The guy is really pissed off - what did I do to him? Ask…

Jamie calls on his killer and they talk. There is a lot to be forgiven and it takes time for Jamie's torturer to truly forgive him for the damage he did in that lifetime. The process of forgiving and releasing this trauma is slow because the hurt is so deep. As Jamie's heart is placed back into his chest and the other priest truly accepts his apologies, Jamie relaxes for the first time in eons.

I feel amazing. Can we leave now?
Not quite…

I notice a much bigger entity standing behind the torturer who is turning to leave. I sense the giant is not happy at the way things are going. A tall, looming, dark skinned, broad shouldered being steps out of the shadows and addresses them both.

"You have vastly exceeded your mandate." The booming, distorted voice growls from the mouth of a black dog, whose head sits on the being's broad humanoid shoulders.

Anubis? My client is incredulous. Were these real beings?
There is more, stay focussed….

There is something behind Jamie. Another large being steps forward. This powerful figure has a hawks head on its strong shoulders, he is not happy either.

Thoth!?

I take a breath, centre myself and suggest that Jamie apologise to Anubis. He sincerity is met with deep and dismissive, mocking laughter, that shakes us to our core.

We care nothing about what you human fools feel or think. This dispute is between us, be gone!

As they square off I address them feeling rather puny. *We take our leave from you great beings, and dissolve all agreements between us, may you find peace.*

This is hard… Jamie is struggling.
What?

Leaving them and dissolving these agreements, I worshipped them. I loved Thoth, they were all powerful Gods. I did their bidding, as did the other priest. I cannot let him go.

I realise the futility of insisting and complete the session. Returning to our time-space we open our eyes. My apprentice is wide eyed.

"How does your chest feel?" she asks.

"Full! And rather emotional."

My apprentice smiles hugging him, pressing her cheek against his as a tear rolls from the corner of his eye.

After he has left my apprentice has questions. "Why didn't you insist he broke all agreements with the gods? They only have power over us if we allow it."

"If he still feels in awe and bound to them it is not my place to insist. He achieved a great deal in this session, maybe in another session he can totally step into his power. He will be ready soon. Until then let him enjoy the new sensation of having emotions. That's plenty to deal with."

Black dog

I am behind my client Andrea as she flees down an sloping subterranean stone tunnel illuminated only by the flickering torch held overhead by her servant, penetrating the thick blackness ahead of us. Andrea is fearful and apprehensive but I know she trusts the person leading us. Without this feeble flame the absolute darkness around would swallow us and we would be utterly lost.

I do my best to help her understand what is happening without leading her.

What are you wearing? I telepath as we hurry along. She looks down at her body for the first time.

A sheer white dress, it's a shame to get it so dirty. Oh, my body is younger than now, this is another time, a long time ago. Why am I so frightened?
Let this play out and see what happens...

There is an almost imperceptible shift in the thick darkness ahead as the dense coal blackness gives way to a soft bluish grey. An opening at last - moonlight.

The older woman leading the way turns and the torchlight illuminates a fleeting smile, which is not as reassuring as it might be. It barely masks the terror concealed beneath it. Still some distance to travel, we hurry on. As soon as it is bright enough to see the floor and walls the torch is extinguished. Our guide steps out into clear night air and immediately holds her hands wide and low, a universal symbol for STOP!

Too late, Andrea is now so close in her enthusiasm to breathe fresh air that she knocks her servant forward and they both stumble into the dappled moonlight. Exposed and vulnerable they face the indescribable half human apparition that awaits them.

Andrea summons all her strength and steps forward in front of her servant.
"You have no business here, you serve ME. Begone!"

The chilling, snarling laugh emitted from the beast is stomach churning. It easily reaches over Andrea and snuffs out the life of her faithful servant. The snap of her neck is is quite audible in the quiet night.

"You have betrayed us and you will be punished." It barks.

I don't understand what is happening, what am I fleeing from? Why am I being punished? Do I have to go though this - again? Andrea looks back at me.

To fully comprehend and release the reasons for your visit you do need to experience it again, yes. But first ask your body to show you what led to this.

Andrea is visiting me to get to the bottom of the endometriosis and ovarian cysts that are making her life a misery. Apart from the constant pain she experiences, she feels that it is now or never in terms of conceiving a child. This shamanic journey has taken her into the core of her being and revealed the moment of trauma in the distant past that triggered her physical condition now. In order to release it she needs to understand it so we have travelled through time and space to experience the lifetime where it all began.

Andrea's body, shows her where it all started, taking her to the start of her past life experience. She is travelling in a magnificent horse drawn chariot next to a handsome man. They are dressed in simple but very fine clothes, wearing heavy gold jewellery and makeup. They are hailed by an adoring crowd as they pass through an ancient city.

This man next to me he is… like a Pharaoh.

He IS a Pharaoh. I contain my own thoughts.

How do you feel about him?

I hate him. This is an arranged marriage and I am married to him solely to produce children. I feel like a cow. There is no love here, from the outside we look fine but behind closed doors he has no respect for me whatsoever. I am his chattel, a child producing female from another high status family.

What is your life like?

Comfortable, but very boring, I love my children, but they have their nannies. My life is meaningless and I want to escape.

Are you ready to see what happens to you at the end of the tunnel?

If we must…

She commands her body to return us the moonlit night and her confrontation with the angry beast with the lifeless form of her servant, a pool of darkness behind her. Her past life self tries to brazen it out, attempting to exert her now abdicated regal authority over the creature before her.

I have never seen anything like this. What is this big black muscular man with the head of a black dog? Focus on what is happening.

I do not want to distract her with explanations but I know dealing with the Ancient Egyptian god Anubis will not be easy.

"By running away from your duty you have abandoned both your Pharaoh and any vestige of power you thought you had. I do not serve YOU. It is the other way around. And now it is time for you to pay the price for your betrayal."

"I do not fear death." Andrea feels the inner strength of her past life self, knowing that her time has come.

"Death is the least of your concerns…" the black man-dog snarls.

He rises to his full height and extending his powerful arms towards her he points at her midriff pouring multi coloured, writhing energy into her womb.

"Henceforth, you are cursed, never to bear children and to experience womb pain in every incarnation from this point forward. Knowing this to the core of your being, now you may die!"

Andrea experiences the terror of her own death, aware of what the future holds for her.

Undoing the curse and negotiating with a recalcitrant ancient god takes all my skills and some time, but eventually it is done and the curse is lifted.

> *One more thing - you must now undo the promise you made to yourself never to bear children ever again. Then you can be free.*

A tearful Andrea voices that promise and we complete the session returning to this timeline opening our eyes.

"How will this affect my life?"

"Nurture yourself and after your regular check up let me know what you doctor says. I am optimistic that you may now bear children."

Seeing the wood for the trees

I have arrived at my studio early and I am in a great deal of pain, I can hardly walk. My young assistant gazes at me in disbelief, her face says it all, she looks like she has seen a ghost.

"You look terrible".

"Thanks. I think I have just had the worst night of my life, and I'm in agony. Please reschedule todays appointments. I think I need to receive the session today, from you."

I sense Jo's excitement at the possibility of actually facilitating a session for me, tempered by her concern for my well-being. Over the past ten days the pain in my back has been escalating to the point where it has become absolutely unbearable.

I have tried alternative, complimentary and mainstream medicine to remedy the situation but nothing has worked. It has taken me over a week to realise the obvious, that this refusal of treatment by any other means, indicates that the cause of my agony is not rooted in this time or space. It is time for for this healer to heal himself.

Jo guides me into an expanded state as we lay in the crystal mandala together. I find myself lying on dry, rocky, desertlike ground. I feel something hard under my lower back, it is primitively made and wooden. It is old, grey, dry and unsophisticated, similar to the kind of yoke an ox might be harnessed to, but I am not tied to it, I am held in place by some invisible force. It is placed under my back causing it to arch, I feel like I am about to be tortured.

The pain in my lower back is so intense in both the physical and non-physical realities I am experiencing, it is hard to remain present in an expanded state of consciousness. Jo reminds me to call on beings who placed this crude wooden slab under my back to step forward. I expect some primitive sadistic beings to arrive, but that is not what happens.

I am surprised when several tall, elegant and refined beings materialise, bending over me. Their skin is translucent, they have long fingers and elongated heads. Whilst vaguely similar in appearance to the ETs we see on kids T-shirts they are not sinister at all. Their demeanour is neutral as they look down at me quizzically.

Why have you called us? They telepath.

Please show me why you placed this thing under my back, I have forgotten.

This slab holds you in place during our implanting procedure...

Implanting! What?

Alarmed, looking down at my body, I feel an intense discomfort in my solar plexus and see another primitive device embedded there. It looks like an old-fashioned radio dial or grandma's bakelite oven timer. They sense my unease.

It is there for your protection.

You can remove it now, I no longer need it.

Are you sure?

Discussion ensues as they look down on me, almost with pity. I realise that to them this device that they have implanted in my etheric body is like a flea collar for a pet, it is designed to repel pests. They reach down and with their slender fingers gently remove it. As they do so the pain in my back and solar plexus releases, immediately and completely.

My physical body was alerting me to its presence as my own vibration had lifted and its presence became obvious. By experiencing the intense pain I felt being pinned across this wooden slab I was able to access the reason for it. At some time in the distant past these beings wanted to help me but it is clear that they do not love me unconditionally. It is appropriate that I dissolve all agreements with them and ask them to leave, but something is intriguing me.

Why does this equipment look so primitive?
Because it looks primitive to us. We lowered its vibration to be effective in your dense reality.

I thank them and tell them they may not return without my written permission. Even though they have interfered with my body I still feel emotional bidding them farewell. I lie alone in this desert wondering what will happen next, when the others arrive…

They gather around me and pick me up. Beautiful elfin beings, playful and exquisite, they take me to lush tropical rainforest and place me in a pool under a magnificent waterfall. They tell me to relax as they dance around me splashing and giggling. They laugh as they tell me to look at myself. I do and not only is my body in perfect shape I it is gold, pure gold.

Congratulations! Your vibration has lifted and you re free of all implants and attachments, we are able to be with you again. You have reached a point of almost total clarity and freedom, where you can be with us in a never ending state of bliss, whenever you choose. We love you and we are here to help you. Just one more thing to clear…

Being with them I feel great, until their statement sinks in and I recall my awful experience from last night.

I had a profound waking dream. I was taken across the planet to an unbelievably decadent place in a big city in America. There I witnessed extreme abuse of power, torture and degradation, all in the name of pleasure. I noticed there was one person orchestrating these activities and feeding off their energy, enjoying the power that he had over everyone. That was bad - but it got worse.

Looking at this man I realised that he was a mirror image of me, my doppelgänger. This confused human even looked like me, but he was the opposite in every way. He was revelling in control he had over people, manipulating them for his own perverse pleasure.

It was then that he became aware of my presence. We looked at each other and were equally repulsed. We turned our backs on each other and walked away disgusted by what we saw in each other, the feeling was totally mutual.

Don't be troubled. It serves no useful purpose. A sweet flying creature whispers to be.

Tears well up in my eyes. *What can I do to lessen his influence on people? Do I travel to the States and confront him? I find it hard to love him. What do I do?* It is rare for me to be at a loss and it feels frustrating.

That would be pointless, there is nothing to be gained by that. You would be vulnerable in his place of power. There are better ways of dealing with this.

How?

The only way! All you have to do is be, here, now - and share your joy in every moment.

How can I allow myself to be happy when there is so much pain in the world, some of it caused by what appears to be me?

Take responsibility for your reality and your feelings here, now. Not somewhere else where you are not. Share the joy that you feel in our presence. Whatever brings you joy follow it and share it. You and your joy affect everything around you. You have reached a point of total clarity, remember your true magnificence, your beautiful, unconditionally loving, infinitely powerful, golden self. It is that simple.

And I realise to my core, that it actually IS that simple.

A healer's choice

I am sprinting across a cold and bleak moor following my client Diane in a past life. She is frantic, literally running for her life. Her hot breath remains suspended in small puffy clouds in the damp, frigid air as she rushes onward, bewildered and barely aware of her surroundings, somewhere in northern Europe.

This dramatic recall has been triggered by her feeling a stone under her foot as we began our session. I am trying to figure out how and why it got there.

Feel into her her, what is going on for her - is there a stone in your shoe? I telepath.

No stone, just abject terror and confusion. Although I can feel everything through these thin slippers.

I am wondering what kind of animal could be chasing her when my question is answered. Her pace quickens as we hear deep, course, threatening male voices in the mist behind us. I catch parts of words, thick with an old Scottish accent.

"Cailleach de'il - she'll be close… Faster neebors… She'll nae outrun us!"

I don't understand what is happening. Why are they after me? What have I done?

My grasp of any Scottish dialect is tenuous, but sense what might be coming. I suggest she ask her body to show her what led to this present situation, so she can understand why her actions have triggered such anger in her perusers.

Command your body to show what your life was like before this.

She is taken immediately to a "bothy", a simple shack in a woodland grove and what she sees there is beautiful…

Diane has come to see me to get to the bottom of her inability to move forward as a healer She is a bright, well-presented young woman who hides her challenge well, appearing confident and forthright, but deep inside things are different.

She knows, after studying a variety of modalities, that she has a great latent ability as a healer and her teachers have reinforced this. The challenge is that she hits a glass ceiling, where she can go no higher or deeper as a therapist in her chosen therapy.

Prior to the session Diane has mentioned recurring physical challenges with her foot from wearing corrective shoes as a child to spraining then breaking her ankle in later life. From a shamanic perspective these persistent injuries are a sure indication that she is holding unresolved trauma there.

In her pre shamanic journey body scan Diane noticed what felt like a painful stone under her foot. Commanding her body to show us when this started has taken us to this desperate moorland chase and vivid recall of what led to it…

Diane sees herself in her simple home, surrounded by plants, herbs and small, gentle, friendly forest creatures. Although her home is basic it is in a picturesque and idyllic setting. Women come to her for remedies and she is well liked by them. She also acts as the village midwife bringing many children safely into this world.

Her life is solitary but not lonely. Her preference not to take a husband or to attend church, creates gossip she is unaware of. Gossip which leads to her present situation, pursued by simple minded, ignorant, fearful and angry men, intent on punishing her for not bowing to their Christian God, or to a man and for other fabricated sins - such as witchcraft.

We are both drawn back to her past life pursuit and its imminent climax.

The mist is lifting and she glances back to see her tormentors and realises they a gaining on her. She comes to her senses and gets her bearings, changing course slightly she cuts across the heath to a place she knows.

My word, this woman's confusion has cleared. Now she has a clear resolve - and boy is she is angry. These bullies and thugs will not get the better of her. She has something up her sleeve.

Accelerating her now exhausted body into one final burst of energy we see what is ahead through the thinning mist. She pushes off hard from the edge of the heath into the sheer drop below. As she does so a sharp stone cuts through her thin shoe and into her foot, condensing this intense emotional trauma into the last physical pain she feels before leaving her body immediately prior to her death on the rocks below.

> Diane is sobbing, Feeling again the emotions of her past life self. *The ignorant bastards… I had a beautiful life, I harmed no-one and I helped so many!*
>
> *How did you feel as you pushed off from the edge of the heath?* I take her into no time-space where she can view the bigger picture.
>
> *Never again! I will never help others through healing ever again - look what it led to!* I can feel the pain of her aching heart as she cries freely.
>
> *You can see clearly now what brought you here and how you created the block to your own healing power that you are looking to clear. You can clear the trauma now and reclaim your power as a healer, affirming that you do so without fear of punishment or retribution. Are you ready to do this?*

There is a long pause as Diane collects herself and feels into her potential future.

> *Yes! Let's do it. I am ready to reclaim my power as a healer and fully be of service to the light.*

I feel joy for Diane's decision but there is one more bridge to cross before we get there and I know she will need a moment to prepare for it.

> *First you must forgive those who persecuted you…*

Mistrust of men

My apprentice and I observe my client Jane as she walks up the driveway to my healing studio, not too steady on her feet.

"It's in her ankles…"

"Which it?"

"Whatever 'it' is she has come to see you about."

"Very helpful!" I smile at young Jo's accurate perception of my client and her deliberately ambiguous answer.

"Tell me more…"

"I see restraints around her legs and I feel rage and despair."

"Good, let's see what the client perceives."

After a brief interview, Jane lays in my beautiful crystal mandala and enters an altered state easily. Immediately she experience discomfort in her ankles.

My legs, I am pinned down and I feel nauseous. She telepaths

Look at your legs, what do you perceive?

I feel calliper-like metal against my ankles and leg straps on both ankles, like I am disabled… No thats not quite right, I can see now, I am strapped to a filthy bed, big leather straps with brass buckles that chafe my ankles. They hurt.

Where are you?

I am in a lunatic asylum, some time ago. I should not be here.

How did you get here?

I have no idea…

Jane likes men, but she can only go so far in an intimate relationship before she starts to have feelings of mistrust and betrayal, usually irrationally and without foundation. Now in midlife, having more or less resigned herself to being single, she has pretty well given up with men, until she came across my work. As a last resort was she has decided to get to the bottom of it through shamanic journey.

Jane's perceptions of her past life are crystal clear but we need uncover the reasons behind her incarceration. Commanding her body to show us, we travel to the deep south of the USA. It is the early 1800's and Jane is the only daughter of a wealthy family, growing up on a huge planation. Life is good for the family who live very well off the hard work of their slaves.

It is a different time and a different sensibility; by their standards they treat their slaves well. They have days off, they are fed well and they are only whipped when they are lazy, insubordinate or try to escape.

The house slaves, the cooks, cleaners and nannies are kind to the child that was Jane and she becomes close to a few of them. Shielded from the more severe degradations they experienced, she does not trouble herself about the rights and wrongs of slavery, they live a comfortable life because of it.

Jane grows into a young woman, not too well educated (as prospective wives did not need to be), but reasonably smart, perceptive and able to run a big household. As a solid looking girl from good breeding stock, she is an acceptable marriage prospect for the right man.

Jane's past life self has romantic ideas about her future husband as a selection of potential suitors visit the house. But romance is the last thing on her fathers mind, when he finally choses a suitable suitor. A lucrative business deal with a wealthy older man in need of a young, healthy wife who could bear him children, finalises his decision.

Wanting to be in love, Jane falls for the older man's charm and worldliness, bearing him several children, but her marriage is loveless. Her husband uses her for his own pleasure and treats her like a baby farm. He ages into a paunchy, balding, disrespectful slob and she grows to despise him. Her revulsion turns into disgust as she notices several pale skinned "mulatto" babies on the estate, born of young, doe eyed, black mothers who are given easier tasks than other slaves.

She tries hard but cannot prove that her lecherous husband is the father of these half caste children, then she realises that nobody cares. She knows that she should feel relief that he no longer bothers her, but she does not. Instead she feels betrayed and with her pride wounded, trapped. She is not strong enough to leave her comfortable life and has nowhere to go, both her parents having passed on.

Feeling utterly powerless, she becomes an expert at nit-picking every single thing her husband does or says. From breakfast to supper he cannot utter one word but to have it quietly derided or turned against him. Over time her sarcasm becomes an incisive, rapier-like weapon, with one sole purpose - to humiliate the man she now detests.

This once beautiful young woman turns into a ageing harpy that would drive any man to distraction.

> *My god, I have urned into a really nasty, resentful woman. I am horrible to be around. He is the one that should be going crazy - not me.*

> *Give yourself permission to remember how you came to be in an asylum.*

We are taken to her sitting room on a beautiful clear morning, she is embroidering, enjoying quiet time, everything is in order: her husband is out and her maid has just brought her morning tea. She is experiencing a rare moment of tranquility when her mind is clear of her husbands infidelities.

> *I hear boots on the verandah outside, I do not recognise them, something is not right.*

The local doctor followed her husband and a petty official. There are no questions and there is no examination.

"You, madam are herby judged to be insane. You have strong opinions and you have obviously lost your mind. These two witness attest to this irrefutable fact. You will be escorted to the local asylum where you will spend the rest of your days. Remove her."

My god I can't believe this is happening to me.

"I damn you all to hell and I curse you, you lying, cheating slob!"

She spits at her husband sobbing with rage as she is dragged out of the room.

And I never got out! I died in that asylum. No wonder I don't trust men.

You had a bad experience with one man. Are you ready to dissolve this pattern of hatred and mistrust and release this man from your curse?

There is a long pause.

No.

As long as your curse is in place and you do not forgive him, you will both continue to suffer and you will both be bound to this trauma. You will not be able to rebuild your trust in men in this life.

I can live with that, he deserves everything he gets.

The awful answer

I am walking next to my client Sharon on her way to work. It is a bright and sparkly blue-sky morning and it feels like spring, although the leaves on the few trees around us appear to have a golden tinge. It has been raining overnight and the city feels fresh, washed clean.

Everything seems perfect and she is happy. We are in a big and busy city, the cars drive on the right and people are well dressed. Apart from the odd beggar it feels like an affluent, clean place. She is walking to work in one of the many office buildings around us.

Why am I here? This does not make any sense, it all feels too modern to be a past life. I feel like I am making this up... Sharon telepaths, resisting her experience.

Please, let's just allow things to unfold.

I sense Sharon's frustration, this is new for her and she is expecting to experience some kind of past life recall. There are many contradictions in her journey so far, which I too am expecting to be a release of past life trauma. But it is playing out as something else, something quite extraordinary. The whole experience has a bright, slightly distorted hallucinogenic feel.

I follow Sharon through what appears to be a fairly routine and mundane start to her day at work. She greets her co-workers as she enters the high lobby of her building with its curved balcony and tall, elegant, almost islamic windows. Heading towards the elevator, in the quiet space that the air conditioning offers, I start to really pay attention to her surroundings, which are both out of time and yet strangely familiar.

Through the windows I notice a type of car that I recognise and tuning into her surroundings I hear people speaking an accented, vernacular form English, but the soundscape is not clear. She appears to be close to our present time but the computer screens and mobile phones look too chunky - almost steampunk by todays standards. People's clothes and hairstyles are slightly off. Could we be in a parallel reality?

The awful answer to my question will become apparent in the next few minutes...

Sharon has come to see me about the irrational despair she has experienced for the last fifteen or so years, she cannot quite place when it started. Her depression has not responded to any other form of treatment and there appears to be nothing in her present life that triggered it. In desperation she has come to see me to experience a shamanic journey to seek the truth of what triggered her despair, which I expect to find in another time and place.

In our interview prior to the session she expressed what appeared to be a genuine open mindedness in seeking the truth of the cause of her depression, but things are not going as she expected. She is experiencing a very genuine "recall" of a past life that cannot possibly be true. It is happening too close to this now for her to be there as a grown woman. Her inability to deal with the lack of logical explanation is preventing her from experiencing all her journey has to offer.

Please just see this through. Experience what your body is showing us. The answer is here, I know it is.

OK I am here, so I may as well.

She sighs and as she surrenders to the process we continue to experience her life as this happy but ordinary woman at the start of her day with much greater clarity.

We witness her take her place at her cubicle, high up in the tower that overlooks the water and the sprawling city beneath her. An early starter, she is the first to her desk. Colleagues arrive and she is settling into her day, when her routine is shattered.

We hear a loud explosion outside, the few colleges who are on her floor start pointing behind her and rushing to that side of the building. She turns to see a similar tower close to hers on fire. Nobody knows what is happening and she looks for her supervisor. Then all the phones start ringing, at once.

She looks out at the unbelievable scene unfolding below her.

"I saw it, a plane hit it - what a terrible accident. Poor souls." Her colleague tears up looking at people leaping to their death to avoid the flames engulfing the higher levels of tall tower next to hers.

Her supervisor tells everyone to stay put but then shortly afterwards the PA advises immediate evacuation and trying not to panic, she joins the ten thousand other office workers trying to leave the building rapidly by the stairs. I realise where we are and I know she has just minutes to live.

This is bullshit I CAN'T be here, it makes no sense! Sharon has realised where she is too.

There is violent jolt and the building rocks wildly as widows are blown out and the second plane hits several floors below us. We are enveloped in intense heat and suffocating smoke.

WHAT? This cannot be another accident! Who would do this? What is happening? WHY? My family, my boys…

She dies an agonising death trying to escape upwards, fully aware that there is no way out, desperate for just a few more breaths of air and a few more moments of life. She despairs, yearning to be with her family. The emotional pain of her death is excruciating.

Sharon, we must step out of this trauma into no time-space so that we can clear it.

How can I be in two places at once? I have never been to New York.

Your higher self can experience more than one incarnation simultaneously. Normally we do not make any contact with ourselves, there is no need, but this is an exceptional case. Your higher self has created this opportunity to clear this trauma, you can choose not to if you wish. If you prefer, you can wait to reincarnate to clear it, experiencing a similar trauma, in some form, to trigger its release, in this life or the next. Or you can clear it now.

I can see she is still having difficulty comprehending the truth of her "impossible" experience. It is a lot to absorb, in just a few minutes.

When did you say your depression started? Fifteen, maybe sixteen years ago, around 2001?

The impact of my question sinks in and Sharon takes a moment to digest its implications. Then she starts crying, allowing herself to fully feel the pain of her parallel self's death.

I was happy. I had a good, simple life… my children. This pain is so intense. What do I have to do to clear it?

In order to be free of this trauma and the despair you have been experiencing for the past sixteen years, you must call on the perpetrators of this awful act and forgive them.

I give her time to collect her thoughts and feelings and be ready to forgive. The people who will step forward when she calls them will not be the ones she expects.

But that is another story…

Vietnam veteran

It is dark, really dark. We are quietly creeping through dense jungle, in single file, next to a fast flowing river. Malarial mosquitos whine close to our faces. Our way ahead is illuminated only by starlight. I can feel the fear emanating from Mark, whose stomach is cramping as he grits his teeth holding back the evacuation of his watery bowels. His reconnaissance patrol is behind enemy lines and every cell of his being wants out.

This is not as I remember it. He telepaths. *Not what I expected, I hurt people, but not here.*

This is where your body has taken us when you commanded it to show where your trauma started. The other things you think are important are not.

Really?

What happened here?

Truly - I don't actually recall...

The soldier in front touches Mark and he passes the signal back. "Stop. Prepare to cross the creek" the touch conveys, the local in front knows the way. But the river looks too fast and deep for an easy ford, His mates have told him there are crocs in there and the area they are in is crawling with Vietcong.

Oh shit! As he enters the water his bowels finally give out and he whole body gives way to abject terror. *Will somebody get me out of there?*

His telepathic cry for help screams out across the Universe, so loud he even thinks he may be screaming.

And then it happened...

Mark is a heavy-set man who would have been muscular in his prime. Now his muscles are soft and his once firm belly, sags, He has the washed out, limp, pasty, slightly vacant look of someone who has been on medication for too long. I ask why he has come to see me.

"I did terrible things..."

His voice trembles as he recalls his activities as a conscript in a hot and steamy war that nobody really wanted and whose heroes were never truly thanked.

I can see his mind is playing and replaying events he had no control over, internalising and repeating guilt and remorse from his forever tarnished youth. Mark was one of the many unlucky young civilians conscripted when his birthday was drawn in the conscript ballots during the Vietnam war.

The Australian government, concerned that the conflict might destabilise the region and affect it's interests in Malaysia, Indonesia and Papua New Guinea could see that it's small standing army would not be enough for a growing conflict being fuelled by its North American ally. So the young 20 something man that Mark was, who had zero interest in being a soldier, found himself kitted out after basic

Spirit World

training, travelling to a place he had never heard of to fight people he had no argument with, whose politics were actually not too far from his own.

I can see Mark is about to start a long dialogue and I realise the best thing is to get him lying in the crystal mandala immediately, rather than regurgitate what he has been through with army therapists and veteran support groups, many times. He has come to see me for shamanic journey not another therapy session.

The process begins and I travel with him into his present life past, where we find ourselves, shuffling through the mud next to a crocodile infested creek. It is crucial that Mark have a clear recall and understanding of what happens next...

Something is happening, I feel the fear easing.

Why?

Something is comforting me, offering me succour.

You must examine it.

Why? It's working, My fear is easing.

This is the key to your depression, it s why you came to see me - to find it.

I don't want to. It's not happy you are here.

OK - let's step into no time-space, away from this immediate trauma and invite it to step forward.

Mark does so, with some trepidation, and the source of all his woes is revealed and it is big.

Oh no...

I take a breath. In my business we deal with every kind of entity but the deal Mark made to be less afraid in Vietnam has led to this being feeding off and perpetuating his depression - ever since.

I greet it formally and politely.

We are honoured to finally meet you. Thank you for helping Mark.

Is this real? Can this truly be a Demon?

More than that, this is a Mother Demon, the biggest and meanest of them all. Please give me permission to speak on your behalf.

Of course.

Thank you for teaching Mark his limitations, he has learnt all he needs to know about fear and depression. Your service is complete and your contract fulfilled, you may leave now. Thank you. I telepath Mark.

Be still, be neutral, do not say a word. Trust me. She cannot stay here without your permission.

I expect a drawn out negotiation, with threats and abuse, but I have dealt with her kind before - and she knows it.

She focusses on Mark.

Spirit World

You want this?

Mark is quick on the uptake.

Th… Thank you I release you - our agreement is complete.

I hope he does not say more and fortunately he doesn't

She turns to leave, addressing me.

I will see you later. Impudent wretch.

Mark, quickly say out loud after me. "You may not return without my conscious written permission. So be it."

Mark complies and now free of negative attachments, I guide him to a place where he may meet those who love him unconditionally.

A cheerful, cheeky 16th century Spanish soldier wearing a steel helmet steps forward and embraces him.

Brother, it has been a long time! You are free now.

We go through protocols to ensure that the man is truly his spirit guide and I give them time to reconnect - it is an emotional reunion.

I notice during their chat the Spanish soldier doubling up with laughter as Mark looks totally askance.

The journey ends with me ensuring they have a way to reconnect outside of the crystal mandala, without my presence.

Opening his eyes Mark wipes the tears from them and looks at me with total disbelief.

"You could not make this stuff up! Unbelievable!"

"Please believe it, your depression stops today, if you choose."

"I get it - I am ready for that, I do believe but… Wow."

"What was the big joke with your friend?"

"Oh - he told me my mates in 'Nam were having me on - the crocs in that part of the world are frightened by people!"

"Very funny."

"And you? That Mother Demon was not happy. What did it mean "see you later"?"

"She will visit me tonight in order to terrify me, but I will be ready."

"Rather you than me."

"All part of the service." I smile as I escort a transformed man from my healing space.

Day tripper

We are in a forest and the pink sky is transiting to purple. The undergrowth around us fluoresces with an other-worldly brilliance. I hear the the plants whispering to each other, the elements also communicate in their own colourful patterns and vibrations. It is overwhelming. It looks like Earth but there is more here, we seem to be having a deeper, expanded, hallucinogenic experience of a reality similar to ours.

Lying in my crystal mandala, Joy has commanded her body to take us to the moment her lung condition started and we are immediately transported to this sensual environment.

Do you recognise this place?

I telepath, as I feel myself being consumed by the richly textured, bright, surreal, moving patterns emanating from the plants around us. Perhaps we are on another planet. Her answer surprises me.

Yes, I remember being here, it was amazing...

My client Joy is lean and muscular, one of the new breed of therapists who really take wellness very seriously. This woman works out. Not for her the wafting layered white fabric of her peers, that creates an air of soft angelic ambience while concealing the softer more rounded form of the less active healer. Joy's preferred style of compression tights and clinging tops screams "I work out, I juice. And I love it!"

I sense under her calm exterior a wired intensity that she hides well from her clients. Although fit, she suffers from an underlying tiredness and an aching in her lungs that will not go away or respond to her own methods of healing.

We are in South America and I am experiencing a sacred shamanic journey led by my guide Juan. It was an incredible experience.... Why do I feel apprehensive? Joy telepaths.

Your body is about to show us the moment your lung condition started.

As a time traveler I witness her shamanic journey, mostly a revelatory expansion into nature that she is happy to revisit. As I observe, my scan of her body reveals several probable reasons for her discomfort. She will not enjoy discovering the cause of her lung pain.

The location of the otherworldly jungle around us now makes sense to me, we are re-experiencing an ayahuasca journey. A potent mix of plants, ayahuasca triggers an experience close to an LSD trip but very much aligned with the plants and animals in the surrounding environment. Now an expanding tourist experience, the use of these plants may not always be used in a traditional sacred space or with an initiated shaman or priest.

In this case her local guide considers his job done once the vomiting has subsided. After that he does not take any responsibility for their guidance or protection, believing that all they experience is perfect.

Joy notices herself becoming distracted by a tiny, playful, dragon-like being that eventually asks to stay with her.

I don't remember this part...

She sees the moment she gives permission, in her altered state, for the playful sprite to stay and play with her some more. Its energy shifts into a less pleasant, almost ravenous being that enters her body through her mouth as she breathes in, making its way to her lungs, where it relaxes into its comfortable new home and energy supply.

Removing it is straightforward, it knows it can only stay as long it has her permission. After pointing this out it offers little resistance and returns to its jungle home

How do your lungs feel now?

No ache, completely clear. Is this possible?

Of course, you have removed the source of the pain.

Does that mean I will no longer feel drained all the time?

Not yet, there is more. Command your body to take you to the moment this feeling of being drained started.

We return to the end of her unprotected shamanic journey with Juan. He walks around the bedraggled groups of westerners in various states of consciousness. Most are unaware of the positions their bodies have assumed during their psychedelic journey. We see him take a particular interest in Joy whose loose skirt has risen up her body to expose her thighs.

He stands over her and closes his eyes, projecting his consciousness between her legs, feeding off her vitality and latent sexuality.

This is disgusting! Joy is flabbergasted.

Rather than removing himself from her as she returns to full consciousness, he pushes deeper inside leaving a hook that will create permanent connection between them. A free energy source for Juan, who the local girls steer clear of because of his reputation as an energy leech. Some even call him a vampire.

Now I understand where my energy is going, no wonder I feel so tired.

How has your sexual energy been since your trip?

Totally depleted. How do I deal with this creep?

We will invite him into no time-space and have a chat. Don't buy into his aggression or threats by becoming angry, that actually makes you more vulnerable and feeds him. Stay calm and please allow me to speak on your behalf.

Juan is not happy about us discovering his free energy ride and threatens me with terrible reprisals for interfering with his abuse of Joy. But I don't buy into threats, I am not one to allow bullies to intimidate. He senses his efforts to destabilise Joy and myself are futile.

In order to complete this healing and be totally free of this confused individual you must forgive him.

Joy takes a moment to compose herself, she is in no mood to forgive. Eventually she feels the wisdom of my words and releases him through forgiveness and he detaches. She completes the process by saying out loud...

"You may not return without my conscious written permission." Sighing as she feels whole again.

Our post session discussion is brief, Joy has learned a lot about discernment and her own naïveté. Her curiosity and desire to experience a drug-induced shamanic journey got the better of her and she did not choose her guide well. She does have one burning question.

"Why was my journey with you so safe. How did we get to such an expanded state without taking drugs?"

"Before your arrival I cleanse and protect this sacred space. The crystals are arranged to gently expand your consciousness and this is the sole purpose of the mandala you lie in. My focus is on your divine highest good. I think Juan may have had other motivations."

Lost Soul

The intense stench of sweat, vomit and faeces is overwhelming. I gag involuntarily, concerned for a moment that I might actually vomit and choke my physical body which lies deep in a trance, in our present time, a long, long way away.

I am in a dark and filthy place that feels like some form of hell. I feel other hot beings pressed against me, the rough, sodden floor beneath us pitches and yaws like a cheap fairground ride. Those around express their terror in a variety of languages and dialects but mostly through screams. Apart from dread, they have one other thing in common. All I can see in the deep gloom that wraps around us like a deathly shroud is their teeth and eyes. Their skin, merging with the gloom is a deep and shiny black.

I did not expect this! Sienna telepaths, overwhelmed with the veracity of her experience. *I thought my shamanic journey would be like a movie. This is too visceral.*

You wanted to discover the source of your present day challenges, step fully into the body you know is yours and feel into it. In order to clear this trauma you must experience it firsthand.

She does so and immediately starts wailing…

Sienna is a mature woman, looking to understand why she has felt constantly lost and ill at ease for as long as she can remember. Unable to form long lasting and meaningful relationships or connect in any way to the place where she lives, she feels adrift in a sea of hopelessness. She hides these feelings under her bright and easy going demeanour. She has no real need to work due to an ongoing allowance from her wealthy family, but wants to contribute in some small way to society. Unable to locate the source of her despair in this life she is seeking answers in other times and places through a crystal induced shamanic journey.

This is awful, I have been abducted and imprisoned on this wretched vessel, wrenched from the land of my ancestors and family. I will never go back. The grief is unbearable!

We are on a slave ship headed for the Americas in the late 1700s and Sienna's prospects do not look good.

Ask your body to show you what happens to you in this life.

We witness her young life play out, a tragic series of events, abuse piled on abuse. Sold to a greedy plantation owner, as a strong looking young male she is given the hardest physical work imaginable. Bullied and whipped the young man, mourning for his homeland and family constantly says to himself, "I am a good person. I. Am. A. Good. Person". He tries hard to feel into this new alien place, full of people who dress strangely and look like ghosts. His attempts to reconnect with the land and the great Mother are futile, it is just so different from the place of his heart.

He is stoic but remains deeply alone. He dies young, worked to death, with a broken heart and back. On his deathbed he is attended to by an older slave who guides his return home to light. The trauma of his abduction and enslavement remain imprinted on his DNA forever - or until consciously cleared through a shamanic journey in a subsequent life.

This explains so much… This feeling of total isolation, abandonment and the emotional pain of separation. It is unbearable.

Time to release this trauma, forgive your oppressor and thank the "Aunty" who helped you.

The forgiveness process takes some time as the feelings are still so raw, but eventually Sienna feels the sense of it and is able to forgive all those involved in her enslavement.

Such a blessed release! I feel so much better, but it feels incomplete…

It is. This is a repeat of a much earlier more intense trauma, which as it was never cleared, re-manifested in your more recent incarnation as a slave.

More intense? Are you kidding?

If you feel able we can go there, I suggest you seize the opportunity now.

Surely, nothing could be more intense that this poor man's awful life?

I choose a silent response. Sienna could not imagine what awaits her, I hope she is strong enough to experience it.

I guess I have to go there.

It's up to you… When you are ready command your body to take you to the primary source of all your feelings of separation and aloneness.

She does so and we are there in an instant.

This is too weird. How can this be?

We are in another part of the multiverse close to this dimension and physicality. Here there is no individual free will. Sienna exists as part of a huge collective of beings that share their consciousness as one. She is experiencing a hive mind.

Strangely comfortable…. But somehow not enough, for me.

Time passes and as she becomes more aware of her own self and its potential, those around her feel it and become restless.

I must escape! This is a painful separation from all I know and love, but I must let go. This existence us suffocating me.

Sienna breaks free and it tears her soul to do so, but she senses more beyond the hive mind, scary - but irresistible.

She pulls away and they pursue her as one. They are many and they are fast. When they catch her they devour her flesh but her soul breaks free from the group consciousness.

How could they do this to me I loved them!

Spirit World

I feel for the gut wrenching pain as Sienna re-experiences her separation and death.

Wandering the cosmos, a free spirit but lost, she yearns for a home she can never return to. After eons of aloneness she finds earth and a way to incarnate here, only to repeat her trauma in human form.

They hated me, they rejected me when they consumed my body.

Call on them and forgive them, you will discover the truth.

The love from the hive is palpable when they arrive in spirit form.

They share their true feelings with Sienna.

They feared me?

They feared what you implied, a disease of individual free will, a threat to the hive mind. They realise they were wrong and beg her forgiveness.

Sienna weeps as she forgives the hive and the final part of her trauma is released, once and for all.

Returning to our time and space, Sienna sits up and dries her eyes.

"This aloneness stops now?"

"Yes, it is finished, you are free to have a normal life, with many happy relationships and to fully enjoy your home here, on Earth."

Bring in the Clowns

I cannot tell what time and place I am in, the furnishings are simple and poor and it is night time. I can feel the terror building around the child in the bed I am standing next to. She is alone in this gloomy space, in a restless sleep. She moans and groans quietly, a fine film of perspiration appears on her brow and neck as she starts to wrestle with the bed covers.

Tree branches outside scratch the windows and the thin steel walls around her as a breeze picks up. I think I hear muffled footsteps approaching, hidden amongst the other night noises. We are in a rural area free of street lamps and the enveloping darkness is moderated only slightly by the thin mist, of partially clouded half-moonlight, that wafts through the small, high window near her bed.

I am alert and ready for anything, I sense this is a repeated experience for the child. Anticipating the door to this isolated room opening to some kind of violator, I prepare myself to help the child as best I can. But the door does not open, something far more bizarre happens as she wakes, sitting upright with eyes wide open, her mouth gaping in a silent scream…

Susan is a mature woman in the midst of a spiritual emergence. Re-assessing her whole way of being, she has changed her job, her home and her relationship, bringing everything into alignment with what she believes to be her life's purpose. She is outgoing, successful and self assured, however she senses a deep seated fear that is preventing her from moving forward into her full potential and power. She has come to me to uncover what it might be.

She has tried various process to unlock this fear without success. Our pre-session discussion covers any kind of trauma she may have experienced in this life. She describes a few instances but assures that she feels they are dealt with.

> "The cause of your present underlying fear may not exist in this time or space. If you allow it, this shamanic journey will take us there," I advise, as she lies in my beautiful mandala of crystals and closes her eyes.

Commanding her body to take us to the source of her present life fear, we find ourselves in this dark room with a terrified child.

> *Oh, I had forgotten about this, this is me as a child, in this life, now. This is terrible, I feel sick.* She telepaths, recoiling from the strange situation before us.

I witness the spirit of a sinisterly happy-faced, small, child-like clown skip through the wall next to the door. He is in full clown make-up and regalia. It is the scariest clown I have ever seen. The child that is Susan is transfixed, petrified and hardly breathing.

> *It's the "Weebie Wobbie" he used to come and play with me. But it was not nice.*

> *Time to PLAY!* The clown laughs jumping up and down on her bed.

> *Oh, this is awful can we stop?*

We can, but this is the fear you came to uncover. Invite this being to step into no time/space and ask it to show you when you invited it to be here.

I invited it... Really?

She asks and is immediately shown herself in the shed a few years earlier, a lonely child, crying, with no-one to play with.

I called for help!?

And for a playmate and this Being answered your call. Tell it not to be afraid and that you won't hurt it. Thank it for its service and release it from your agreement. Its service is complete.

Oh, it is so sad, that I want it to leave. It's making me feel sad too.

It has been with you since then and you have become familiar with it. Its presence offers you a kind of reassurance. Your spiritual growth and expanding self-awareness frightens it. It senses you won't need it anymore and wants you to stop, so it is triggering your irrational fear.

The overly playful energy of the clown has changed, it is crying real tears.

I see through the clown's make-up and have my own realisation of what this Being actually is.

Ask it to show itself in its true form.

Susan does so and the transformation is immediate and profound.

Oh! It's just a little boy just a bit older than I was then... He answered my call, he wanted to play with me.

Why did he appear as clown?

He thought it would make me happy, he knew I wanted a playmate. He did not mean to frighten me and he did not know how to change his appearance back to a child. He is such a lovely little boy...

Ask him what year it is and what is the last thing he remembers.

The boy shares that it is 1953 and he members being in a car accident with his parents. It is the year he died. We call on his parents and they come and take him home to light. It is a joy-filled reunion. Susan is very emotional as she finally releases him to find peace.

We complete the session and Susan sits up drying her eyes.

"I was SO scared of that clown. It seems silly now I know what was really happening."

"You can see how his presence has affected your life?"

"Oh yes, whenever I took steps towards empowerment and self-realisation I felt this deep inexplicable fear in the pit of my stomach. It was that little boy, frightened that I might discover him and ask him to leave."

"How do you feel now?"

"Crystal clear! Thank you."

"By the way, how come you were locked in that shed?"

"I wasn't locked in. My parents were fixing up a dirty old house and they figured the old tin garage was a cleaner, nicer place for me to be. They thought they were doing the right thing, but they felt a long way away when I was a child. I never told them what happened or asked to be moved. I thought they might not believe me."

Death and Birth

My client Kirra is screaming, her face contorted, her dark skinned right hand pushed hard into the futon beneath her, fingers spread wide. Something invisible is pinning her wrist down as her body writhes around it, she is in excruciating pain.

Her screams are so loud they have brought me back to this time and space to glance for a moment at her contorted body in my healing studio. Fortunately I am in a rural area and those nearby know I am some kind of healer. Reassured she is not actually dying, I allow myself to return to the time she is experiencing with such a visceral recall.

Just allow yourself to be here. I telepath

Do I have any choice? The pain is unbearable. Why are they doing this to me? My hand!

Let your awareness expand outwards from your hand. What is happening around you?

Her breathing moderates, a little.

I am in a musty place, underground, faded whitewashed walls, curved arches, crumbling bricks. The people in uniform who are hurting me despise me. I am female, my skin is white, I feel heavier than I am now. Why am I here? Why am I not Aboriginal, with my ancestors? What did I do to deserve this torture?

Your incarnation into the Aboriginal bloodline is recent, you have incarnated elsewhere at other times. Command your body to show you what led to this...

As we travel through time and space I can see both before and after this incident and feel deep compassion for Kirra, who has come to see me because of her inability to conceive. After trying many other processes she has been referred to me to help her uncover why. Our shamanic journey has plunged us straight into this trauma, when we commanded her body to show us the reason she could not have a baby.

She relaxes as we are transported to another era. A period where everyone looks thinner and the few cars on the streets are bigger than they are now and mostly black. The air feels clean and fresh and the locals who are going about their daily business push carts, walk or ride bicycles. It feels peaceful, almost mundane but there is an undercurrent of fear, hidden by people trying to make the most of a bad situation by carrying on as normal.

For a moment Kirra forgets her recent pain, she is fascinated by the clarity of her recall.

This feels like Europe, France maybe. The buildings, the people they look pre-war. People look good without much effort, the women have style, on a shoestring by the look of it. This is like a movie...

Where are you? Do you recognise yourself anywhere?

Yes, thats me! That busy woman over there, she looks happy, but something is not right.

Spirit World

Step into her body and allow yourself to be her, how does she feel?

She has a secret, an important secret. She feels scared but defiant, she is a big woman.

Oh no…

Kirra has noticed the grey uniforms of her torturers that walk in small groups through her community.

I feel like they know who I am.

And who are you?

I see myself writing, I have access to information and I am helping the resistance, with good reason. I don't look it, but I am Jewish. They have taken everyone I know.

So it's not pre-war France is it?

No, it is occupied France. Oh… I feel it now. I am not fat, I am pregnant. I did not mean to fall pregnant, but I love him so much!

Kirra sobs quietly, re-experiencing the intense connection she felt with the leader of the local resistance.

He is such a loving, brave and gentle man. They captured me and because I won't talk they are cutting off my fingers one by one. My writing hand! I did not tell them anything, but they found him and they have him standing here before me now, witnessing my torture.

I cannot believe that anyone could do this to another human being.

We are beneath the largest Chateau in town, in the wine cellar, recently repurposed. The resistance leader is stoic, denying all connection with his pregnant lover, now witnessing her intensifying torture and coldly refusing to acknowledge her, in the vain hope that it will stop.

I have seen many things in my time travelling practice but what happens next is beyond revulsion.

After repeated threats they execute Kirra in front of her lover by opening her womb allowing the foetus to spill out before them both as she bleeds to death, now well beyond feeling any physical pain. Her stony faced lover is then taken outside and shot.

Never! Never will I get pregnant ever again! Her last thoughts and feelings spread out across the universe and soak into her DNA.

Are you ready to release that promise to yourself? You see how it is affecting your life now?

She is still in a state of shock. I give her some time, then she agrees.

Please repeat after me out loud… By speaking we add the greatest power to her affirmation.

"I now dissolve any and all agreements I may have made with myself regarding my ability to bear children. These agreements no longer serve me and I release them once and for all. My reproductive area functions perfectly and I can conceive easily, as I choose. I do this of my own free will across time and space, now. So be it."

As she finishes this powerful affirmation, her whole being releases a deeply relaxing out breath, permanently changing her present reality.

I feel it! I feel my womb, my ovaries opening, easing... Unbelievable.

In order to totally release the trauma you must also forgive those who tortured and killed you...

This takes a little more time and counselling, but eventually she is ready and does so.

I cannot believe how free I feel. What about my lover what happened to him?

Call on him.

She does so and he appears immediately, still very distraught, locked into the nightmare of their deaths, as if it were a moment ago. Deeply traumatised he has become Earthbound; we talk with him and I help him understand that all is well, that he is not responsible for the death of his lover and unborn child.

Calling on the beings who love him unconditionally to help him journey home to light, Kirra has one question of them, as they help him find peace.

Will I ever get to be with him again?

You are free of your death trauma and are able to bring new life into your world, you will now conceive easily. Once he has been counselled and healed, you may incarnate together again.

He will be your first born.

Forbidden Love

My usually calm young apprentice, Jo, is agitated. I have never seen her this animated before a session. We are gazing into the parking area next to my healing studio as my client, Georgia, steps out of her polished, black Range Rover. Even the tyres are shiny.

"She looks much smaller in the flesh... Beautiful dress, she is SO pretty."

Jo rushes to the door and greets the well known TV personality who is also welcomed into several million living rooms each week. I smile to myself as Jo unconsciously almost curtsies as Georgia enters, bowing her head as the media royalty crosses our threshold.

"Apologies for overdressing, I've just come from another function. I hope that's OK?" Georgia breezes in.

I reassure her that we will be lying down and as long as she is comfortable that is fine; she slips off her shoes as we chat. Our interview reveals that she is ready to deal with her well concealed anger and resentment, which is affecting her wellbeing and work relationships.

She tells me she has experienced no major trauma in her life and I catch Jo's eye. She has made a smooth transition from a starstruck fan into focussed healer. We both sense that Georgia is concealing something. As Georgia lies in the mandala of crystals next to me, I confirm that she understands the power of the journey on which she is about to embark.

"We will be uncovering and resolving the source of the feelings we have discussed, this process reveals *everything*. All you have to do us surrender and allow me to guide you. Are you OK with that?"

"I am." She nods, after a slight hesitation. Georgia's journey will be far deeper than she anticipates.

Both Jo and I know that whatever she is hiding will surface once the crystals laid around her head work their magic. I watch her eyelids flutter rapidly as the enters a light trance.

"Please say after me: Body I command you - take me to the source of my anger."

Her body obliges, immediately transporting our consciousness to another time and place. We find ourselves in a beautiful bucolic setting, we could be in any time when fields are cultivated. It is a clear sunny day with a powder-blue sky and a light, warm breeze - a great day to be alive. Georgia is standing next to me in the body of a young girl.

She is so happy, so innocent. So free. Georgia telepaths.

Why so happy?

She feels very loved. Life is wonderful!

A man calls her and she runs to him across the lush, green paddock, propelling herself headlong into his open arms. I feel an intense bond between them as they embrace. He loves her deeply and unconditionally and there is great joy between them. It is moving to witness such profound love.

I don't want to be here anymore. Georgia telepaths, distressed.

Why not? This recollection of deep love is beautiful, we have not located the time and place, the nature of this relationship and what happens next. Please allow it to unfold.

She is reluctant to observe what comes next, but nonetheless allows the process to continue.

Ask your body to show you where this relationship leads.

I feel her resistance to the experience grow as we observe the relationship develop. The child that she is approaches puberty and their embraces become more intense, they hold each other closer and kiss each other longer than before. They are almost furtive when they do so. Still, I can feel the man has pure intentions in his love for this child.

Then things change.

Another beautiful, playful day filled with love and embraces, they lie together looking up at clouds in the sky, laughing at the shapes they make. His hands behind his head, her head on his chest, hand on his stomach. She moves her hand slowly down and touches his penis through his trousers. He is startled.

"No, my love you cannot touch me there, it is not allowed." She persists and rapidly, naturally, without any overriding thought his body responds.

"We cannot do this. I love you but I am your father, it is not allowed." He hugs her close and she cries deep, mournful sobs.

"I want it to be like it was before."

"Before? We have never done this before." Her father is perplexed.

"I love you SO much." The child cries, hugging him. He comforts her, reflecting on her words.

Over a period of years we see her persist with her advances, until, against his better judgement her father allows their relationship to become sexual. Their passionate, illicit affair continues for years until her mother, his wife, discovers them 'in flagrante delicto.' The family falls apart and becomes fragmented, her father is disgraced and the teenage girl is shamed beyond redemption. She leaves and they never speak to each other again.

Ask your body to show you when this happened.

There is no need to ask, I know… It was this lifetime, now. I seduced my own father. Georgia's sobs are deep and full of remorse.

I hear a sharp intake of breath from Jo, I can guess what she is thinking.

Call on the beings who love you unconditionally and ask them show you why this happened.

The atmosphere in the room brightens as several beings of light join us.

Dear child, please do not be so hard on yourself. You set yourself a big challenge to reincarnate with this man so soon after your death. He was killed suddenly, when you were very passionately in love, your relationship felt incomplete and you yearned to be in a loving relationship with him again. Incarnating together in this life as father and daughter, you were not able to move from Eros into Agape love for him and that is understandable. It is time to beg forgiveness of those you hurt and most of all forgive yourself and move on. Remember that he had free will too. There is much joy in store for you if you allow it.

I take Georgia through the forgiveness process, calling on the higher consciousness of all those involved. We complete the session by affirming that she has learnt all she needs to know about self-loathing and needs never to repeat the experiences that led to it, ever again.

A much brighter Georgia sits up and opens her eyes.

"I truly understand what happened and why and I am at peace with it. Thank you."

"Your life enters a new phase today, take your time. Jo will take you for a walk before you drive."

As the bright, black car leaves, Jo returns, looking a little bit sheepish.

"Thank you for not speaking during the session, I know you wanted to. The big lesson for you today is to let go of all judgement. We are here to facilitate peace and freedom, for all beings - without judging them."

Heaven and Earth

"Raym, she has stopped breathing, we should do something!" I hear my apprentice's rising tone, faintly, in the distance. She has been observing my session and has collapsed into fear and panic.

In the tranquility of a healing centre, alarm is not a good thing, I feel it prickling my energy body as I take a deep breath, return to full consciousness and open my eyes. I gaze at my clients inert and supine form, spread on the floor next to me, surrounded by crystals. At her request we have taken a long and deep journey into her future death. As I return to my body and my out of focus vision adjusts, I perceive a pale, flaccid form next to me, that is my client Anna.

Did we travel too far?...

Anna is a mature, wealthy woman in the final chapter of her life, looking to understand more about her focus and community service as she ages. She is particularly interested in the implications that her lifelong yoga and meditation practice may have on her next life. In our pre-session interview she mentions that she had found a guru whose unconditional love touched her deeply, it is clear she still mourns his passing some ten years ago.

Anna wishes to visit her immediate past life death and her approaching death in this life in the hope of understanding her soul's journey and choices. With some reservations and several repeated promises from Anna to return to her body at the end of our journey we travel together across time and space, as she lies in my crystal mandala and I command her body to take us to her most recent incarnation.

We arrive in an Asian country and she experiences a life as a male peasant working hard to feed his family. By Western standards the living conditions seem harsh and primitive. He spends long days under a fierce sun in a humid environment, planting, tending and harvesting his rice paddies in an interminable cycle of hard labour. His body is lean and his muscles ache but he is happy. He is a devout Hindu and his faith and daily practice help him rise above the limitations of his birth.

We witness his love for his family as he tries hard to give them the opportunities for a good education that he did not have. They grow and leave home for jobs in the city, returning occasionally, driving cars and wearing Western clothing. He feels proud of their achievements. He grows old with his wife and his focus on daily devotion, offerings and community service increases as he ages. He dies, body worn out but at peace with everything, his practices helping him transit into greater consciousness as he leaves his body surrounded by his family.

Anna is emotional as she telepaths. *Such a simple humble life, so beautiful... I guess I understand my choices to live a more comfortable life this time around. It was harsh. I see too how I fell easily into my yoga practice and spiritual path in this incarnation. It always seemed so natural to me. I sense his purity of heart and simple devotion made his death transition easier.*

Anna also sees clearly that she has learnt all she needs to know about poverty and hard work and so incarnates into an affluent Western family.

May we look at my future now?

You promise to return to your body afterwards?

I do.

Commanding her body to take us to the moment of her future death, I realise that the circumstances and date of her death are irrelevant as her consciousness spreads outwards from her dying body. It touches the people close to her, then the trees, the land, the sky, the continent, the seas, the planet, the sun and the stars. Her awareness expands exponentially, connecting via a matrix of light with the Milky Way, the Universe and Multiverses beyond that, into infinity and All There Is. She becomes one with everything and the beauty of the moment is beyond words.

After an age I gently remind her of her reason to visit this time, her question echoes outwards mingling with the music of the spheres. *What happens next?*

From the vastness around us a deep and resonant knowing responds.

In your now you say you are ready to be of service to humanity, your choices in the coming years are important. You have been touched by unconditional love in this life and you wish to share that. You may do so, you may express it in every interaction with every being you encounter from this moment onwards refining your essence with each interaction.

Like my guru? I can do that?

If you wish. However it is enough to just be love and share love in your daily life. In doing so you will attune your own vibration to the limitless love that holds reality together. If you do so you will reach this point of limitless expansion and bliss that you are witnessing now.

Anna hesitates. *How will I be able to compress this into a human form, when will I reincarnate?*

If you reach this state of interconnectedness and love, you will have passed the need to return to the cycle of death and rebirth on this planet.

If Anna does not reach this state? I enquire on her behalf.

Then she will reincarnate as a less aware being or thing, until she does.

Please show us her potential if she fulfills her desire to be of service based on love.

You may become anything that pleases you...

Moving into a profound understanding of the nature of reality, we are shown Anna's consciousness becoming form again as a planet or a star and its magnificence is humbling. The communication between us becomes faint as Anna is drawn into the immersive experience of her probable future.

Oh so beautiful.

I know that her body will be looking devoid of life as her consciousness stretches into the distant reaches of the cosmos as I hear Jo's distant panicked voice calling from another time and place pulling me from a deep and reverent state into the dense reality I call home. Jo has never seen a client in such a deep state before and does not completely understand what is happening, Anna's very shallow breathing and state of utter surrender appears far more distressing than it actually is.

Nonetheless I realise it is time to call Anna back to this time and place and I do so as gently as I can, knowing it will be hard for her to leave the exalted state of bliss she is experiencing. I calm Jo as she returns. It takes some time for her to become fully present in her body, her voice thin and her eyes still closed, I hand her a grounding stone and as colour returns to her cheeks, she whispers.

"That was the most profound experience of my life... Is that truly possible? That I may become that? Is it that simple?"

"It is."

All that Glisters is not Gold

It's an Angel. An Angel!

My client Sheila is in a mossy place that shimmers with bright and playful rainbows, created by the sunlight refracting through the clear, sparkling waterfall beside us. We have arrived in a sacred, other-worldly place at the end of her shamanic journey.

She is teary and cannot believe her eyes, her journey has not been an easy one.

So beautiful... She telepaths.

Ask her does she love you?

She does. And she has a gift for me...

A translucent, mystical mandala, fluoresces before us, hovering in the hazy gloom of the moist and misty cave.

This will bring you peace. Touch it, gaze into it and whenever you need solace think of me. We will be forever connected. The Angel smiles.

Sheila steps towards the beautiful hovering yantra.

Just a moment, before you go any further, please say out loud after me, "I have learnt all I need to know about suffering and pain, I choose now to be totally free of all trauma."

You cannot be free of it. The Angel sounds stern.

Why not? Sheila is surprised

Because you are evil.

This sounds a little judgemental to me; Angels are beyond judgment. I stare hard at the being before us.

Touch the mandala and I will always be with you. The Angel gazes at Sheila. as she reaches out her hand.

Ask this angel, does it love you unconditionally?

What? Of course it does.

Ask.

She asks and we sense a microsecond of hesitation revealing a hint of anger on the radiant smiling visage before us, like a momentary flicker on a TV screen.

Say after me quickly, "I challenge your truth as a being of light. Show yourself in your true form!"

Sheila follows my instructions and things change rapidly. The cave is filled with the stench of sulphur and a loud, hideous, cackling laugh.

Spirit World

You will suffer for eternity, I promise you that. A voice emanates from the dark cloud that was the Angel.

Sheila is picked up and thrown across the cave by this dark force which has her by the throat and is strangling her. I know her physical body in our time/space will also be gasping for air and I must act quickly…

Sheila has come to see me because of her inexplicable weight loss. She weighs about half of her normal weight. She looks frail and overwhelmed as she recounts her life. She describes being placed in psychiatric care by her family for being anorexic, when she wasn't. She tells me about a series of physically abusive lovers, a mother who repeatedly told her she was worthless and a violent father.

I do not mention it, but she presents as a textbook case of major karma ready to be cleared, unpleasant, but a blessing in disguise. She lies in my crystal mandala and I prepare myself to plead her case to the karmic court, after witnessing some awful past life deed. I end up doing neither.

One after another we clear layers of multiple traumas held in different parts of her body: the pain in the side of her face reveals a motorbike accident later in life where her face hit the ground but actually relates to the emotions she felt being slapped as a child by her father. Trauma held in the throat first manifests as an abusive partner choking her but when it is cleared it exposes an earlier forced promise not to speak of childhood sexual abuse. Her body has been repeating traumas to draw her attention to the primary emotional wound, creating an opportunity to clear the held emotion at its source, once it is revealed.

And so it goes on, witnessing then clearing layers of extreme related traumas in this life and in others until finally I feel that she is clear and we arrive at the glistening waterfall. Wondering what could have caused so many layered, traumas without any apparent karmic connection, I am just about to relax into an angelic vibe and hopefully hear an explanation, when Sheila is attacked and strangled.

I address the being pinning Sheila to the wall. *Do not fear us we will not harm you.*

Stay out of this, you fool.

I gaze into the black form and understand more.

Do you realise you are dead?

It pauses. *I am not dead. I travel through time to perpetuate this curse. You know nothing.* It hisses.

Once you were a good and wise woman; accused of wrong doing you were starved, tortured and burned alive.

Her form stabilises into what she once was and her grip loosens on Sheila's throat.

And I cursed the descendants of the bastard who imprisoned and raped me. This is one of them! I have cursed you all for eternity. Your ancestor destroyed my family and humiliated me in front of the townspeople! You will feel unimaginable pain, you will starve, you will be raped and abused and your skin will burn!

Sheila finds her own inner strength and stands up to the spirit of the woman throttling her.

No need to talk in the future tense, I have experienced all of those things. My life has been torture: despised by my parents; betrayed; physically, sexually and emotionally abused. This has gone on for long enough!

An eternity is not long enough to redress the wrong your ancestor did to me and my children. Yes, I realise I am dead. I recall my tortured death now, with great clarity. And I still see your ancestor's smiling face in YOU. You carry it still. Her grip tightens.

The negotiation for Sheila's release is long and protracted but eventually I help her tormentor realise that enough is enough, that Sheila is not responsible and it is time for the curse to be lifted. The heartfelt apology from Sheila's ancestor also helps and the woman finally lifts her curse and is taken away for counselling by those who love her unconditionally.

A magnificent ancient god steps forward and congratulates Sheila for her forbearance.

Ask him to complete the session by clearing all residue of trauma you are holding onto in all realities, across all time/space. He does so.

Addressing Sheila, the Ancient One transmits a resonant vibration.

You are strong not to have collapsed under the strain of this life. It was not your fault, it was not Karma. It was a curse placed a long time ago with such venom and intensity it was well hidden and hard to discover, let alone break. Your entire lineage has suffered from it.

How will this session affect Shiela's life? What should she do now? I ask on her behalf.

I feel his deep compassion as he addresses her. *You should rest now. All your physical ailments will fade away and you will be able to put on weight and retain it. All the traumas you have experienced will now stay in the past where they belong, you do not need to repeat them or be affected by them ever again. There is a partner waiting for you and you may have children, if you wish. Until today this curse would have affected your children too. This is no longer the case, you are free.*

Thank you. I speak for Sheila who is too emotional to communicate.

Sheila allows herself the deepest sigh as she opens her eyes to her new reality.

"I feel at peace - for the first time in my life!"

And the blind shall see

My client Bob is very quiet, he is in a state of awe and wonder.

How is this possible? This is so clear, SO clear. I see everything! Bob telepaths, a tear slowly seeping from each eye, his chin creased, dimpled and quivering from holding the well of deep sobs begging to be released.

We stand together in a lush river plain, rich with fruit and vegetables, not the desert that it is now. A broad silty river flows past us, languid but with purpose, it carries nutrition and life giving water to the surrounding fields and valleys below. It is humid and hot, if we had bodies we would be sweating profusely, but we do not. We are time travelling, seeking to uncover the source of what my client believes to be a curse placed on him in this time, that has affected his life profoundly.

He hopes to release it and I feel optimistic as we have arrived at this point in time and space with no interference to our journey, a good sign so far. Nothing and nobody is trying to stop us uncovering the truth.

Please explore and let me know if you recognise anyone who feels like you. He or she will look different, but you will know when you see yourself.

We wander through the marketplace of the town that sits on the riverbank, invisible to the locals. Bob is fascinated by everything he sees, staring at fabrics, food and people, stopping to admire the intricate work of a jeweller.

This is Lapis isn't it? He admires both the setting and the stones, *such a lovely blue.*

We sense a disturbance approaching. Before anything has even set foot in the market an invisible vanguard of fear pushes ahead of it, announcing its imminent arrival. Fear mixed with awe. The locals do their best to carry on as normal but their gaze is downcast and their conversations muted. They truly fear for their lives and the anonymity of normality offers them some protection, they do not want to be noticed.

Then we see it, moving slowly through and above the crowds, lurching, higher than the rough awnings that flap in the soft breeze created by the nearby body of water. Its lumbering gait is semi-human and its colour the most startling and precious of all, the most regal Lapis Lazuli.

We observe as it approaches and realise this is no strange creature but a figure carried like a holy relic, a statue sitting on platform, bedecked and bejewelled by precious stones, gold and silver, carried shoulder high, by well dressed slaves.

Bob is transfixed, staring at the lofty, regal figure. *This is not a statue, this is a living being and it's me! Why do they fear me so much?*

You may step into his body and experience being him again. How does he feel?

He feels semi-human, extraordinarily powerful, godlike and extremely paranoid.

> *He thinks everyone is out to get him. His advisers and court, fearful they may themselves be accused are happy to spread blame well away from anything they touch. He is terribly alone, born into a life of limitless wealth and luxury without any choice in the matter. He is deeply depressed, he can trust no-one.*
>
> *His parents were poisoned and he fears the same fate himself. And yet the common people are in awe of him and because of their conditioning they love him, but he cannot see that.*
>
> *How does this affect your life now? Why was he cursed?*
>
> *Oh no...*

I too sense impending dread, but encourage my client to re-experience it in the hope that we may be able to seek forgiveness, negotiate with the cursers and change his present situation.

> *He brought this on himself.*
>
> *Command your body to take you to the moment this started.*

We travel forward in time to a balmy, clear, moonless, starlit night. He and his servants are upstream and he is almost hysterical. He has them pour a greenish-white powder into the river. They obey reluctantly having some inkling of what they might be doing, but too afraid to disobey.

As they make their way back to the city they are met by the palace guards who promptly kill everyone accompanying the king, obeying orders put in place by the king himself earlier.

Over the next few days and weeks we see a horrible purging of the riverside population. A fever and blindness followed by an excruciatingly painful death is experienced by about one third of the population.

> *This neurotic fool has killed his own people convinced that the poison would seek out only those who conspired against him. I am responsible for this. Bob is disgusted.*
>
> *So who cursed you?*
>
> *Nobody! No-one knew it was me. I was very clever, I went around blessing and healing people from my platform and they loved me all the more for it!*

I see clearly now where this leads, unfortunately I will not be able to reverse Bob's present challenge, this is not what I was hoping for.

> *Command your body to take you forward in time to your death, how do you feel?*
>
> *I live a long time! But I am wracked with guilt, guilt that pushes me into doing good things for my people, but it is not enough. I die a miserable, lonely death without an heir.*
>
> *And when you leave your body?*
>
> *I attend the karmic court and I am forgiven by those whose lives I took. To balance my own karma I insist on living a whole life with my disability. There could have been an easier route to redemption, but I was so full of remorse. It was my choice to experience this limitation.*

"And are you at peace with the decision you made then?" I ask as Bob returns to his body.

"I am, it makes so much sense."

"I am sorry I could not do more."

"You did a great job, thank you. I understand so much now."

He sits up and rubs his eyes, and although agile and aware, he is dazed. I help him stand when he is ready and walk him slowly outside, where his partner is waiting for him. He is still shaken by the visual clarity of his lucid experience but now calm, he completely understands the reason for his condition and is at peace with it.

He steps outside and feels the breeze caress his soft skin, his opaque and sunken eyes look up to the sky he will never see. He has been blind since birth.

CIA interference

I am in a vast, cool, limitless, dark space, which fades to black below me. I am weightless with my client Megan suspended next to me. I search for stars, trying to orientate myself, but there are none. I am disorientated and my client is confused - she has asked to be taken to the core of the interference with her work, but we appear to be nowhere.

I sense something huge, slowly approaching us through the gloom. It is accompanied by a slow, deep, otherworldly moaning that we feel rather than hear. As I become aware of its vastness an enormous eye focusses on our small forms and my consciousness is probed. I find myself balancing on a knife-edge of panic. Trying to remain calm, I gaze back into the eye examining me and I collapse into a most unexpected emotion…

I feel Megan's tension as she looks over her shoulder after parking her car outside my healing studio. Her fear has created an unconscious reflex reaction that she is no longer aware of. A wiry, middle-aged woman her walk is erect and purposeful: she approaches smiling. She greets me with a happy, brave face but within her I see the fading spark of a once passionate, young activist fading into despair.

Recently returned from her crusading work in the States, I can see she is close to burnt out. A rest would be good for her, but she is driven. Not a woman to mince words, she sits and cuts to the chase.

"There is ongoing government interference with my work and I want to get to the bottom of it. I have been told you can help."

"How are you being interfered with?"

"You are familiar with my work?" I nod, having seen her both on the news and in several documentaries about climate change and environmental degradation.

"Over the past year so many things have gone wrong, it is beyond a joke." She tears up, her stoic visage crumbling momentarily. "I have been betrayed, malicious and unfounded stories leaked to the media and expedition finance has fallen through. I know I was being followed in the States and I have had inexplicable health challenges. It can only mean one thing - the CIA is out to stop me."

I sense she is on the edge of paranoia but I choose not to judge, her journey will reveal the truth.

"Are you willing to enter this shamanic journey without expectation? Can you release all attachment to outcomes? Things may not be as they seem."

She hesitates then nods. "That's why I am here."

It takes some time to clear her busy mind but after a few exercises she surrenders to the power of the crystals around her and lets go of thought. Moving into an expanded state of consciousness we find ourselves drifting in this empty, endless space, confronted by a being whose form is so large it disappears into the gloom behind it....

Thank you. It telepaths to Megan whose face contorts through a gamut of emotions. I too am deeply moved by this being's profound love, vast intelligence, and endless patience with humanity.

You have spoken for us in many forums and your voice has been heard, you HAVE made a difference. The form before us becomes clearer and I realise we are communicating with the rarest, largest and gentlest of mammals - a great blue whale.

I speak for all of us. Your service is complete, you may rest now.

No! There is more to do! I have just begun, who else will speak for you and our environment? Megan seems almost frantic.

There are others. We love you, it is time to rest.

What about the interference? Who has been trying to stop me?

The great being pauses. *Mmm... I would like to introduce you to someone...*

In an instant a glowing figure descents from above us. It is a radiant younger version of Megan, who exudes wisdom. Megan stares at herself blinking in disbelief.

You must let go of anger.

Who are you?

You know that I am your Higher Self. You sense that but find it hard to believe. I am you.

Megan turns to me. *Is this some kind of CIA hologram? Are you on their pay role? I know they want me to stop.*

No, they do not have access to me or my space. Please listen to her...

The anger you are generating is giving the destroyers of your environment energy. You are feeding them and other beings like them by engaging in conflict with them. You are being manipulated. Megan's Higher Self gently reveals the truth.

But they have being trying to stop me! I am sick!

Your health challenges are your own responsibility, you are burning yourself out. Your despair has attracted some low level interference. But mostly that was me, trying to attract your attention.

Ha! Pretty unsubtle.

Well, it worked, you came to see Raym and through him, me.

Megan pauses. It is a lot to take in for a person who has been engaged in worldly conservation campaigns and more recently direct conflict, since she was a teenager. Megan's life has been dedicated to a worthy cause, but her increasing anger and despair are creating their own challenges.

Spirit World

Your work has been valuable - priceless, but it is time to disengage. Wearing yourself out serves no useful purpose. Feeding the destroyers with your anger is counter-productive and the energy that generates can be used against you and the beings you love. You must trust me. Everything is perfect.

I can feel Megan's frustration about to boil over, I guess she has heard the "Everything is perfect" phrase before and I know it's hard to swallow. Then something wonderful happens…

Whilst we have been communicating we have been silently surrounded by other beautiful sea creatures, every one of whom has been touched by Megan's dedication.

Feel them. Her higher self commands. *Allow yourself to feel their gratitude. Rest now, your work is complete.*

Megan sobs as she is caressed by waves of unconditional love and for the first time in a very long time I feel her being totally relax. It is a profound and beautiful experience.

However, feeling into Megan's core I sense that her passion will get the better of her and after this session she will continue her work, regardless of its consequences.

Sorry Business

We walk beneath a starry, starry sky. The stars fill the firmament above us, the milky way clearly visible like a thick strand of the wild, flowing hair of a goddess. There is no moon, but the billions of distant suns are bright enough for us to just see what lays before us: we are in the bush somewhere in the outback.

I smell woodsmoke on the cool night air, the gentle warming, welcoming smell of a small campfire. I hear it's distant crackle and sense its glow in the bush beyond us.

A young Aboriginal woman walks lightly before us, almost skipping through the darkness. She turns and her heart stopping, radiant smile seems to lighten the atmosphere around her. She is beautiful.

This way...

She telepaths moving silently and gracefully ahead, finding a path where I can see none, I trust her and follow.

What are we doing here? Where are we? My client Suzette is confused.

I have brought you here to meet some very special people. Our young and playful guide walks purposefully towards the distant crackling fire.

Why can't I feel my body? Suzette looks at her hands waving them in front of her face.

Because you're not in your body, silly. The young Aboriginal girl's smile is luminescent.

You're in the space between worlds. She giggles. The place you white-fellas don't believe in. Her private joke turns into a full blown laughter. *Time stopped when your friend brought you here, remember? You're in our sacred spiritual space, our Tjukurpa .*

We approach the small campfire which sheds a flickering pool of light on the rough ground around it. Next to the fire is an old Aboriginal man with a younger Aboriginal man standing next to him. The older man sits warming himself, enjoying the night. His skin is very black, making his white beard and hair appear like pure white, curly candy floss. His face looks careworn, although eyes have the same playful glint as our young guide's.

He acknowledges us as we approach, a subtle nod in my direction. His thoughts touch mine, he is surprised to see two non-Aboriginals in this sacred place.

The younger man next to him is an imposing figure: clear, lean and intense he stands proud and free, leaning on a long spear. He is not a man you would mess with.

Our guide approaches, they exchange glances and the Uncle smiles, sharing some kind of private joke about us, I sense Suzettes tension building. Her apprehension transforms into fear as the young man steps towards her, his spear held loosely in his hand.

We have been waiting for you mate, long time. You want to know why you don't like black-fella? I show you…

Suzette steps back as I step forward ready to deal with whatever happens next…

Suzette is a striking young French woman who has fallen in love with Australia, particularly the remote outback. Before our shamanic journey she tells me of the intense feelings of joy and homecoming she felt the first time she set foot in the red centre, when she knelt and pushed her hands deep into the orange ochre sand, sobbing.

Fiercely French, she is surprised at how much she adores Australia and wants to understand more. She tells me quietly that she is embarrassed that she is repulsed by indigenous Australians. She would like to understand why she feels that way and be free of that feeling. She finds it both distressing and confusing as in Paris she has several black French friends, whom she loves.

Laying in my crystal mandala, the depth and speed of our shamanic journey has taken her by surprise and she has temporarily forgotten why she came to see me and take this journey, the tall man with the spear has just reminded her.

French to the core she quickly regains her composure and stands resolute.

Who are these people? She asks our young guide, who then points at the Elder.

This is my Uncle, he is a wise man. This fella… She points to the spear carrier smiling, but her sentence trails off as the Uncle catches her eye and signals her to stop.

Let him show you, you came here for answers, he has them. The old man telepaths smiling.

Suzette looks to me for guidance. I feel the young man's power - but I also sense that he is not threatening. I encourage her to go with him.

He takes her to the past and they witness a tragic story play out. A story of forbidden love which ends with a trial by a council of Elders who make a harsh decision. The young black man is accused of murdering a woman's husband and will suffer traditional, rigid justice. He will be speared in front of the gathered clans.

The woman he loves is devastated. He innocent and is enraged at the blind injustice of tradition. Often when a man is speared the wound is not life threatening, sometimes it is more of a symbolic gesture, but in his case the spear severs his femoral artery and he bleeds to death surprisingly quickly. His punishment is severe because he is a trainee Medicine and Lore man who should know better.

The spear carrier turns to Suzette, *You carry this pain still. You were born a long way away, in another land but Biame called you back.*

Spirit World

As he communicates he becomes more eloquent, searching Suzettes current vocabulary for the right twenty-first century words to communicate clearly.

Suzette is sobbing. I feel her grief. Such a cruel end. I want nothing to do with this harsh justice and you people, ever again.

I have forgiven. It is time for you to forgive and let go of the contracts you made with yourself not to be all you can be. Its time to remember who you are and what carry in your... DNA.

What do you mean? Who I am? I was the woman then and I have had enough of being Aboriginal. I am a proud French woman now, I do as I please.

No, it is not that simple, it is time to remember what brought you back to this land. You are with your people again and we love you.

Suzette's tear ducts well up as she absorbs his words.

You carry our Lore with you, it is in your blood, please don't waste it. It is time to leave this trauma in the past and continue your work as spiritual Lore man, we have work to do.

What?

You were not her, you are me.

A Christmas present opens a Christmas past

I stand next to my client Eleanor as young girl, she is lying peacefully asleep in a comfortable bed, in a comfortable house. The night is bright and clear and she looks angelic, illuminated by starlight which caresses her sweet, innocent face. There is a red and green Christmas stocking at the bottom of her bed, yet to be filled.

Her peaceful sleep is disturbed when her door opens and a man lurches in. Groggy she opens her eyes, trying to understand what is happening. He is a blurry silhouette illuminated by the light from the open door behind him. He sits heavily on the bed and leans over her, his breath smells of alcohol and stale cigarettes.

"Your mummy is asleep…shhh!"

She tries to hide under the covers dumbstruck, but he throws them back pulling her out of bed. It hurts and she starts whimpering.

"Quiet! We don't want to wake mummy!" He slurs his words slightly. Dragging her across the plush carpet past her toys and into the hall, heading towards the living room, away from her mother's bedroom next door.

"We have something to do in here…"

This is me as a child, I recognise my room but I do not remember this happening… Eleanor telepaths.

Sometimes to protect ourselves we hide challenging memories or we may have made promises not to remember.

I feel repulsed.

Who is the man? Do you know him?

He is my stepfather and I really do not want to see what happens next…

Eleanor is a renowned folk singer who is experiencing a well concealed crisis.

She sits and shares her reasons for coming to see me before our shamanic journey commences, I sense interrelated traumas as she speaks.

"I have taken a break from singing… I just don't feel motivated. More than that… it's hard to express, but I just don't feel *worthy* of singing these beautiful songs any more." Her eyes brim with tears. "I just don't know what to do, I can't think of a reason…"

"There may be several reasons. When did this feeling start?"

Eleanor takes a deep breath. "It's hard to say, it has crept up slowly, maybe after Christmas. I had a busy schedule but I always make time to be with my daughter, this year we decorated the tree together, usually her nanny does it with her. It felt good - but on reflection, there was something strange about it. I felt uneasy afterwards."

"Anything else I should know about?"

"Yes, I have asthma, hard to believe in my profession I know, but it is true."

Lying in the Crystal Mandala Eleanor moves into an expanded state easily. She feels tightness in her chest and asking her body to release the cellular memory she is holding there, we are transported to a damp and dingy tent on an overcast afternoon. We see a young woman lying awake, legs akimbo, she looks bored.

This is me! Eleanor telepaths.

Eleanor is a teenager in this life, snoozing on top of her sleeping bag in her wet tent. The environment is gloomy and musty, the weather has closed in.

Oh no, this is so creepy, it was my boarding school camp, I had forgotten about this. We were sent to bed early...

A man quietly unzips her tent and creeps in touching her leg as he enters. She responds immediately and instinctively by kicking him hard in the face. He muffles a cry and scuttles out. From that day onward the lecherous house master turns her whole house against her. She is ostracised and contracts a severe chest infection, which he deliberately ignores. Because it was left untreated for so long, it leads to the asthma that has plagued her ever since.

In order to release the trauma I lead Eleanor in the following affirmation.

"I forgive your ignorance and your selfishness, I forgive your lack of consideration and your cruelty. I forgive you for assaulting me. In forgiving you I release us both from this trauma. We are no longer bound by it, we are both now released and I do not need to repeat it. Go in peace. So be it."

My chest feels more open. That is so much better. And I can breathe! But there is something else here, deeper. Its hidden in my heart and when I probe it I feel sick.

Commanding her body to take us to the moment this feeling started, we see her decorating a Christmas tree as a child putting out presents with her mother. Eleanor is singing happily and the scene looks perfect.

I can't see any problem here I look like a happy little girl...

She looks longingly and the delicious wrapped chocolates on the tree, a special annual treat.

"You know you must wait until Christmas Day before you touch them don't you darling?" Her mother smiles as her stepfather joins them and they admire the decorations.

Later that night her drunk stepfather enters her room and drags her down the hall.

Oh! I am starting to remember what happened, this was well hidden... Eleanor observes the scene with some trepidation.

Spirit World

He hauls her to the Christmas tree, pushing face towards the shiny chocolate decorations - one is missing.

"You couldn't wait could you?" We feel his irrational, alcohol-fuelled anger.
"You ate one, didn't you?"

The young Eleanor is mystified. Sobbing, she tries to tell her stepfather that she had been asleep, but he will have none of it. He takes her back to her room, tosses her on her bed and lurches out mumbling, slamming the door behind him.

In the morning her mother backs her stepfather up and her punishment is that she is not allowed to eat any of the chocolate decorations that Christmas. She is crestfallen, confused and ashamed. Her heartache lodges in the centre of her chest.

After Christmas the cleaning lady finds the missing sweet that had dropped behind the tree and offers it to Eleanor who bursts into tears, feeling totally betrayed by both her parents. Her mother is not interested in the news and dismisses it. Putting out presents and decorating the tree this last Christmas triggered the hidden memory of her childhood abuse and the feelings of unworthiness that went with it.

I cant believe such a small thing has affected me so deeply.

The abuse was a profound betrayal of trust that has affected you emotionally, as much as any other, more physical abuse. It is time to forgive them and let it go.

It is emotional but Eleanor forgives and is immediately transported to a beautiful, sacred place, a timeless temple of great stillness and peace.

I feel amazing. Clear, empowered...

A stunningly beautiful woman with a dusky complexion is waiting for her. She looks Ancient Egyptian and wears a pale blue tipped lotus with a yellow centre in her hair. Eleanor does not know who this radiant being is, but her imposing presence and unconditional love are sublime and humbling.

I am Meret, the Goddess of song. You served as my high priestess, do you remember? You are now free of all limitations you may call on me again, when you sing, if you wish.

How?

When you sing from the heart and your clear intention is to uplift, I will be with you again. You will embody my voice and you will affect others deeply, whatever you sing.

Eleanor is overwhelmed and I give them time together before I call her back into full consciousness. She sits up and stares at me in disbelief.

"How do you feel about singing now?"

"Totally worthy and... limitless!" She smiles with a deep knowing.

A big man

Johno edges awkwardly into my healing space, he is a big, broad-shouldered, muscular man who seems to barely fit through the door, over-filling my small client interview seat; as he sits down, it creaks under his weight. He greets me with a surprisingly gentle handshake.

"My girlfriend said you might be able to help me. I haven't done anything like this before…"

He is out of his comfort zone, in an alien environment. His last healing experience was in a hospital, he has never set foot in an alternative healing centre. Assessing his state of being, I look into his large brown eyes. They are deep, almost black and they don't give much away, but I sense pain and confusion underneath his calm and gentle exterior. I ask why he has come to experience a shamanic journey with me.

"My girlfriend thinks I might be depressed, but she doesn't really know how angry I get. I work it out at the gym and boxing helps, but sometimes… I have this intense rage. It just wells up. I am frightened I might hurt somebody… her. That would be unbearable, she is lovely." His voice breaks and eyes brim with tears that surprise him.

"You are in a safe place here and if you are willing we can get to the bottom of it and change how you feel. Have you experienced any trauma in your life?"

"I reckon all things considered, that life has not been too bad. I know something bad may have happened when I was little but I have no memory it."

I have no doubt we will find out what it is and how it connects with his rage once he surrenders to the power of the crystal mandala that he will lie in.

"What do I have to do?" He looks at the crystals, puzzled.

"Not much," I reply. "The crystals will open parts of your consciousness that are normally closed, all you have to do is relax, allow it and follow my guidance, I will be with you."

The big man lies down with a shrug, his head surrounded by crystals. His body fills the futon and spills onto the surrounding carpet. I look down at his pumped physique and pray silently that this session does not get too physical; sometimes they can, especially where there is hidden rage.

When a client has no expectations or resistance, laying in the crystal mandala for the first time can trigger a very rapid, profound and intense opening into the superconscious and All There Is. Johno's naiveté and openness create just such an opportunity as I follow him down a tunnel of light, emerging into the vast cosmos beyond - never ending consciousness and love. I sense his vertigo as his awareness touches the infinite.

Spirit World

I had no idea... He telepaths awestruck.

This is where your higher consciousness resides, always, in a never ending now. It is not a place we usually visit, but it is just a breath away. By accessing no time-space we can access all time-space.

I sense his confusion. I have used my own esoteric vocabulary without thinking, I rephrase...

We can travel through time and space and find out what is causing your rage.

What do we do now?

Just allow your heart to open to the infinite love that surrounds you, that will trigger the response I am looking for.

Johno does so and simultaneously we both sense an aggressive, lithe and spiky figure flitting around on the periphery of our consciousness. Its form is like a living rendering of a wiry, medieval imp from a Hieronymus Bosch painting. It emanates hatred.

It is not something Johno has encountered before and big as Johno is he becomes fearful, which not something I can allow. The fear will feed the imp which in turn will fuel its rage which it will then channel through Johno's inert body, in my healing space.

Don't be frightened we are not going to hurt you.

Johno and the imp both look surprised, which buys me some time.

Show me the moment you attached to Johno.

Its foul mouthed response is immediate and clear in any language - no chance. It is on its haunches, wild but focussed and ready to pounce - on me.

Johno say after me: "Body I command you to take us to the moment this being attached to me".

We are immediately transported to Johno's childhood, we look at him in bed sleeping peacefully, a beautiful, innocent, little cherub with black curly hair.

That's me, when I was little...

The bedroom door opens spilling light into the room, a figure lurches in and sits on Johno's bed.

Uncle Jim...

"Hey little fella wake up. Be quiet now, or something bad will happen." Jono's uncle slips into bed next to him, his cold hands undoing the boys pyjamas, touching his warm little body.

The abuse and threat terrifies the child who cannot escape. His frantic silent cries for help attract the spiky entity, which attaches to him filling him with rage. He kicks and shouts biting his uncle.

The noise wakes the household and the uncle pretends that he is the first responder to the child's "bad dream".

I always knew there was something off about uncle Jim, good for nothing, scumbag… So this thing came when I cried for help?

What is it, a demon? Is this what makes me so angry? How do I get rid of it?

It is manifesting its rage through you, you have an agreement with it which you must dissolve. It is not quite what it appears to be. First we must calm it so we can help it.

Following my instructions Johno calls on the entity and thanks it for helping him, which calms it a bit. We then explain it can no longer stay here without Johno's conscious written permission. It gets agitated again.

It's frightened! It has nowhere to go. Johno starts to feel compassion for this being.

Tell it that it is beautiful and that it is loved. Use your own words to reassure it, ask it to show you what happened to it.

Johno does so and immediately starts sobbing.

It's a little boy, he was abused like me, but much, much worse. Poor little fella, it went on for years, his teachers, the men he and his family trusted! This is so sad. He killed himself, poor kid, I feel so sad for him.

I tell the tortured earthbound child that some high level perpetrators are being found out and sent to prison in our now and this calms him a bit. His form changes to the frightened boy he was as I call on the beings who love him unconditionally to escort him safely home to light and peace.

He leaves, grateful for our intervention and I then call on Johno's ancestors to join us. They offer him guidance on his future life and also thank me for helping him.

Returning to this time-space Johno sits up drying his eyes.

"You couldn't make this stuff up!" He is stunned by his experience. "Is that it? Is my anger gone?"

"You tell me…"

He shakes his head and laughs, a big, free, joy-filled laugh from a big man, with a big open, anger-free heart.

Predator

My client Josie is composed, if a little nervous; she has the kind of elegant good looks that are supported by a good bone structure. She is well dressed in a casual Boho kind of way and exudes an air of quiet stoicism. I sense she is not totally comfortable around men and it turns out she has good reason not to be. As she talks about her present situation I sense shame, guilt and resentment as undercurrents that pull her through the flow of her life, subtly affecting everything she encounters. She describes being psychicly stalked by a local "healer".

"He is a powerful man, a shaman. He is considered an Elder among his people. He has strong magic."

"Then he should know better." I respond.

"You don't understand. He comes to me at night and he gets *inside* me. It's repulsive and exhausting fighting him off. I have tried everything to get rid of him. I have been to other shamans and healers but nothing works, it just turns into another battle. I am worn out and frightened - I did not ask for this."

Maybe you did. I try not to reveal my feelings.

"Tell me how this all started."

"He is traveller I have met over the years at different festivals and events, I heard he was homeless and looking for place to park his van. I called on him energetically and spoke to him as clearly as I see you now. I said, 'If you need to you can stay at my place.' That's when it all started."

"So effectively you invited him in and gave him permission to be with you, right?"

"That's a bit harsh… but yes, I suppose did. And he took it all the wrong way, he thought it was a sexual invitation…"

"Was it?"

"No way, I was just trying to help a brother in need, but now I can't get rid if him. I've done, ceremonies, rituals, I have dissolved all agreements with him, I have done my best to erase him from my life. But still every night there he is, trying to have etheric sex with me. It's hopeless."

She takes a breath and composing herself, Josie wipes away the tears forming in the corners of her eyes.

"I have been told you're the one who can undo this, that you are fearless. And that you are a strong magic man yourself."

I can't believe I am blushing.

"So how do we fight this?" *I sense her vision of duelling shamans, which is not my preferred reality.*

Spirit World

"We don't fight it. We do not match this with aggression, it just does not work, if anything it makes things worse."

"Yes, but he is using magic, I need stronger magic to fix this don't I? It's wearing me out."

"You are here to find a solution, it may not be where you expect it to be. If you allow me, I can help you. But you must let go of all preconceptions."

She shrugs as she lies in the crystal mandala. Eyes closed we scan her body for anything unusual or uncomfortable and I notice lumps on her hands. I point them out and I immediately encounter resistance.

Oh, that's nothing, they have always been there. It's physical, it's arthritis and I get treatment for it. She telepaths.

Yes, but right now, in this expanded state of consciousness, we have asked your body to show us anything not totally aligned with unconditional love and this is what your body shows us.

What's, this got to do with my stalker?

We won't know unless you allow the process to proceed without resisting it.

I sense scepticism in her agreement to continue, as we move deeper into our journey and she commands her body to take us to the moment these lumps materialised.

Oh no, not this again... Josie becomes emotional.

I witness her punching walls as a young girl.

I feel so disgusted with myself.

How old are you?

I am nine years old.

Give yourself permission to remember exactly what led to this.

We witness Josie as an innocent, little girl being sexually abused: first by her father, then her uncle and then her school teacher. I try not to get involved with clients' trauma, but for a moment I feel sick to my core and ashamed to be a man. But my shame will not help her, I need to remain centred.

I thought I had dealt with this...

Not quite, or it would not be surfacing now.

How can this affect my predator?

We will see. I know its hard but in order to be free of this trauma and the way it affecting all of your bodies you must forgive the perpetrators.

Josie takes a some time and little persuasion, to understand the power of my suggestion, she completes her release by stating out loud...

"In forgiving your selfishness and ignorance I release us all from this trauma. I choose never to repeat it and It no longer binds us, we are all now free of it."

How does that feel?

Much better, like a load has been lifted from me. The lumps on my hands are disappearing.

Josie sees clearly that this trauma and self loathing led to her teenage promiscuity and later work as a prostitute. She truly releases all feelings of low self-worth and guilt connected with that time and feels better for it. To complete this part of the healing I suggest she bathe in a crystal clear waterfall and describe how she looks and feels. I witness her radiant higher self materialise in front of her.

I feel sensational! I feel totally clean and pure. Who is this? Wow!

They merge and Josie immediately feels her power.

I feel expansive, so big! Who is this Goddess? She is powerful, impenetrable!

This is your higher self and you have become one with her. Ask her how the merging will affect your life and your current challenge.

I hear her Higher self clearly...

Your time of vulnerability is past. You have learnt all you need to know about being a victim. Now you are truly at peace with all your choices, there are no lower vibrational energies attached to you, so the man who has been bothering you will no longer be able to access your consciousness. Provided you accept the truth of who you are and remain whole unto yourself, he will have no leverage, no way in. You are safe now.

We complete the session with clear suggestions from her Higher Self on Josie's lifestyle changes and a vision of how she may help others as a healer herself in future, if she chooses. She sits up opening her eyes.

"So this interference stops today?"

"He could read you and was using your own self loathing as a way into your consciousness. Now that you have let go of that, he cannot access any part your consciousness - or any of your bodies."

"What else can I do about him?"

"Erase him and your experiences with him from your consciousness and do not interact with him in anyway. You are far more powerful than he is. In fact you always were, you were just not aware of that power, until today."

Dead twin

Ron allows the mandala surrounding his head to open his consciousness to a deeper understanding of why he has felt so alone for his entire life. He has told me that he lost his twin in the womb and that he has seen scans of them holding hands. What we discover reveals a totally unexpected terror.

My hands are heavy. Ron telepaths, looking down at his body as we access no time/space in search of answers.

Command your body to take you to the moment this feeling started.

We are immediately taken to a beach where he is playing as a child. He seems wholly preoccupied with all the sensations of being at the seaside: The bright hot sun; the sweet scent of sun cream cutting through the distant smell of seaweed, his father's smooth, shiny bathers; his mother's partially hidden smile, lurking beneath a broad brimmed hat and big black sunglasses; the sea-salty taste in the air; the repetitive, sleepy breathing sound of waves crashing on shoreline pebbles and the rolling exhalation of them being combed seaward.

Then, as he looks down at his perfect little hands making marks in the sand, the terror and the feelings of emptiness start. His younger self's vision is sharp and clear, he gazes at what he has done, the significant, unconscious marks he has made in the sand. And his hands. Then turning his palms upwards he focuses on the terrible thing that they prove to him.

Why do I feel so afraid?

We witness his parents' concern as the child starts screaming staring wide eyed at his perfect little hands.

Give yourself permission to remember. It's OK to go there again - just for a few moments...

His parents pick him up, wrap him in a towel and comfort him, perplexed, looking at the strange podlike shapes he has drawn in the sand and at his hands, having no idea what has created his tangible terror.

My hands... Ron gasping at the implications of his terrifying childhood realisation and its subsequent effect on his life, starts sobbing...

Ron presents as a relaxed and thoughtful man who appears a little withdrawn as he explains his feelings of isolation, which he tells me led to thoughts of suicide earlier in life. He has had a stable and loving upbringing, with no major trauma apart from his birth. He mentions that his twin died in-utero and that he also had a childhood friend, invisible to others, that he could see clearly and that he talked to constantly, right up until kindergarten. A classic symptom of an earthbound spirit attached to a child.

Ron has spent his entire life feeling out of place, disjointed, uneasy and separate from the rest of humanity. At 32 he has finally decided to look into it with me. A friend has told him that his feelings may have something to do with the fact that he survived his twin.

I have dealt with this situation before, where the surviving twin discovers during a shamanic journey that their dead twin is still with them, earthbound and confused. Not understanding that they died in the womb and wanting to continue living with the surviving twin. The dead twin's presence and neediness creates feelings of anxiety and disconnectedness in the living twin which can play out as a life that lacks connection with others.

I try not to influence the session by presuming that this will be the case, knowing that apart from anything I might say - my thoughts have the power influence outcomes too. I remain in neutral, ready to understand what might be causing these feelings, without preconceptions.

Our interview is brief and we move straight into our shamanic journey - arriving on the beach, where Ron re-experiences the mysterious terror in his hands...

My hands... he stares transfixed and terrified.

I am baffled, trying to figure out what is different about them.

My fingerprints...

I gaze intently at Ron's little hands, looking for any indication of anything that should not be there. Yet I know the child that Ron was sees more.

They are unique!

As they should be...

But that means that I am unique! I am different from everyone else. I don't want to be different I want to belong! I want to be with my pod! How awful, this aloneness is terrible, I do not want this. I want to go home!

Where is home? Ask your body to take you there.

Ron calms down, his sobs change pitch, moving from terror to joy as he has another realisation. He is immediately among a group of large blue pod-like beings floating in what could be water or space.

We are one!

I witness his consciousness merge with the beings that surround him as he returns to group consciousness and it is beautiful. I am mindful not to lose him, but before I can even communicate my thoughts the group responds.

Don't be concerned, Ron is not becoming less or getting lost. He is becoming more. This is where he belongs, it is SO beautiful that he has returned to us.

Could one of your group step forward so I can communicate with you? I have some questions.

No, it is not possible, we are one.

I feel a fool for not realising the obvious, but things are moving quickly.

You may address us as one.

Spirit World

I do so, enquiring initially about the well-being of Ron's dead twin, who I am advised, transitioned home to light from the womb. Ron's invisible childhood friend is described as a temporary guide provided by the beings he is with now and I accept that. So all is well.

I am shown that this is Ron's first time incarnated as a human, which is why it has been so hard to be separated from his group consciousness. This realisation brings great peace to him now as he truly understands the deeper reason for his feelings of isolation.

It all makes so much sense… They express his feelings.

Why did Ron come to Earth?

To learn about separation! They laugh.

How will this session affect his life on Earth?

Peace! Ron now understands everything and after today may return to this group consciousness whenever he chooses. Being separate is hard! They laugh.

I call Ron back into his body as we complete the session. As he opens his eyes I can see he is having difficulty being in his human body again. He smiles.

"The terror of being isolated and separate has left me. For the first time ever I feel connected to this planet and those who love me. I can enjoy being human. It's OK to be here! Thank you."

Slave to love

Martin is a handsome young man who is confused about his relationships. Looking every inch the metrosexual he exudes a gentle charm blended with an intense physicality: he works out and he likes to show it. Describing himself as pansexual, he confides that although he enjoys the company of all sexes and "loves to love" he can never really give himself completely in a sexual relationship. He tells me he feels something is holding him back and he wants to get to the bottom of it.

"I am looking for a totally fulfilling sexual relationship but I just can't seem to find it. I go through the physical routines to please my partners but something is missing. I love them all, I love their intelligence, their bodies, their wit and their energy but..."

Seeking answers, our shamanic journey commences. Laying in my crystal mandala Martin is surprised by how quickly we are taken to another time and place. I stand beside him in a farm field: the humid, afternoon air and the woodsmoke from cooking fires pinching our nostrils as we sense the purposeful activity around us. It is harvest time and what appear to be white snow-covered fields around us are alive with activity.

That's me! Martin telepaths, gazing at the muscular, good-looking man easily lifting heavy sacks of cotton onto a cart.

My word, I was strong and good-looking... His past life self exudes his same winning smile as now - this time directed at the master's wife as she passes in a horse-drawn carriage. She smiles briefly before averting her eyes.

"Oh boy Elijah, if youse knows what's good for yer, yer'll stop that right now."

The man working next to Martin's past-life self shakes his head, sweat dripping off his nose, his tight, curly black hair appearing patchy white with cotton fluff.

"I think she loves me!" Martin lets out a belly laugh which attracts the attention of the overseer, who, too far way to use it, waves his whip at them both, threatening action.

"Head down yer fool!" His companion is afraid and makes a show of working faster, smiling to himself. "She sure is a pretty one..."

"Sure is." Elijah sighs.

Over period of months we see Elijah grow closer to the master's wife. She is flattered by his attention and any chance she has, when her husband is away on business, she finds things to do close to Elijah. She instructs her staff to remain silent and they do so, knowing they would be punished by both her and her husband if they spoke up.

The feelings between them are mutual and genuine, they are both attractive enough to pick any lover they choose, but there is a timeless, irresistible something about forbidden love that affects them both, intensifying their stolen, passionate moments together.

Elijah is a big man and he is skilled in lovemaking, he takes her to peaks of pleasure she could never have imagined possible. In turn her sweet smelling, soft, white skin, long red hair and willowy body drive him to distraction. They make for a passionate couple and as time passes they cannot get enough of each other. Everyone on the plantation knows what is going on, except the master, who, busy making money and buying more slaves, is blissfully ignorant. His wife is smart enough to fulfil his needs in the bedroom with alacrity, so the cuckold really does suspect nothing is amiss.

The other slaves disapprove and those close to Elijah let him know, but he just laughs it off with his big broad, winning smile. He feels invincible.

I really do love her, she is so special. So… exotic.

Martin ponders his past-life's self's infatuation, as another winter approaches and the master's wife falls pregnant. They have been trying for a baby for several years, so her husband is overjoyed with the possibility of a dynasty opening before him.

His wife however is afraid: there is a good chance that the baby is Elijah's and if it is, it will be obvious and there will be no denying it. Although nagged by fear himself, Elijah moves into denial, convincing himself that because they are in love it will work out. They will escape together or, disgraced she will be sent away with the child.

It is a gothic night full of sultry spring thunderstorms, when the baby is born. It does not live long, murdered by the midwife under instructions from the master: the midwife is in turn murdered by the overseer for a botched birth. She will never share her secret.

His wife, desperate to survive, explains in terror and tears that she was raped by Elijah nine months prior but was too ashamed to speak up.

Enraged, the Master sends men to capture and punish Elijah. Although powerful he is overwhelmed: they drag him to a tree and tie him up, spreadeagled, beating him almost to death. The master looks on, not soiling his hands, enjoying his righteous revenge. But Elijah is strong, he clutches on to the thread of life within him as the beating brutes tire themselves out, pointlessly pulverising him trying to break his body and his will.

"Hand me that knife, I'll fix him." The master steps forward repulsed by the gory mess that is his wife's 'rapist'. "Grab his cock."

An overseer does as instructed. The master reaches down and with one swift merciless move unmans Elijah, who stares defiantly at the master.

"She loved me…" Elijah whispers at the master who becomes apoplectic cutting off Elijah's testicles as well, throwing them to the pigs.

"Leave him to die!" rage spent, the master turns his back and walks off.

But Elijah does not die; once he is left alone his people come and staunch his wounds and he does not bleed to death. Mutilated, he lives and the master, when he hears of it, decides that he will allow it. Elijah will become a living example for the others and he will torture him by working him to death.

Elijah survives for three more years, living with the coldness of his ex-lover, the never ending taunts and brutality from the overseers and the indignity of squatting to piss. A broken man physically and emotionally, he dies vowing he will never, ever, truly love again.

Martin is in tears. *I understand now what prevents me from loving, what a foolish, brave man I was.*

It is time to undo the promise that you made you to yourself on your deathbed, but first you must forgive.

It takes time, but Martin forgives both his lover and her husband, then I lead him into the affirmation that he speaks out loud, that will change not just this life but his soul's journey…

"I now dissolve all promises I have made with myself not to truly fall in love. I will not be punished for loving someone with all my heart. I have learnt all I need to know about betrayal, brutalisation and being punished for loving. I do not need to repeat it. I leave these traumas in the past where they belong. I choose love, I choose freedom and I open my heart to true and passionate love. Nothing can prevent me doing this, now. So be it."

Martin senses a profound change in all of his bodies rippling across time ands space, particularly in his heart and base chakras.

He sighs, *My heart is open and I am free.*

Birth of a Guru

"Do not judge this book by its cover," I advise my rebellious, indigenous apprentice. I can see her eyes rolling as a sleek shiny new Tesla, hums to a stop next to our studio. I find myself experiencing a rare moment of envy.

Jonathan is an affluent advertising executive. After overwork and a messy divorce took him to an emotional rock bottom, he is here to find out why it all happened, so he can be at peace.

"Wealth does not always equal corruption and desecration of the land." I am almost speaking to myself as I gaze at his very expensive "green" car.

"In my world it does," she grumbles. Putting on her sweet and innocent, child-of-the-bush face, she greets my client.

Surprisingly, for such a left brained person, Jonathan enters an expanded state of consciousness easily. We clear past life trauma and attachments, each taking him into a deeper understanding of his choices and experiences in this life.

I sense my apprentice is becoming bored with what to her has become a routine session. We feel close to completely clearing Jonathan when I hear my apprentice's thin, wavering voice...

"The sun isn't usually this bright at this time of day. It is getting really bright and hot in here... Sorry, I just feel so... happy! I can't say that I have ever felt like this before."

"Observe what is happening with Jonathan in no time-space and you will understand."

Jonathan telepaths me. *My whole body is tingling, I feel very clear, expanded.*

How far does your consciousness reach?

He starts crying.

It stretches forever. I am connected to everything.

How does that feel?

Indescribably beautiful. His sobs fall into a strange unison with my apprentice.

Call on the beings who love you unconditionally. Invite them to join us now.

They are telling me I am now clear and that there is someone here to meet me...

I start to feel emotional myself as a radiant being steps forward: I think I recognise him.

I recall reading a poem just before I left, about my beloved Ganges, the Himalayas and... The youthful looking, long haired, round faced Master sounds wistful.

I am honoured. The usually cocky executive expresses himself with true humility.

Let us walk together... The Master places his hand on Jonathan's shoulder as they stroll through a beautiful garden, chatting.

"Pay attention," I whisper to my apprentice.

The Master explains to Jonathan that prior to birth they made an agreement that when Jonathan reached a point of clarity and oneness in this life that they could merge, becoming one, working together for the greater good of humanity, if he chose to do so.

"Soul braiding!" My apprentice is pleased to be witnessing what was, until today, a concept.

Jonathan, if you feel ready we have work to do. The Master embraces him.

It is clear that Jonathan has a choice; to embody the Master he is aligned with and walk together - or not. He may continue as a prosperous businessman or radically change his life and take a totally different path.

We return to our current time and place. A very different Jonathan opens his eyes.

"Wow. That was a lot to take in. Does this mean I am him?"

"You will have worked together in the past. Now if you wish, you may work together again, only this time you will embody his wisdom and love. It is entirely up to you. Take your time to integrate this experience. This could mean making some big changes in your life."

My stunned apprentice shows him to his flashy car and waves goodbye.

"I know you have seen this before; what usually happens?" Her focus has returned to learning.

"For a few it is a major shift but for many it is all too much and very little changes. Some are able to embody the love and teachings of the Master concerned in their interactions with others in their daily lives. Without anybody knowing who is involved and what is happening, that is enough."

"What are the chances of him truly embodying this being and sharing his teachings based on unconditional love again? He looks pretty materialistic to me."

"Many things will conspire against him; his mind, ego, family obligations, community status and the fear of being judged can all undermine his potential. However, Jonathan stands an excellent chance of becoming a great teacher and ambassador for peace. He has a clear mind and and the right kind of worldly experience to make this work. He knows his experience here was authentic. Let's keep an eye on him, I believe he may follow through."

"Really? Wow, a guru is born…" She looks genuinely starry eyed.

"So what about you?" She turns, looking into my eyes.

Reflections of Spirit World

What feelings arise for you when you read these stories?
What is an Earthbound Spirit?
How may an Earthbound spirit may attach itself to a person?
How do people give permission for this to happen?
Why is possession such a serious concern? How can it affect people?
What is the best way to deal with possession?
How does any person allow this to happen?
What do demons feed on? What were demons before they became demons?
Why is it important to show compassion to confused beings?
How can past life trauma affect this life? How does it play out?
What is the key to releasing unpleasant past life experiences?
When you call out for help how specific should you be?
What key question you might ask a spirit claiming to be your spirit guide?
Is it possible for spirit guides to love us but still have their own agenda?
How might you be abducted by aliens?
Is this more likely to be a physical or etheric abduction?
Is any crystal implant a good thing?
What is the best way to work with indigenous spirits?
How can they affect the occupants of the land they are custodians of?
Is it possible to experience and release trauma from another reality or from another person in this timeline? How and why?
How can unresolved past life trauma affect our emotions now?
Can the release of past life trauma affect our physical body now?
In what way can this happen?
What type of pain does past life trauma really relate to?
Is it possible to retrieve future technology and build it here and now?
How are curses placed and how can they be released?
When we enter the superconscious how might we appear?
Why are we vulnerable to spirit attachment when we experience great physical or emotional pain?
Can we experience the physicality of being a member of the opposite sex?
Or another species altogether?

Spirit World

Can we work with a highly evolved being that loves us unconditionally?

How may we cohabit the same body and still have free will?

Is it possible to negotiate our way out of a Karmic debt?

How do we do this? How do past life agreements affect us now?

Is it possible for us to experience life as a totally different type of being?

Is time linear? Can we time travel? If so what is the point?

May our ancestors make agreements on our behalf before we are born?

How does this work?

How do binding past life agreements affect us now?

Are past lives relevant to our journey here now? If so how?

Can multiple past life traumas affect our bodies now? If so how?

Why do repeated traumas happen in the same part of the body over a series of incarnations?

How might the Dark Lord appear? What is the best way to deal with him?

Can anything have power over us? If so how?

We all aim to exist in state of unconditional love, can this create challenges? If so how?

Is it possible for us to be from another part of the universe and still be incarnated here as humans?

If so - how might this complicate our life now?

Is it possible for entities to have entities attached to them?

What does repeated traumas in the same part of the body indicate?

How can we deal with it?

What can prevent us from reclaiming our past life skills and activating our life plan?

Can we make pre-birth agreements with the Masters to embody their wisdom?

How might that play out?

How can you reclaim your power?

In a present life recall can we see more than our memories? Why?

How can you align yourself with unconditional love?

How might that affect your life?

For in-depth answers please - read the book again!
If these stories resonate please consider becoming a Crystal Dreaming™ practitioner., all you need is compassion and fearlessness. To study the process or to experience a personal Crystal Dreaming™ session you will find licensed teachers and practitioners here... **www.CrystalDreaming.com**

About the Author

Raym was born Raymond John Richards, in Merseyside, UK on July 26, 1953, he is a Shaman and Crystal Master. Since 1994 Raym has specialised in connecting people with their own higher guidance, the spiritual realm, bliss and beyond, through drug-free, deeply altered states of consciousness, triggered by his advanced healing technique Crystal Dreaming™. His stories are based on actual, real life experiences. He teaches this process worldwide.

Raym holds a Bachelor of Arts Honours Degree in Fine Art and enjoyed many years as a visual and Performance Artist. He has been happily married for over 40 years and lives in the hinterland of Byron Bay, Northern NSW, Australia. He takes annual tours of sacred sites in the UK.

For more information about the Crystal dreaming process visit...
www.CrystalDreaming.com

Raym has written two other popular books:

Spirit Guide

A guidebook for a new life in the Golden Age.

> *"Raym's very comprehensive introduction to holistic thinking and living leaves no stone unturned. If you are just embarking on the journey of discovery for yourself, you will be lightly and often humorously guided in every facet. Contrasting the light style, some of the concepts covered are deep, but Raym at all times has your welfare uppermost in his approach. A master healer himself, he is there to guide you in deep meditative and healing experiences, and it may be that these are the real gems of this excellent primer of holism."*

Elizabeth Stephens, Editor, LivingNow magazine

Alchemy of Crystals

The complete Crystal Dreaming™ technique summarised in one volume, in this thorough practitioner's handbook.

> *"Raym has developed a powerful and truly transformative therapeutic method that rapidly resolves the emotions, cognitions, physical ailments, and behaviour associated with trauma - often within a very short period of time. I can confirm, as a scientist, as a doctor and as a psychiatrist that what I experienced was life changing."*

Dr David Burton MB.BS B(sci)

Spirit Guide and **Alchemy of Crystals** are available from the publishers by mail order or as ebooks through Amazon and iBooks.

For more information visit... **www.CrystalDreaming.com**

Dairy of an Urban Shaman

For updates, new stories and to subscribe to Raym's blog visit...
www.DiaryofanUrbanShaman.com

www.ingramcontent.com/pod-product-compliance
Lightning Source LLC
Chambersburg PA
CBHW051942290426
44110CB00015B/2075